UNIVERSAL HISTORY,

ANCIENT AND MODERN;

FROM

THE EARLIEST RECORDS OF TIME,

TO

THE GENERAL PEACE OF 1801.

IN TWENTY-FIVE VOLUMES.

——◆◆◆——

BY WILLIAM MAVOR, L. L. D.

VICAR OF HURLEY IN BERKSHIRE, AND CHAPLAIN
TO THE EARL OF DUMFRIES.

Factorum est copia nobis.

. . . .

Res gestæ regumque, ducumque, et tristia bella.

VOL. III.

——◆◆◆——

New-York:

PRINTED BY STANSBURY AND GIRD,
FOR SAMUEL S. BRADFORD, NO. 4, SOUTH THIRD-
STREET, PHILADELPHIA.

——

THE
HISTORY
OF
G R E E C

---❈---

IN TWO VOLUMES.

---❈---

BY *WILLIAM MAVOR*, L. L.
VICAR OF HURLEY IN BERKSHIRE, AND C
TO THE EARL OF DUMFRIES,
AUTHOR OF THE BRITISH NEPOS, &c.

---❈---

VOL. I.

---❈---

New-York:

PRINTED BY STANSBURY AND GIRD,
FOR SAMUEL S. BRADFORD, NO. 4, SOUTH
STREET, PHILADELPHIA.
———
1804.

CONTENTS.

Page

Chap. I.—*From the earliest Accounts of Greece, to the general Abolition of Royalty in that Country.* - - - - - - - - - 1

Chap. II.—*The Government of Sparta, to the Subjugation of the Messenians.* - - 10

Chap. III.—*The Government of Athens, from the Establishment of the Archons, to the Expulsion of Hippias.* - - - - - 23

Chap. IV.—*The Transactions of Greece, from the Expulsion of Hippias to the Death of Darius.* - - - - - - - - - 35

Chap. V.—*The Grecian Affairs, from the Accession of Xerxes to the Throne of Persia, to the Return of that Monarch into Asia, after his Expedition against Greece.* 49

Chap. VI.—*From the Retreat of Xerxes into Asia, to the final Event of the Persian Invasion.* - - - - - - - - - 70

Chap. VII.—*The Affairs of Greece, from the final Overthrow of the Persians, to the thirty Years Truce.* - - - - - 87

Chap. VIII.—*The Affairs of Greece, from the Truce for thirty Years, to the Peace of Nicias.* - - - - - - - - - - 125

2 A

CONTENTS.

Chap. IX.—*From the Peace of Nicias to the total overthrow of the Expedition against Sicily.* - - - - - - - - - - - - - 167

Chap. X.—*The Affairs of Greece, from the Defeat of the Expedition against Sicily, to the Conclusion of the Peloponnesian War.* - - - - - - - - - - - - - I - 252

PREFATORY MEMOIR

*Relative to the Geography of ancient Greece,
and illustrative of the Map.*

IN order to give a distinct idea of this celebrated country, which was broken into so many rival states, it appears necessary to prefix to its general history, a geographical account of its component parts.

Greece, in the early periods of history, comprehended Peloponnesus, Græcia propria, Epirus, Thessalia, and Macedonia; but when subjugated by the Romans, it was divided into two provinces, Achaia and Macedonia; the former containing the first and second of the ancient divisions, and the latter the other three. We shall review the original divisions in order.

PELOPONNESUS.*

This peninsula derived its name from Pelops, the son of Tantalus king of Phrygia, and in its general form resembles the leaf of a palm tree. It is joined to Græcia propria by the isthmus of Corinth, which is only about five miles over. On this spot the inhabitants of Peloponesus usually intrenched themselves when in dread of an invasion; and here the isthmian games were triennially celebrated. Demetrius, Cæsar, and others, attempted to cut through this isthmus, but constantly failed in success.

* Now called the Morea.

The subdivisions of Peloponnesus were Achaia, Elis, Messenia, Laconica, Arcadia, and Argolis.

ACHAIA—The chief towns of Achaia were Corinth and Sicyon, the latter the most ancient city in Greece, and once the head of a kingdom.

Corinth was long and justly celebrated. It stood at the foot of a high hill, on which was built the citadel, including which it was about ten miles in circumference. The navigation round the capes of Malea and Tænarus was reckoned so dangerous on account of storms and pirates, that merchants generally transported their goods over the isthmus, whence Corinth became the mart of Europe and Asia. The natives of this city were distinguished for their skill in working in metals. The Corinthian brass, a mixture of copper with some small quantity of Gold and silver, formed a composition extremely brilliant and durable. The ornaments on pottery—ware, were also executed here with inimitable art.

Corinth, after lying long in ruins, was rebuilt by Julius Cæsar. In removing the rubbish, an immense quantity of vessels of brass and earthen ware was found, and carried to Rome.

The other cities of Achaia were comparatively of little consequence; their names were Phlius, Pallene, Ægira, and Helice.

ELIS—Of this district the chief cities were Elis on the river Peneus, and Olympia on the river Alpheus. Near the latter, the Olympic games*, so famous throughout all Greece, were celebrated every fourth year; hence a period of four years was called an Olympiad. Near the site of Olympia stood

* Among the Greeks there were four solemn games, consecrated to religion; the Olympic, Pythian, Isthmian, and Nemean. Of these the Olympic were reckoned the chief. The contests at each were nearly similar. Running, leaping, wrestling, boxing, and throwing the quoit, were alternately displayed for the exercise of strength and agility. The spot on which these contests were exhibited was called the STADIUM. That division of it where the horse and chariot races were run, was called *Hippodromus*; where the course began, *Carcer*; and where it terminated, *Meta*. At each of these games the prizes were somewhat different. In general, however, the victors at either were presented with a branch of the palm-tree, which they carried in their hands; but at the Olympic games they wore a crown, or wreath, of olive; at the Pythian, laurel; at the Isthmian, pine; and at the Nemean, parsley. Those who bore away the palm were called Hieronica, and were carried with great pomp and solemnity to their native city, which they entered in a chariot drawn by white horses through a breach in the wall made purposely for their passage, and were for the remainder of their lives maintained at the public expense. Even kings did not consider it derogatory to their honour to contend for the prize; and no person branded with infamy was admitted as a combatant.

The Olympic games derived their origin from Hercules, but falling into neglect, were afterward renewed by Iphitus. These proved an excellent preparative for youth to bear the hardships of war, as well as to improve their bravery and adroitness.

§ The year in which Coræbus of Elis won the chief prize (which was that of the chariot race) was the period when the Greeks first regulated their time by Olympiads. This corresponds with the 776th year before Christ, and is a remarkable æra in ancient history.

the ancient city of Pisa, which was demolished by the people of Elis*.

MESSENIA. The chief city in this division was named Messene, by which appellation the whole country was formerly known. It was built by Épaminondas, and stood at a short distance north from the top of the Messenian gulf. Being under the immediate protection of a strong fortress, exclusive of its own peculiar fortifications, it was almost impregnable. The ancient capital was Pylos, the city of Nestor: the epithet Messeniaca was afterward added, in order to distinguish it from two other places of the former name.

Pylos of Messenia was situated on the Ionian sea, near the small island Sphacteria; where a large party of Lacedæmonians in the Peloponnesian war were, after a valiant resistance, compelled to surrender to Demosthenes and Cleon.

There were several other towns in this district, among which Cypanissa, Methone, and Asine were the most important.

* The people of Elis generally had the regulation of the games, and occasionally the inhabitants of Pisa, prior to the destruction of that city. Their duration was for five days. The day on which they commenced was the eleventh of the month called Hecatombeon. During their celebration there was a general suspension of hostilities. An immense concourse of people attended, not only from all Greece, but likewise from the neighbouring nations. Here also works of genius were displayed; and it was here that Herodotus read his history, which so affected Thucydides, then a boy, that he shed tears, and on that account he attracted the notice of the author.

LACONICA, or Laconia. No portion of the Peloponnesus was more celebrated than this. It contained the famous city of Lacedæmon*, or Sparta, the most powerful in ancient Greece, which stood at the bottom of Taygetus on the banks of the river Eurotas. This city was about six miles in circumference but had no other walls than the bravery of its inhabitants, till it fell under the dominion of tyrants. The prevailing manners were inimical to external splendour, and therefore the houses were small and destitute of ornament.

South of Lacedæmon, on the west bank of the Eurotas, was Amyclæ, abounding in trees, and honoured with a splendid temple of Apollo.

Gythium, the port of Lacedæmon near the mouth of Eurotas, which falls into the Laconic gulph, was a very strong place. Not far from this was the site of the ancient Helos, which the Spartans having taken, reduced the inhabitants to slavery, and hence all their slaves were called Helotes.

The promontory of Malea, so dangerous to mariners, bounded the gulph of Laconia on the east, as Tænarus did on the west. This was the most southern point of Europe, and here stood the inviolable temple of Neptune, and near it the cave through which Hercules is fabled to have dragged Cerberus from the infernal regions.

* Now called Misitra.

The other towns and places of Laconia were Selasia, Delium, Epidarus, and some others of inferiour note.

ARCADIA—The enchanting descriptions of Arcadian scenes in the Greek and Latin poets, have rendered this country dear to the lovers of nature and simplicity. There is scarcely a spot within its precincts, that has not been the subject of fabulous invention, or beautiful description.

Arcadia was the country of shepherds, and therefore sacred to Pan, the pastoral god. It abounded in lofty mountains, and was agreeably intermixed with sylvan and champaign scenery. Its chief cities were Tegæa, whence Pan has the epithet of Tegæus; Pallentæum; Mantinea, where Epaminondas fell; Megalopolis, Belbina, and a few others. Arcadia was very populous, and was said to contain three hundred thousand slaves.

When the natives had occasion to confirm any engagement by an inviolable oath, they proceeded to Nonacris, near which issued a deadly stream called Styx, and to swear by its waters was reckoned binding both on gods and men. This water corroded every substance, except the hoofs of certain animals; and by means of it Alexander the Great is said to have been poisoned. The fabulous river of Hell took its rise from this source.

ARGOLIS. The principal city in this district was Argos, supposed to be the favourite residence of Juno. It was situated on the river Inachus, and was defended by two citadels. The inhabitants were denominated Argivi, a name by which the Greeks in general were often designated. Nauplia was the harbour of Argos; and to the south of this was the lake of Lerna, where Hercules slew the monstrous hydra.

To the north of Argos stood Mycenæ, the city of Agamemnon, after whose death it gradually declined, till at last it was destroyed by the Argives. In a neighbouring grove the Nemean games were celebrated every three years.

At the bottom of the Argolic gulf stood Trœzene, so called from its founder Trœzen, the son of Pelops. Opposite to this city lies the island Calauria, to which Demosthenes being pursued by his enemies, he swallowed poison.

West from Trœzene, was Epidaurus, and at the distance of five miles from this last mentioned place stood the famous temple of Æsculapius.

The promontory of Scyllæum on the Saronic gulph was the burial-place of Scylla, the daughter of Nisus. Near Scyllæum was the town of Hermione, from which the passage to the shades below was supposed to be so short, that it was not necessary to put money into the mouth of the dead to pay Charon's fare.

VOL. III. B

GRÆCIA PROPRIA.

This grand division of Greece was bounded on the north, by mounts Othrys and Oeta, which divided it from Thessaly; on the west, by the river Achelous and Epire; on the south, by the Corinthian and Saronic gulphs, and the isthmus of Corinth, which separated it from Peloponnesus; and on the east, by the Ægean Sea, the boundary between Europe and Asia.

The subdivisions of Græcia propria were seven; Attica, Megaris, Bœotia, Phocis, Locris, Doris, and Ætolia.

ATTICA. No part of Greece was so celebrated as this; and from the interests which will ever be attached to it, in the estimation of every polite scholar, it will be proper to notice some of the principal circumstances connected with it. Athens*, the capital, was long the most illustrious seat of learning, arts, and sciences, and deserves to be described at some length.

In very early times this city consisted of little more than a citadel, built on the top of a rocky eminence about seven miles round. This fortress was surrounded by a strong wall, and had only one entrance, the ascent to which was by stairs. Within its precincts were several magnificent edifices, the chief of which was the temple of Minerva, called Parthenon. After being burnt by the Persians, it was rebuilt of the finest

---

* Now Setines

marble by Pericles, and still exhibits one of the most splendid remains of antiquity, being two hundred and twenty-nine feet long, one hundred broad, and seventy high. The colossal statue of Minerva, made by Phidias of gold and ivory, was thirty-nine feet high. In the citadel there were also a number of statues in honour of that goddess; among the rest, that which was believed to have fallen from Heaven: it was, however, merely a shapeless mass of olive wood, though held in the highest veneration.

Adjoining to the Parthenon was the publick treasury. The chief of the prytanes, or the president of the senate, who was changed daily, had the charge of the key; but some of the treasurers, having embezzled part of the publick money, burnt this edifice to the ground, in order to conceal their peculation.

At first the Athenians attended chiefly to agriculture, particularly to the cultivation of the olive; but afterwards following commerce, they built a joint temple to Minerva and Neptune, with a chapel consecrated to each. On one side stood the olive tree, which was said to have sprung out of the earth at the command of Minerva; and on the other was a fountain of salt water, fabled to have been produced by the stroke of Neptune's trident.

As the inhabitants of Athens began to increase, it was necessary to build on the level ground round the citadel; and in process of time the lower city became embellished with many splendid edifices. The temple of Jupiter Olympus, of Theseus, built by Cimon, and the Pantheon, or temple to all the gods, both which are still standing nearly entire; the temples of Castor and Pollux, and of Apollo and Pan; the Prytaneum, where those who had merited well of the state were supported at the publick expense; the Odium, or musical theatre, and the theatre of Bacchus, were among the most remarkable.

Near the citadel was the fountain Callirrhoe, the water of which was used in nuptial and sacred rites; and on an eminence at a small distance, was the place where the Areopagus assembled.

The Ceramicus, however, or the place where pottery was made, is one of the most famous quarters of Athens. In it was the forum or market-place, surrounded with temples and various other publick buildings. Here were the porticoes of Hermæ and Pœcile, in the latter of which, Zeno the philosopher used to teach, and from this circumstance his followers were called stoics, stoa signifying a portico in Greek.

Athens had three harbours, the Piræus, Municia, and Phalerum, all very strong, and united to the city by two walls, called the long walls, which were projected and partly executed by Themistocles.

Independent, however, of the memorable places within the limits of the city, some of which have already been cursorily noticed, the Athenians had several Gymnasia, either in or near the city, the principal of which were the Academia, Lyceum, and Cynosarges. The Academia lay about three quarters of a mile north-west of the city, and contained a gymnasium, a garden, and a grove surrounded with walls, and adorned with delightful covered walks. Here Plato taught his scholars, whence his followers are called academics; and such decorum was observed in the place, that it was forbidden even to laugh in it.

The Lyceum* lay on the opposite side of Athens, on the banks of the Ilissus, and was remarkably salubrious. Aristotle, the disciple of Plato, chose the Lyceum for the place of youthful institution; and because he taught his followers while walking, his sect was called peripatetics.

The Cynosarges was situated on the north of the Lyceum, on an eminence, and contained a gymnasium, a temple of Hercules, and a sacred grove. It is said to have received its name from a white or swift dog, which snatched away part of the sacrifice offered to Hercules. In this place foreigners or citizens of half blood, that is, who were born of an alien mother, performed their exercises; and here Antisthenes taught his philosophy, whence, as some say, he

---

* So called from Lycus the son of Pandion, who also gave name to Lycia, in Asia.

was called the cynic; though others imagine, and perhaps with greater probability, that he obtained this epithet from his snarling disposition, which certainly some of his followers deserved.

The inhabitants of Athens were properly divided into three orders: citizens, sojourners, and slaves. The number of citizens seldom exceeded 20,000, of sojourners or foreigners 10,000, while the slaves amounted to 400,000. The last two classes had no share in the government; but to enter into the civil and political institutions of this famous republick, would carry us beyond the bounds prescribed.

About ten miles north-east of Athens stood Marathon, illustrious for the defeat of the Persians by Miltiades. In the same direction from Athens was the fortress of Phyle, the first place seized by Thrasybulus with only thirty men, when he emancipated his country from the tyranny of as many usurpers.

West from this lay Acharnae, the chief borough of Attica, which is frequently mentioned in history; and not far from this stood Eleusis, famous for the celebration of the mysteries of Ceres.

Other memorable places in Attica were Erchia, Gargettus, Decelia, and Oropus.

MEGARIS. This was a small tract of land lying at the top of the Saronic gulf, between the territories of Attica and Corinth. The chief city was Megara situated on a rising ground, and possessing a good harbour called Nisæa. The other towns of Megaris were very inconsiderable.

The people of Megara had twenty gallies at the battle of Salamis, and three hundred men at the battle of Platæa. They even ventured sometimes to enter into hostilities with the Athenians; but their country is more justly entitled to distinction for having produced Euclid, than for all their other advantages combined. This great mathematician had conceived the highest respect for Socrates, and during a war between the Megarensians and the Athenians, he frequently visited that philosopher by night in a female disguise, and returned again before day break, though the distance was twenty miles.

Bœotia. This country stretched along the west of Attica and Megaris, from the Euripus to the Corinthian gulf. The soil was fertile, but the air was gross, and the inhabitants in general reckoned characteristically dull, though there were many splendid exceptions.

The capital was Thebes, built by Cadmus, who first introduced letters into Greece.— It was situated on the river Ismenus, and had seven gates, with walls upwards of seven miles in circumference.

The other states of Greece were long indignant against the Thebans, for their perfidy in joining the Persians, and for this they were severely punished. Under Pelopidas and Epaminondas; however, Thebes was the most powerful city in Greece. It was destroyed by Alexander the Great, after a terrible carnage of the inhabitants; but was rebuilt by Cassander.

About nine miles south of Thebes stood Platæa, at the foot of Mount Cithæron, on the banks of the Æsopus. Near this place the Persians, under Mardonius, met with a signal defeat from Aristides and Pausanias.

To the westward of Platæa lay Leuctra, the scene where the Lacedæmonians experienced a dreadful overthrow from Epaminondas; in consequence of which, they lost their pre-eminence among the Grecian states.

On the west side of an extensive morassy plain, where the river Melas loses itself, stood Chæronea, the birth-place of Plutarch, and remarkable for the defeat of the allied states of Greece by Philip of Macedon, which they never afterward recovered.

Not far from this was the cave of Trophonius, where oracles were delivered, and which rendered such as entered it melancholy for the rest of their lives.

Thespia, sacred to the muses; Ascra, the birth-place of Hesiod; Aulis, whence the Greeks set sail to the siege of Troy; Tangara, infamous for its cock-fighting exhibitions; Delium, where stood a temple of Apollo; and some other places, are memorable in the history of Bœotia.

This country is further illustrious for its

connection with the muses. The mountains of Helicon and Pimpla, the fountains of Aganippe, Dirce, and Hippocrene can never be mentioned without exciting poetic imagery.

PHOCIS. This district, or rather its capital Delphi, was conjectured by the ancients, not only to be the centre of Greece, but of the whole earth; but Delphi is still more illustrious for the temple and oracle of Apollo, which stood on an eminence above the town, at the foot of mount Parnassus, and near the Castalian fount. In the middle of this temple was a chasm in the ground, whence issued a subtile vapour, that threw such as breathed it into convulsions. It is said to have been first accidentally discovered by some goatherds. The priestess, or pythia, being placed on a tripod over the aperture, and becoming gradually intoxicated with the vapour, proceeded to utter her oracles, generally in hexameter verse, but sometimes in prose. To this oracle not only the Greeks, but many of the neighbouring nations used to resort for advice on any critical emergency.

The revolutions which the temple and oracle at Delphi underwent are too numerous to particularize. In the time of Cicero, the pythia and her predictions had fallen into contempt, but she did not wholly give up her very lucrative vocation, till after the period of Nero's reign.

At Delphi, as being most central, was

held the meeting of the Amphictyonic council, or deputies from the confederated states of Greece. In its vicinity likewise were celebrated the Pythian games, at first every ninth, and afterward every fifth year.

Cirrha, the port of Delphi, lay in the Corinthian gulf, about eight miles distant; and near this stood Anticyra, famous for the production of hellebore, once reputed specific in maniacal cases.

In latter times Elatia, situated on the river Cephissus, became the principal city of Phocis. Its other towns were inconsiderable.

LOCRIS. - The country of Locris was divided into three parts, but no very satisfactory account is given for this. Amphissa, defended by a strong fortress, was the principal town of the first district; Opus of the second; and Naryx, the native place of Ajax, of the third.

Not far distant from the last mentioned town was the famous pass of Thermopylæ, so called from its hot springs. It was justly reckoned the key of Greece, and is immortalized from the self-devotion of Leonidas. Where narrowest, there is only room for a single carriage between Mount Oeta, which here terminates in a precipice, and the Malian gulf.

DORIS, or DORICA. This country was of small extent, it lay along the foot of Mounts Oeta and Parnassus. Its inhabitants were one of the most ancient tribes of Greece, from Dorus, the grandson of Deucalion. It contained four cities, Erineon, Boion, Pindus, and Cytinium; none of them remarkable.

ÆTOLIA. This was the country of a very warlike people, and extended from the top of the gulf Naupactus* to the river Achelous.

The towns were few, but of considerable note. Calydon on the river Evenus, was an ancient and beautiful city, and the birthplace of Tydeus. At the efflux of the Evenus into the Ionian sea stood Chalcis, not far from a mountain of the same name; and on the north-west extremity of the Corinthian gulf lay Naupactus, so called from the number of ships built there; but its very site is now overflowed by the sea.

When the Athenians and Lacedæmonians had enfeebled themselves by mutual contests, the Ætolians became a very powerful people, and possessed themselves of several cities beyond their original limits. They were esteemed the best cavalry in Greece; but were always turbulent and fickle in their disposition.

EPIRUS.

The principal subdivisions of this country were into Acarnania, Thesprotia, Molossis, and Chaonia.

ACARNANIA. Extending from the river Achelous to the Ambrocian gulph, was an-

---

* Now Lepanto.

ciently included in Greece proper, but afterwards added to Epire.

Near a promontory of the same name, at the mouth of the Ambrocian gulph, lay the little town of Actium, celebrated for its temple of Apollo, and still more for the decisive naval fight between Augustus, and Anthony and Cleopatra. In commemoration of his victory, Augustus built the town of Nicopolis on the opposite side of the strait, and instituted the Actian games, which were celebrated every five years.

The chief city, however, of Acarnania was Stratus, about twenty-five miles from the efflux of the river Achelous; and in latter times Leucas, built by a colony from Corinth on the isthmus which joined the peninsula of Leucadia to the main land. Near this was the rock of Cephalonia, or the lover's leap, which Sappho and others tried, to cure their hopeless passion.

THESPROTIA. The chief city of this country was Ambrocia, the royal residence of Pyrrhus, situated near the head of the gulph of the same name. It was built by a colony from Corinth.

On the strait which separates Corcyra from the main land, lay Posidium, Buthrotum, Portus Pelodis; and to the south were Chimærium and Ephyra, near the lake Acherusia, through which ran the river Acheron; and into the latter flows the muddy Cocytus, at no great distance from the lake Avernus.

Indeed it is generally supposed that Homer copied the names of his infernal lakes and rivers from those of Thesprotia.

MOLOSSIS, the country of the Mollossi, lay to the north-east of Thesprotia. The most remarkable town of this district was Dodona, at the foot of Mount Tomarus, famous for the temple and oracle of Jupiter. It was built by the Pelasgi, who justly designated their gods as the rulers of all things.

The other remarkable places in Molossis were Tecmon, and Passaron, where the kings of the country at their accession used to swear that they would govern according to the laws; and the people, that they would defend their native soil.

CHAONIA. The chief towns of this district, were Oricum, situated in a champaign, north of the Acroceraunian mountains, so called from their tops being struck with thunder.—Palæste, where Cæsar landed when in pursuit of Pompey, Cassiope and Phalacrum. Among the inland towns were Antigonea and Phænice.

Chaonia is said to have received its name from Chaon, the companion of Helenus, the son of Priam, who was inadvertently killed in hunting. The celebrated mount Pindus, which consists of several ridges, ran partly through Epire.

THESSALIA.

According to Herodotus this country was wholly enclosed by mountains, on the east by Pelion and Ossa; on the north by Olympus; on the west by Pindus; and on the south by Othrys and Oeta. The intervening champaign, constituting Thessaly, was watered by numerous streams, all of which uniting in the river Peneus, devolved their waters into the Thermaic gulph* by a narrow passage, supposed to have been opened by an earthquake, between Olympus and Ossa.

Along the banks of the Peneus was the delightful vale of Tempe, the subject of every poet's theme. This was about five miles long, but of various breadth.

At the foot of mount Oeta, and north of Thermopylæ, stood Heraclea, so called from Hercules, who is said to have consumed himself in a burning pile on the top of Oeta near this place. Lamia and Hypata, Larissa, the city of Achilles, Pegasæ and the post of Pheræ, the capital of the tyrant Alexander, whom Pelopidas conquered, also lay in this quarter.

About three miles from Pegasæ stood Iolcos, the city of Pelias and Jason, and not far from the latter, Aphetæ, whence the Argonauts set sail. Near Iolcos likewise was Demetrias, built by Demetrius Poliorcetes, which soon became very populous, on

* Now the gulph of Salonichi.

account of its local advantages. North of this lay Meliboea, the city of Philoctetes, famous for the manufacture of purple.

At the bottom of mount Othrys, the abode of the Centaurs, stood Alos, washed by the river Amphrysus, along the banks of which Apollo used to feed the flocks of Admetus; and near the reflux of this stream lay Thebæ, which some have confounded with Thebes in Bœotia.

South from Larissa, already mentioned, lay Pharsalus, near which the ever memorable battle took place between Cæsar and Pompey, when the latter fled to Larissa.

Towards the confines of Macedonia was mount Pierius, sacred to the muses, and from which they are called Pierides. Many other places in Thessaly are mentioned by the poets and historians, but they do not deserve a particular indication in this memoir.

The Thessalian women were said to possess remarkable skill in magick. By their charms or spells they pretended to perform the most wonderful things; to raise or allay tempests, to recal the dead, to destroy the living, and even to arrest the sun in his course.

MACEDONIA.

From the different form of government which for a long period prevailed in this country, it scarcely appears to be a legitimate Grecian state, though usually included within its limits.

Macedonia is made to extend from the mouth of the Peneus to the river Nessus in Thrace; including on the east the countries bordering on the Ægean sea, and surrounding the Thermaic, Toronæan, Singitic, and and Strymonic gulfs; but the precise boundaries on the other sides are not ascertained.

The country lying between the mouth of the Peneus and the Ludias was called Pieria; the towns on this coast were Heracleum, Phila, Dium, and Pydna, near which last Paulus Æmilius defeated Perseus.

To the north of Pieria, the country obtained the name of Pæonia, or Emathia-Pella. The chief town of this district was the birth-place of Philip, and of his son Alexander. It was washed by the Ludias, and was a place of great strength. At some distance lay Edessa, once the residence of the Macedonian kings, and afterward their place of sepulture.

Near the mouth of the Axius and Chidorus stood Therma, which gave name to the Thermaic gulf, afterward called Thessalonica, and now Salonichi, where the illustrious Cicero spent the time of his exile. The principal towns in early periods of history on the north-east of the Thermaic gulf were, Ainea, Simila, Campsa, and in latter times Antigonia and Potidæa.

At the head of the Toronean gulf stood Olynthus, a very considerable city, which was long either subject to, or in alliance with, Athens. Being treacherously taken by Philip, it was destroyed, and the inhabitants carried into servitude, which gave rise to the fatal war between the Athenians and the Macedonian prince.

Between the Singitic and Strymonic gulfs lies Mount Athos, which projects many miles from the plain into the sea. On this vast hill stood several towns, the inhabitants of which received the appellation of Macrobii, from their longevity. Towards the west side of Athos, the two gulfs approach each other within a mile and a half; and through this isthmus Xerxes dug a navigable canal, so wide and deep that two ships could pass at once. In its vicinity stood Stagira, the birth-place of Aristotle, whence he is called the Stagirite.

Near the place where the Strymon divides into two branches, was built Amphipolis. About 30 miles north-east of this city stood Neapolis, and above it Philippi, in the plain adjoining which Brutus and Cassius were overthrown by Antony and Augustus.

The interior part of Macedonia, called Macedonia Superior, was possessed by various tribes. This district was rough and mountainous, and consequently cold.

The country south of the Ceraunian mountains, along the bottom of the Adriatic sea, being chiefly inhabited by Greeks, was named Illyris Græca. The chief towns were Apollonia, a place where learning was much cultivated, and Dyrrachium, now

Durazzo, the common landing place from Brundusium. Not far from this is Petra, where Pompey pitched his camp, and suffered a circumvallation to be drawn round him for fifteen miles, rather than venture an engagement with Cæsar.

GRÆCIAN ISLANDS.

To this geographical description of the continent of Greece it appears of manifest utility to subjoin a brief account of its islands.

CORCYRA, now CORFU, &c.

This island lies in the Ionian sea, and is separated by a narrow strait from Thesprotia. Here were the celebrated gardens of Alcinous, which produced fruit twice a year. ·

Corcyra contained a city of the same name, which was the residence of Alcinous; and near the northern extremity of the island stood Cassiope.

A few small islands, called Sybota, lie between the south-east part of Corcyra and Epirus; and near Leucadia, which has already been mentioned, are the little islands of Paxæ.

Before the mouth of the river Achelous are scattered a number of small islands, called the Echinades, the principal of which is Dulichium. · It was subject to Ulysses; and to the west of this lies Ithaca, the residence of that hero: it was about 25 miles in circumference, rocky and sterile, and contained a town of the same name, at the foot of mount Neius. ·

CEPHALONIA.

This island, called also Same or Samos, lies about fifteen miles from Ithaca, and is 93 miles in circumference. The principal town, named Samos, was taken by the Romans after a siege of four months, and plundered. The other towns were of little note. Between Cephalonia and Ithaca is the small island of Asteria.

ZACYNTHUS, now ZANTE.

South of Cephalonia lies Zacynthus, about 20 miles in circumférence, sylvan and fertile, with a town of the same name. South-east from this were the Strophades, fabled to be infested by harpies.

CYTHERA.

This island was sacred to Venus, and its name is frequently used to designate that goddess. It lies about five miles from the promontory of Malea, and contained a city of the same name, and another called Scandea, both excellently fortified, and furnished with commodious harbours. Cythera was alternately under the power of the Lacedæmonians and the Athenians.

ÆGINA, &c.

The island of Ægina, about twenty-two miles in circumference, lies in the Saronic gulf, about ten miles from Attica. On account of its hidden rocks, it was difficult of access on all sides. The inhabitants were anciently rivals of the Athenians by sea; and, in the battle of Salamis, the prize of valour was decreed to them. In the event they experienced many revolutions of fortune, and submitted to various masters.— They are famed for being the first people that coined money.

West from Ægina is Salamis, containing a town of the same name. It was the island of Telamon, the father of Ajax and Teucer, and is about ten miles long.

Round Salamis and Ægina are several small islands, but none of them of any consequence.

Euboea, now Negropont, &c.

This island lies along the north-east coast of Attica and Bœotia, and is about 150 miles in length, and 40 in breadth. It is separated from the continent by the Euripus, remarkable for the irregularity of its tides. Several of the promontories of Eubœa are mentioned by historians, namely, Geræstus, Caphareus, Carystus, and Amarynthus.

Chalcis was the capital of the whole island, then ranked Eretria, and lastly Artemisium, near which the Greeks first engaged with the fleet of Xerxes.

East from Eubœa lies Scyros, where Achilles lay concealed, and where Theseus died in exile.

The Cyclades.

These islands received their Greek appellation from lying round Delos, in the form of a circle. Some authors reckon twelve of them, others more : the principal are as follow :

DELOS. This island, called also Ortygia, was the birth place of Apollo and Diana. It was anciently said to be a floating island, and was fabled to be chained by Apollo, who bound it to Mycone and Gyaros. Delos abounded in brass; and vessels of that metal fabricated here were held in high estimation. To some of the desert islands in this vicinity the Roman emperors used to banish criminals. CEOS, near Sunium in Attica, was a small but fertile island, and deserves to be particularized as being the birth place of Simonides, the first elegiac writer. This great man being asked by king Hiero, what God is? he demanded a day to consider it: when the same question was put to him the next day, he required two days; and so went on, always doubling the time. The king surprized, asked him why he did so? " Be-" cause," said Simonides, " the longer I " consider the matter, the more difficult it " appears to me."

South of Ceos lies Cythnos, and still farther in the same direction is Seriphus, then Siphnus and Melos. East of Seriphus is PAROS, the birth place of Phidias and Praxiteles, and farther celebrated for producing the finest marble.

To the eastward of PAROS lies NAXOS, fruitful in vines, and therefore sacred to Bacchus. Ios, Thera, now Santorin, and some other small islands lie in the same quarter.

CRETE, now Candia, is by far the largest of the Grecian islands, extending 270 miles in length, and about fifty in breadth. It is extremely mountainous and woody, but has many fertile plains and vallies. In the middle of the island stands mount Ida, and its eastern extremity is mount Dicte, in a cavern of which Jupiter is said to have been nursed.

The three chief cities of Crete were Gnossus, Gortina, and Cydonia. The harbour of the first was named Heracleum, and here the present capital of the island, Candia is built. A number of islets surround Crete, but none of them are remarkable.

The SPORADES.

These islands obtained their original appellation from their scattered form. They lie chiefly on the coast of Asia, to which quarter of the globe they belong.

Carpathus, which gave name to the Carpathian sea, stands eastward of Crete. In the same direction, and near the coast of Lycia, is RHODUS, about 125 miles in circumference, which contained the cities of Lindus, Camirus, and Rhodus, the latter famous for its maritime force, and likewise for the brazen colossus or image of the sun, about 105 feet high. This was the workmanship of Chares, a native of the island, and employed him twelve years. It was overthrown by an earthquake eighty-five years after its erection, and lay on the ground till Rhodes was taken by the Saracens, A. D. 653, when the metal which composed being sold to a Jew, furnished sufficient to load nine hundred camels.

North of Rhodus lies Cos, now Lango, about 100 miles in circumference: it was the native country of Hippocrates, the physician; of Apelles, the painter; and of Philetas, the poet.

PATMOS, now Palmossa, lies in this vicinity. Here St. John wrote the book of Revelation.

SAMOS, the favourite island of Juno, and the country of Pythagoras, stands opposite to mount Mycale, on the coast of Ionia. West of this is ICARUS, which gave name to the Icarean sea; and north of Icarus is CHIOS, famous for its wine and earthenwares.

About 60 miles north of Chios lies LESBOS, an island of considerable extent, and famous for its wines. The chief city was Mytilene, by which name the island is now known.

To the north of this is LEMNOS, now Stalimene, the island of Vulcan, about 112 miles in circumference. It contained two cities, Hephæstia and Murina. On the forum or market-place of the latter, mount Athos, though distant 87 miles, casts its shadow at certain seasons.

Upwards of 60 miles to the eastward of Lemnos, and five from the coast of Troas, lies TENEDOS, about ten miles in circuit. It had one town, where stood a temple of Apollo Smintheus.

The other Grecian islands are scarcely worth an enumeration in this rapid survey.

Universal History.

HISTORY OF GREECE.

CHAPTER I.

From the earliest Accounts of Greece to the general Abolition of Royalty in that Country.

THE history of Greece, like that of every other country, has its origin clouded by fiction, and replete with errors and absurdities. The artless song, or the rude and shapeless monument, was the only commemorative which man employed in the infant state of society, to record his martial exploits, or the memorable destinies of his nation. To attempt, therefore, to trace and depict the several monstrous and improbable accounts, which the Grecian poets and historians of antiquity have transmitted to mankind, would be a task not only useless and insipid, but unworthy of the dignity of historical writing. The fictions of those men must not be blended with the palpable demonstrations of truth. In an ignorant and barbarous age, some degree of credit may have been, and certainly was, attached to them; but they have been too long exploded to merit our slightest attention. Many indeed are the writers, who, by the assistance of strong and lively imaginations, have endeavoured to clothe fable in the garb of probability, to separate truth from falsehood, and to describe, in an uninterrupted series, the history of ancient Greece, from the most remote antiquity. But the affairs of the heroic ages present to our view such a motley and mythological picture, as explained by ancient authors, that every modern writer has been under the necessity of adding some new conjectures of his own. Unsatisfactory, however, and improbable, after all, are most of the interpretations given of those poetical and allegorical compositions; and the former, no less than the latter, appear to be merely the ebullitions of fancy, varied as to their object.

We shall therefore dwell as little as possible on the fabulous age of Greece, for the reasons already assigned. Facts that are more probable, and which have been better substantiated, can alone demand the historian's attention. Ancient Greece, which, at this time, constitutes the south part of Turkey in Europe, was comprehended within the thirty-sixth and forty-second degrees of latitude; extended about 380 miles from north to south, and 310 from east to west; and was bounded on the east by the Ægean sea, now called the Archipelago; on the south by the Cretan sea; on the west by the Ionian sea, or Adriatic gulf; and on the north by Illyria and Thrace. It contained the following kingdoms: in Peloponnesus, Sicyon, Argos, Messenia, Corinth, Achaia, Arcadia, and Laconia. In Greece, properly so called, those of Attica, Megara, Bœotia, Locris, Epichnemidia, Doris, Phocis, Ozolæa, and Ætolia. In Epirus, were the Molossians, Amphilochians, Cassiopæans, Dræopians, Chaonians, Thesprotians, Almenians, and Acarnanians. In Thessaly it comprehended the countries of the Thessalians, the Estiotees, the Pelasgians, the Magnesians, and the Phthiotes. But the most considerable kingdoms were Argos, Attica, Thebes, and Sparta.

The Greeks are said to have derived their name from Græcus, the father of Thessalus; and all those nations are affirmed by the learned Bochart and others, to have been descendants of Javan, the son of Japhet, and grandson of Noah.

Greece is in general an excellent country, situated in a temperate climate, in which none of the necessaries of life are wanting, and to which the seas that surround it waft in abundance every superfluity.

The manners of the first inhabitants of Greece were rude and savage; they fed on herbs, fruits, and roots. The time when they first began to lay up a store of acorns for a season of scarcity, to clothe themselves with the skins of beasts, and build huts to dwell in, is pointed out as the era of civilization. Till then they remained in the open air, or lodged in caves. It is observed, that the more feeble retired to sterile places, that their enjoyments might not be envied; and thus Attica became peopled. The fabulists have endeavoured to point out the age in which those lived, who first taught agriculture, or attempted to make voyages by sea; and it results from their chronology that the invention of these arts is of a very early date. By their voyages and military expeditions, a number of the Greeks made their way into countries more advanced in the sciences and every kind of knowledge. They brought from Phœnice the art of alphabetic writing; and from Persia and Babylon, geometry, astronomy, and magic.

For want of laws the Greeks were long governed by oracles. It is the property of every religion, whether true or false, to act as a restraint on the people. The most celebrated oracle was that of Delphi, where Apollo himself rendered answers through the medium of a priestess named the Pythia. It was at first required that she should be a virgin, but in process of time a matron was substituted. She was seated on a tripod, placed over an opening, whence issued a vapour that inspired the priestess with a sacred fury. In this paroxysm she pronounced, with the tone and gestures of a maniac, answers almost always intricate and ambiguous, but the true sense of which was discoverable after the event. It is to be observed, that the heroes, kings, and even sages, appeared to have a firm faith in the oracles, and consulted them with great solemnity. Those who may think that they only affected this credulity, must at least confess, that they apparently considered it as necessary to inculcate it on the people by their example.

B. C. 2764. Sicyon was the most ancient kingdom of Greece, of which we have any account in history; and Ægialeus was its first king.

B. C. 1846. Inachus founded the regal government of Argos in Peloponnesus. Acrisius, one of his successors, transferred the seat of government to Mycenæ. After which the Heraclidæ, or descendants of Hercules, made themselves masters of it and of the whole peninsula.

B C 1556. Athens was formed into a regular government by Cecrops, an Egyptian, who carried thither a colony of people from the mouths of the Nile. He married the daughter of Actæus, king of that country, established a new monarchy, and founded the afterward so much celebrated city of Athens. Cecrops is said to have taught the Greeks the several arts of peace and war, to have instituted the laws and rules of marriage, and to have appointed religious and civil offices. He is also supposed to have been the founder of the Areopagus, a court of justice, on the plan of the Egyptian tribunals. The reign of Amphictyon, the third king of Athens, is chiefly remarkable for the establishment of the council of the amphictyons, a deputation from the twelve Grecian states, that assembled twice a year at Thermopylæ, to consult the common interest of Greece. Theseus, one who succeeded to the throne of Athens, is said to have founded a more perfect equality amongst the citizens, in which the state rather resembled a republic, than a monarchy. Notwithstanding his many public and private virtues, he fell a sacrifice to the inconstancy of the people, and suffered banishment by ostracism*, a mode of judgment he had himself instituted. Codrus was the last Athenian king ; during his reign the Dores and Heraclidæ had regained all Peloponnesus, and encroached on the Athenian territory. The Delphic oracle declared, that the Heraclidæ should finally prevail, if they ab-

* Ostracism; so called from *ostrakon*, a shell or tile, was a kind of popular judgment or condemnation among the Athenians, whereby such persons were banished as had power and popularity enough to attempt any thing against the public liberty.

The process in this condemnation was thus: the people being assembled, every man took a tile called *ostrakon* and carried it to a certain part of the market place, surrounded with wooden rails for that purpose, in which were ten gates for the ten *tribes* to enter distinctly : in this place the tiles were deposited by each person, and numbered in gross by the *archons*. If the tiles did not amount to 6000, the ostracism was void. Then laying every name by itself, the archons pronounced him, whose name was written by the major part, banished for ten years, with leave to enjoy his estate.

stained from injuring the person of the king of
Athens. This being known to Codrus, he disguised himself in the habit of a peasant, proceeded to the quarters of the enemy, and insulting one of the soldiers, was slain by him in combat. The next day the Athenians sent to demand their king, and the Heraclidæ despairing
of success, suspended all farther hostilities. The
inimitable merit of Codrus was held in so much
veneration by his subjects, that they considered
no man worthy of succeeding him, and therefore
abolished royalty.

B. C.
1448.
Cadmus, we are told, founded the kingdom of Thebes, in which the monarchical form of government was more des-
potic than in any other of the Grecian states.
This prince is supposed to have been of Phœnician extraction. He is universally allowed to
have introduced into Greece the knowledge of
alphabetic writing. To him are ascribed sixteen letters of the Greek alphabet. But as the
order, names, and form of the Greek characters
greatly correspond with those of the Phœnician,
there can be no doubt, that the Greek letters
were formed from the Phœnician, and that Cadmus did not invent, but copy them. He is also
said to have taught the people navigation and
commerce, the method of cultivating the vine,
and the art of forging and working metals.
Many of his descendants act no inconsiderable
part in the writings of the ancient poets ; and
the tragical occurrences that befel them are
universally known.

B. C.
1514.
Sisyphus has been generally reckoned
the founder of the kingdom of Corinth.
He is said to have been the son of Æolus,
and grandfather of the celebrated Ulysses. His

successor Glaucus is commonly supposed to have instituted the Isthmean games. The Corinthian monarchy, however, did not long continue in the lineal succession of Sisyphus. His family became extinct; or, as others affirm, was driven from the throne; when the Bacchidæ seized the reins of government. Subsequent, however, to this, Corinth fell under an aristocracy; and a supreme magistrate, whom they called prytanis, was annually elected from the body of the nobles. The aristocratic government continued until Cypselus found means to usurp the regal power, who transmitted the same to his son.

B C 1104. The Spartan, or Lacedæmonian government was at first monarchical. Its founder was Lelex. The little that is known of the origin of this monarchy, must be ascribed to the contempt in which the Lacedæmonians always held literature and learning. Helen, the daughter of Tyndareus, the seventh king of Sparta, is famous in story for the ten years war which her beauty and infidelity occasioned. She was first stolen away by Theseus; for which reason Tyndareus bound all her suitors by an oath, to allow her to make choice of her own husband; and that if she should be carried off a second time they would join all their forces, and endeavour to restore her. Whereupon Helen married Menelaus, the son of Atreus, and brother of Agamemnon. They had not long enjoyed the sweets of conjugal union, when Paris, son of Priam, king of Troy, universally accounted the handsomest man of his age, and adorned with the frivolous accomplishments that usually captivate the female mind, arrived in Sparta. His person, attainments, and address, seduced the affections of Helen; and she abandoned her country, her husband, and relations; and was transported with all her treasure to the Trojan land. Menelaus, by the advice of his brother Agamemnon, demanded the performance of the promise made by the princes her admirers, and their assistance in the expedition against Troy. It cost the Greeks, however, much bloodshed, before ample revenge on the perpetrator and abettors of this dishonourable act could be executed by the taking of Troy. The kingdoms of Argos, Mycenæ, and Lacedæmon, were afterward united under Orestes.

B. C. 795. Caranus, an Argive by birth, and a descendant of Hercules, established the regal government in Macedonia. Royalty, in spite of the dangers that had proved fatal to it in most of the Grecian communities, subsisted in this kingdom for the space of six hundred and forty-seven years.

Such are the general outlines of the Grecian nation, after it was first formed into regular administrations. Each particular state, assuming to itself the power of modelling its own form of government, might be properly considered as an independent sovereignty. The regal power, as we have seen, was the first that was established in Greece. In the politics of the heroic ages, superior opulence and extensive property were no marks, or cause, of distinction and preeminence. The warlike tribes knew no difference amongst men, but what personal merit and abilities effected. But if we examine minutely the power and authority of each sovereign, in matters appertaining to his own dominions; or if we carefully observe the influence of the chieftain over his people; we shall discover, that the regal jurisdiction was, in general, limited and moderated by the wisdom of a mixed government. In each particular kingdom, the will of the prince was fettered by the prudence of his counsellors, or the voice of the people. It is, however, reasonable to infer, that, had the Greeks never known oppression, nor experienced the insolence and tyranny of their kings, their regal power would have still continued. But the republican government, in most of the states of Greece, succeeded monarchy; and on the ruins of royalty was the freedom of man, though not always his happiness, more fully established.

. Beside the same language, religion, and interest, which prevailed throughout the Grecian territory, and tended to unite the several small and independent states, and to consolidate them into one body politic, games were instituted in different parts of Greece, and prizes adjudged to the victors. At these sports all the inhabitants of the Grecian communities assembled; and the youth were exercised in feats of activity and strength, and thereby enabled the better to endure the hardships and fatigues of war. The council of the amphictyons was, however, the most indissoluble bond of their union. The amphictyonic institution was at first established in the northern parts of Greece, for the purpose of repelling foreign invasion; and had been found equally useful, in promoting concord and unanimity at home. In process of time, however, the amphictyons became a representative assembly of the whole Grecian nation. The states that sent deputies to this council were twelve. Each independent community deputed two members, one of whom was called the pylagoras, and had charge of all civil concerns; the other was named hieromnemon, and to him were committed the interests of religion. After the abolition of royalty, the number of amphictyons was increased to about a hundred. The vernal assembly was held at Delphi; and the autumnal meeting at Thermopylæ. After the deputies had met at the place appointed, they took an oath, guarded by the most solemn imprecations, " That they would never subvert any amphictyonic city, or stop the courses of its water; but punish to the utmost of their power all who should dare to commit these outrages, and oppose every attempt to depreciate the reverence of the gods." To this council was committed every thing pertaining to peace and war, to religion, and the interests of the state. The deputies who composed this august body had full powers delegated to them from their constituents, to act and resolve whatever appeared most conducive to the common weal. Nor was their authority limited to the decision of public affairs, as a dernier resort.... they could even raise troops, and proclaim war, in the first instance.

CHAP. II.

The Government of Sparta, to the Subjugation of the Messenians.

THE Heraclidæ, or posterity of Hercules, having expelled Tisamenes, the son of Orestes, from the throne, divided the countries they had subdued, and of which the principal leaders became sovereigns. Temenes had Argos; Chresphontes, Messenia; and Aristodemus, Lacedæmon. But Aristodemus dying about this time, his two sons Euristhenes and Procles succeeded to the sovereignty of Sparta. These princes neither parted the kingdom between them, nor did they reign alternately. Whether this were owing to the commands of their father, or to some other cause, of which we are ignorant, certain it is they governed conjointly, and with equal authority; each of them being styled king of Sparta, and acknowledged in that capacity. What renders this more astonishing is, that these two brothers entertained the strongest aversion for each other; and their whole lives were spent in continual broils and disagreements. The same misunderstanding likewise prevailed between their successors. And nevertheless this singular and seemingly inconsistent form of government existed for several centuries, until the two families became extinct.

The revolution, which had driven the descendants of Pelops from the throne, had caused all the horrors and miseries of war to be felt in Peloponnesus; and the inhabitants had been obliged to seek an asylum in some of the neighbouring states. In order, therefore, to repeople the kingdom, Eurysthenes and Procles bestowed on all strangers, that would fix their abode in Lacedæmon, the rights and privileges of citizens. This decree was afterwards reversed by Agis, the son and successor of Eurysthenes, and a tax imposed upon all peasants. The Helotes were the only people that would not submit to this impost; but waged war against the Spartans. The citizens, however, finally prevailed, and the wretched Helotes and their posterity were doomed to perpetual slavery.

Lycurgus, the tenth in descent from Hercules, received the Spartan sceptre upon the death of his brother Polydectes. But his sister-in-law proving pregnant, he resigned the crown. The widow of Polydectes, however, intimated to Lycurgus, that if he would consent to marry her, the child should be destroyed; and thus no posthumous son of his brother would disappoint his succession to the throne. Lycurgus was shocked at the proposal, but feigning to comply with her wishes, exhorted her not to procure an abortion, for fear of injuring her own health. He commanded, however, some of his confidants to bring the child to him, as soon as it was born, if it should be a boy. This was accordingly done, and Lycurgus receiving the infant, whilst at supper with some of the principal persons of the city, presented him to them, saying. " My lords of Sparta, here is a king born to us." Then placing the child upon the chair of state, and perceiving how much the people were overjoyed at this disinterested action, he named him Charilaus. Thus did this great and good man sacrifice every proud and ambitious view to the performance of his duty; and laying aside the regal authority, exercised that of protector only. This conduct conciliated the esteem and admiration of the people; but extremely irritated the queen and her partisans. Whereupon Lycurgus, that he might suppress all the calumnies and insinuations published against him by the faction of the queen, determined upon a voluntary exile.

He first visited Crete, an island famous for its laws, and for that polity by which it had been governed in the most early ages. From it the Greeks learned navigation, and derived many of their legal institutions. After that, he sailed to Egypt, and carefully examined the civil and religious establishments of that ancient kingdom. Thence he passed over into Asia, and there found the valuable works of Homer. While thus employed, Lacedæmon having become a prey to anarchy and confusion, he was requested by the people and princes of Sparta, to return to his native country, that his presence might quiet faction, and promote harmony.

Upon his arrival in Greece, finding all things in confusion, and the people weary of their present rulers, he determined to execute the plan he had long designed; and to substitute a more popular form of government. Having first, as a necessary step for insuring the future success of his undertaking, obtained the approbation and assistance of the Delphic oracle, he made his intentions known to a number of his friends, and explained to them the plan he was about to adopt, and the method intended for accomplishing it. Accordingly, when his project was ripe for execution, he commanded thirty of the principal men to appear armed in the market-place, at break of day. Charilaus, fearing a conspiracy against his person, fled to the temple of Minerva; but being informed by Lycurgus of their B. C. real design, he became one of the confederates. Thus was a form of government established, that has excited the admiration and applause of the world.

705.

In the political institution established by Lycurgus, the kings were permitted to rule, and had still the shadow of royalty; but their power was greatly weakened and circumscribed. They had no considerable influence in the government, or credit in public deliberations. They were merely the first citizens in the state, and acknowledged the superior authority of the ephori and the people, to whom they were accountable for their conduct. But they possessed privileges sufficient to distinguish them from the mass of citizens; and their persons were held in the greatest respect and veneration.

The senate, which was intended to serve as a counterpoise between the kings and the people, consisted of twenty-eight members, who sided with the people, when the regal power appeared to preponderate too much; and, on the contrary, espoused the interests of the kings, when turbulence and licentiousness prevailed. By these means the power was equally balanced, and neither the sovereign nor the populace could obtain an undue preponderancy.

The ephori formed a court consisting of five members, annually elected out of the body of the people, with authority to arrest and imprison their kings, if they acted improperly.

The people also had their assemblies and conventions; and possessed a nominal share in the government of Sparta. But, as the senate convened and dismissed them at pleasure, and they never held any offices in the state, it is evident their real power must have been very insignificant.

In order, however, to depress the insolence, pride, and luxury of the great and wealthy, and to banish misery and want from the dwellings of the poor, Lycurgus distributed the lands of Sparta and Laconia in nearly equal portions amongst the inhabitants of each district. The whole territory was divided into thirty-nine thousand shares, of which nine thousand were assigned to the city of Sparta. The principal landholders, on a supposition that resistance would not only be ineffectual and vain, but might perhaps tend to their utter ruin, were easily persuaded to give up their property. In this manner was effected by Lycurgus that extraordinary division of lands, which banished from Lacedæmon all distinction and preeminence, excepting what virtue and merit naturally obtain.

This regulation, however, did not appear to introduce an equality sufficient between man and man. Lycurgus, therefore, withdrew all the silver and gold then in circulation, and permitted nothing but iron money to be given in exchange for every commodity. This coin was made of iron heated in the fire, and quenched in vinegar, in order to render it brittle, and unfit for any other use. From that time all commerce with foreign nations was annihilated, and the ships of another country never entered the ports of Laconia.

The next ordinance which the Spartan legislator established was, that all, even the kings themselves, should eat at publick tables only, where moderation and frugality were to be exercised; and that thenceforth no man should be permitted to take his meals at home. This law was intended to destroy every the least desire of wealth, and to stop the progress of luxury. This innovation, however, was opposed by the people with the utmost violence, and a tumult ensued. Lycurgus found himself obliged to quit the assembly, and to flee to a sanctuary for protection. On this, Alcander, a young nobleman of a generous but hasty disposition, pursued him, and struck out one of his eyes. Lycurgus exhibited to the multitude his face covered with blood; at the sight of which they immediately relented, entreated his forgiveness, and delivered up Alcander to punishment. But, instead of condemning him, Lycurgus, by affability and kindness, made Alcander become his most steady friend and strenuous partizan; and the change thus wrought in his opponent engaged the people to receive as oracles the instructions of this legislator.

‘ ‘ Thus undaunted amidst the opposition with which he was encountered, Lycurgus proceeded in the business of reformation. We must, however, attribute it to the ignorance and barbarity of the age, that some of his laws so evidently militate against the feelings of humanity, and the ties of nature. All children, as soon as born, were commanded to be brought by their parents, and examined by persons appointed for that purpose. Those that were well made and vigorous were preserved; but such as were weak or deformed were exposed to perish at the foot of the mountain Taygetus. And, that prejudice and partiality might not impede the progress of reform, the children that were healthy, and deemed worthy of preservation, were committed to the care of nurses provided by the state. As no Lacedæmonian was permitted to have his children educated after his own manner, the boys, at the age of seven years, were sent to the publick schools. Letters were taught them for use only, and not for ornament. They appreciated things solely by their utility; rejecting the vain and the specious. And, therefore, if they wrote what could be read, or spoke that which might be understood, they judged it quite sufficient, and after more than this they did not seek. The masters endeavoured to give their pupils just ideas of men and of things; to avoid all matters of a trivial or abstruse nature; and to confine themselves to points of the highest importance in civil life. Harmless raillery was encouraged amongst the boys; and a quickness of wit and repartee was equally commended. Their bodily exercises were of the most violent nature; and the youths were particularly enjoined a fatiguing and laborious kind of life. Every art seems to have been made use of, to render them patient under the hardships that might happen to them. Theft was encouraged, in order to prepare their minds for the stratagems of war; but if they were caught in the fact, they were punished severely. Plutarch tells us of a boy, who had stolen a fox and hidden it under his coat, and who rather chose to suffer the animal to tear out his bowels, than to discover the theft. At thirty years of age, they were allowed to marry, to enter into the army, and to bear offices in the state.

The discipline enjoined the virgins, was equally strict with that of the boys. They were accustomed to running, wrestling, and throwing the quoit and the javelin naked before all the citizens. Nor was this deemed indecent or disgraceful, as it might serve to check every lustful and inordinate desire. An education so manly, could scarcely fail of producing manly sentiments. One of the Spartan women, whose son was going to battle, gave the shield to her son with this advice, *Return with it, or upon it;* implying, she had rather see him borne upon it dead, than that he should throw it from him in flight, or resign it to the enemy.

The cryptia, or secret act, was an institution most inhuman and detestable, by which the Lacedæmonians were permitted to kill the Helotes, or slaves, whenever they became too numerous. Plato justly condemns this law. Plutarch denies that it was made by Lycurgus; but Aristotle expressly charges it upon him.

Such was the general purport of the institutions of Lycurgus. If there be some laws among them which we cannot approve, there are others that appear highly meritorious; and they were, no doubt, on the whole calculated to change and meliorate the condition of the Lacedæmonians, and to make them a great and potent people.

When Lycurgus had thus perfected, as he imagined, the form of the commonwealth which he had planned, his thoughts were employed in rendering it fixed and stable. For this purpose he obliged the Lacedæmonians by an oath, that they should strictly adhere to the laws he had promulged, until his return from Delphi, whither he was going to consult the oracle, relative to something of which he would afterwards inform them. Being arrived at Delphi, he inquired of the oracle, if the laws he had given the Lacedæmonians were sufficient to make them happy; and was answered, that nothing was wanting to render them perfect. This response he sent to Sparta, and then voluntarily starved himself to death. Different accounts are, however, given of the place and manner of his death. Some say, he died in Crete, and that he commanded his ashes to be thrown into the sea, lest they should be afterward carried to Sparta, and the Lacedæmonians thereby consider themselves released from their oath.

The state thus instituted was soon at war with the Messenians, a neighbouring people. The causes of this war are not certainly known; the Messenians accusing the Lacedæmonians of promoting it, and the Lacedæmonians retorting the charge. But as the assigned causes tend to mark the manners of the age, we shall briefly notice them. Some Spartan virgins had repaired to the temple of Diana, situated between Laconia and Messenia, and to which the inhabitants of both states were wont to resort. These virgins were violated by the Messenians; and Teleclus, one of the kings of Sparta, was slain in attempting their rescue. The Messenians, on the contrary, asserted that the pretended virgins were armed youths in disguise, who, with Teleclus, had come thither to assassinate their chiefs. To this quarrel another provocation was soon after added. Euphænus, a Lacedæmonian, had received some cattle into his pastures, belonging to a Messenian of high birth, named Polychares. Euphænus sold the cattle, and pretended they were lost. Polychares sent his son to receive the money for them; whereupon Euphænus caused him to be assassinated. The Messenian went several times to Sparta, to demand justice and redress, but experienced only insults and derisions. He therefore retaliated his wrongs upon the Lacedæmonians, and slew all of that kingdom, with whom he happened to meet. These private outrages naturally produced national animosity; and occasioned an open rupture betweeen the two states. After expostulations had passed between the two kingdoms, a publick war commenced, which private justice might have prevented. It was carried on for many years with various success, and the issue was doubtful. At length the Messenians, prompted by the desire

B. C. 743.

of freeing themselves from an oppressive state
of hostility, sent to consult the oracle at Delphi.
The answer returned was, that a virgin of the
royal family of Æpytus should be sacrificed to
the gods, otherwise the utter ruin of the whole
Messenian nation would inevitably follow. Upon
this, lots were cast, and the daughter of Lycis-
cus was the virgin on whom the chance fell.
She, however, being considered as supposititious,
Aristodemus voluntarily offered his own daughter to be the devoted victim. But her lover,
who was present, asserted, that the mariage between them was already consummated, and that
she was with child by him. This enraged Aristodemus so much, that he instantly slew her;
and, that he might vindicate the honour of his
family, by proving the falsehood of his assertion, caused the body to be dissected. Publick
rejoicings followed the sacrifice of this virgin;
and the Messenians concluded they should now
be victors. After a war, however, of twenty
years continuance, in which the Lacedæmonians and Messenians were by turns conquerors,
B.C. 724. Aristodemus, finding all things desperate, slew himself on the grave of his
daughter; and the kingdom of Messenia
became tributary to Sparta.

Among the events of this war, we must not
omit to mention one, which, extraordinary as it
may appear, is affirmed by many ancient writers
to have been authentick. The absence of the
Lacedæmonians from Sparta, in consequence of
the oath taken at the commencement of the war,
not to return until their designs were accomplished, was for a long time supported by their
wives with great fortitude. But after the lapse
of several years, and their being no prospect that

Messenia would be shortly subdued, the wives sent to represent to them how much they neglected the city. In consequence of this message, the Spartans decreed, that the Lacedæmonian youths who were under age, and had not bound themselves by the oath, should return to Sparta, and, associating themselves promiscuously with the young women, preserve the city from falling into decay. When the war was at length terminated, the offspring of these promiscuous embraces found themselves contemned by the other citizens. They thereupon joined in a revolt with the Helotes, some of whom, dreading the consequences, divulged the conspiracy. They were, therefore, permitted, under the conduct of their leader Phalantus, to sail to Italy, where they settled, and founded the city Tarentum.

After the Messenians had been tributaries to the Spartans for thirty-nine years, they endeavoured to shake off the yoke; and the Argians and Arcadians having promised them their assistance, the war was begun a second time. Aristomenes was commander of the Messenian forces. He defeated the Lacedæmonians in the first engagement, which continued for a long time, and was obstinately contested. The oracle being consulted, the Spartans were advised to seek a leader from Athens. The Athenians, envious of the glory of Lacedæmon, sent them Tyrtæus, a schoolmaster and poet, lame of one foot, and suspected of insanity. As soon as the Spartan kings appeared in the field, they offered the enemy battle; and were a second time routed by Aristomenes. A third defeat followed soon after. And the Spartans growing weary of the war, dissatisfied with

B. C. 685.

their kings, and diffident of their own power, sunk into the greatest dejection and despondency. Now it was that Tyrtæus became useful to them: he encouraged them by his poems; directed them by his counsels; and recruited their armies by men chosen from among the Helotes. The Messenians suffered a discomfiture soon after, in which their general Aristomenes was taken prisoner. With many others of his countrymen, he was thrown into a deep cavern; and was the only person not killed by the fall. Perceiving a fox gnawing a body near him, Aristomenes seized the animal by the tail and mouth, and followed him until he came to a small crevice, through which he forced himself, and opened a passage to the light. He was received with joy and amazement by the Messenians; and falling upon the Corinthians, at that time the allies of the Spartans, he put them completely to the rout. He was, however, seized again by some Cretans; but they being made drunk, he stabbed them with their own daggers, and returned to his troops. He is said to have celebrated three times the hecatomphonia, or sacrifice appointed for those, who had killed a hundred of the enemies with their own hands. But he could not avert the ruin of his country. The city of Eira was taken, and Messenia annexed to the Spartan territory. Tyrtæus, the Spartan general, was made free of their city, the highest honour they could confer; and Lacedæmon, by the accession of the Messenian country, became one of the most powerful states of all Greece, and inferior only to Athens.

B. C. 664.

CHAP. III.

The Government of Athens, from the Establishment of the Archons to the Expulsion of Hippias.

THOUGH the Athenians refused to have any other king but Jupiter, after the death of Codrus, they nevertheless made his son Medon their supreme magistrate, under the humbler title of archon. This office was at first for life, but was afterward rendered decennial. The extinction of the family of Medon, however, gave the Athenians an opportunity of making the archonship annual. Nor did they commit

B. C. 634.

the whole power to one person, but created nine archons yearly; and by these means made the supreme magistrate dependent on the people. Before the time of

B. C. 623.

Draco, who succeeded to the archonship, the Athenians had no written laws. He therefore undertook to alter the judicature of his country, and to compose a code of laws. Every crime, from the most enormous to the most trifling, was considered as equally heinous, and therefore punished with death. The severity of such a system defeated its own purposes. Aristotle tells us, Herodicus used to say, "That his institutions seemed rather to have come from a dragon than a man;" and Demades rendered himself famous by observing, "that Draco's laws were not written with ink, but with blood."

In this state of things, the character of Solon attracted the attention of all parties. Beloved by all for his private virtues, his wisdom and learning procured him the respect and admira-

B. C. 594.

tion of the publick. He was therefore advanced to the archontic office, with full power to reform the laws and constitution of the state. His friends advised him to endeavour to procure the regal power, but this he absolutely refused; alleging that "tyranny resembled a fair garden; it is a beautiful spot while we are within, but it wants a way to get out." Rejecting, therefore, the idea of royalty, he resolved to give the Athenians the best laws, which they were capable of receiving. Wherever he found things tolerable in the constitution, he refused to change them* ; and was at considerable pains to explain the reason and necessity of the alterations he made; laying it down as a maxim, that those laws will be best observed, which power and justice equally support.

The first act of this great man, after he was advanced to his high office, was to cancel the laws of Draco, those only excepted which related to murder. He next abolished the debts of the poor, by a law of insolvency. To do this, however, with the least injury, he lowered the interest, and increased the value of money. In the midst of this transaction, some of his intimate friends, betraying the trust reposed in them by Solon, borrowed large sums of money, with which they purchased estates, before the edict was published. This fraud was, at first, supposed to have been by the connivance of

---

* How vastly would it have redounded to the honour of reformers in all ages, and to the happiness of individuals who are the victims of their innovations, had they carried in their minds, and adopted in their practice, the prudent caution of Solon

Solon; but the suspicions were soon found to be without foundation, when he himself appeared to be a loser by the law he had passed.

He next proceeded to regulate the offices, employments, and magistracies of the state, all of which he committed to the care of the rich. But as the desire of Solon was to act with moderation and prudence, while he intrusted the execution of the government to the nobles, the supreme power was placed in the people. For this purpose, he distributed the Athenians into four classes: those that were possessed of five hundred measures yearly, whether of corn or liquids, were placed in the first rank, and paid an annual sum of money to the publick treasury. The second class consisted of those, who were worth three hundred measures. And those that had two hundred measures, and not more, constituted the third rank. The fourth and last class, comprehended all those whose incomes did not amount to two hundred measures; and to them no office or employment in the state was assigned. They had, however, the power of voting in the general assembly of the nation; and though this was at first considered as a matter of little or no importance, it was afterward found to be productive of the greatest advantages to the people. For, as Solon had purposely drawn up his laws in obscure and ambiguous terms, an appeal from the decisions of the magistrates to the general assembly of the nation was always permitted; and, therefore, in process of time, all affairs of importance came before them, and awaited their ultimate decision.

But, in order to guard against the influence of this democracy, he conferred greater power on the court of Areopagus, which had been deprived of much of its authority during the archonship of Draco. Before the time of Solon, the Areopagus was composed of persons conspicuous in the state for their wealth, power, and probity. But he passed a law, that none should be created members of this court, unless they had previously filled the office of archon. This had the desired effect; and the reputation of this tribunal was thereby raised to such a height, that for several ages, the judgment and integrity of its decisions were never called in question. The power of the Areopagus was very great; and it is said to have been the first court that ever sat upon life and death. It was the custom, to hold their sittings in the night only, and without light. The purpose of this singularity is said to have been, that the members might not be prejudiced for, or against, any accused persons, by seeing their gestures and their looks. Truth only was regarded; and no attempt to warp the opinion of the judges was permitted. Solon also formed a senate, to consist of four hundred persons. These had the cognizance of all appeals from the Areopagus, and the examination of all causes, before they could be proposed to the general assembly of the nation.

Such were the general institutions, which Solon established for the government of Athens. The particular laws, which this legislator enacted, were more numerous. In the first place, all those who, in an insurrection or schism of the people, should retire from the evils which had fallen upon their country, and observe a blamable and dangerous neutrality, were condemned to perpetual banishment, and their estates and property were confiscated. This law has been highly and justly commended, as tending to bring matters to a speedy and safe conclusion, and deterring the seditious from exciting discord and dissension in the state. For, as honest and good men would naturaly espouse the part of those, who appeared to act conscientiously and uprightly, the wicked and factious would dread their opposition. And, by making every man considered as an enemy to his country, who should appear indifferent and unconcerned in times of public danger and tumult, he consulted the good of the state and provided against the most pressing emergencies.

. He abolished the custom of giving portions in marriage with young women, unless they were only daughters. The bride was to carry no more with her than three suits of clothes, and some household goods of trifling value. The intent of Solon by this was, to render marriage no longer a traffic; but to promote a union of congenial minds and mutual affection.

. It would be tedious and unnecessary to enter into any farther details of the subordinate institutions of this legislator. They have since become the basis of the civil law of Europe; and we may with reason affirm, that his constitutions are still partly in force.

. After his laws had been promulged, persons were coming to him daily to have them explained, to know the reasons on which they were founded, and to advise him to alter certain particular parts, according to their own humour or interest. Wearied, therefore, with these importunities, and to afford means to his great work of settling into firmness, Solon determined to travel ; and having bound the Athenians by an oath, that his institutions should be changed in no part for the space of ten years, he departed on his journey.

Soon after Solon had left Athens, three different parties appeared among the people : those of the highlands, the lowlands, and the coast. They inflamed the minds of the Athenians against one another, and endeavoured to subvert and usurp the government. Lycurgus was at the head of the country people ; Megacles was the chief of the inhabitants upon the seacoast ; and Pisistratus, in order, as he pretended, to protect those in the highlands from tyranny, declared himself their leader.

Pisistratus was of these the most powerful. He was courteous and affable, generous without profusion, and beneficent without ostentation. Two or three slaves constantly attended him, with bags of silver and gold ; and when he saw any one out of health, or heard of a person dying insolvent, he was ready to do every thing in his power to relieve him. He appeared to be a lover of equal rights, and of the constitution. Solon, however, saw through his dissimulation, and was wont to say, " Sir, were it not for your ambition, you would be the best citizen in Athens." This man was at the eve of success, and upon the very point of attaining the summit of his ambition, when Solon, after an absence of ten years, returned to Athens. All the factions pretended the greatest reverence and respect for their legislator, and requested him to resume his authority, and to compose the differences in the state. He left no means untried to bring the chiefs and their followers to reason, and to moderate the spirit of opposition ; but in vain. Solon, now arrived at an advanced age, was not able to quell the factions, and direct the helm of government in the storm; and Pisistratus, by artifice and duplicity, became master of the commonwealth.

B. C. 561. Having purposely wounded himself, he drove his chariot into the market-place, as if pursued by his enemies; and, exhibiting his mangled and bleeding body to the populace, requested their protection. A general assembly was immediately convened, and Ariston, one of his partizans, proposed to decree a guard of fifty men for the security of the friend of the people, and the martyr of their cause. Solon opposed the motion as much as he was able; but finding his efforts were vain and fruitless, he withdrew. And so great was the popularity of Pisistratus, and such the indignation excited by the visible marks of ill-treatment, which he bore, that the proposal of Ariston was immediately agreed to. Having obtained the guards, which was all that he aimed at, he seized the citadel, and assumed the sovereignty of Athens.

Pisistratus, however, did not change any thing in the Athenian constitution. On the contrary, he endeavoured, with all his power, to provide for the better execution of the laws. Nor did he lose any of that moderation, for which he had before been so remarkable. And not only the assembly, council, magistracies, and courts of justice, remained with their full constitutional powers, but Pisistratus is said to have shown his respect for the laws, by obeying a citation from the Areopagus on a charge of murder.

Solon did not survive the assumption of the regal power by Pisistratus, above two years.

He died at Cyprus, in the eightieth year of his age. After his death, the Athenians paid him the highest honours, and erected in the forum, and at Salamis (of which he was a native), a statue of him in brass, with his hand in his gown, the posture in which he was accustomed to harangue the people. Beside knowledge of legislation, he was a very eloquent speaker, and excellent in poetry.

After the death of Solon, Megacles and Lycurgus, the chiefs of the other factions, who had been disappointed in their designs upon the government, uniting their interests together, drove Pisistratus from Athens. Megacles, however, finding his hopes a second time blasted by the faction of Lycurgus, offered to reinstate Pisistratus in his kingdom, provided he would marry his daughter. To this proposal Pisistratus readily assented; but a majority in the Athenian assembly must be obtained, otherwise this compact would avail little. To effect this, therefore, a very ridiculous project was resolved to be attempted. They found, we are told, a woman, whose name was Phya, the daughter of Socrates, a man of mean family and fortune. This woman, being of a prodigious size and very handsome, they placed in a chariot dressed in armour; and having made her appear to all possible advantage, conducted her towards the city, and sent heralds before to address the people in these words, "Give a kind reception, O Athenians, to Pisistratus, whom Minerva honours so much, that she condescends to bring him back to the citadel." When the heralds had published this intimation in several parts of the city, the multitude believing the woman to be the goddess Minerva, worshipped her, and received Pisistratus, who thus recovered the sovereignty.

After this, however, he was deposed by Megacles, with whom he had quarrelled about domestic affairs. Retiring, therefore, to Eretria, in Eubœa, with his two sons, he consulted the means of recovering the kingdom. Hippias proposed to his father to attempt Athens by force of arms. This was accordingly agreed upon, and some of the other Grecian states affording him their assistance, he defeated the Athenians in an engagement, and a third time possessed himself of the sovereignty.

Some anecdotes are related of Pisistratus, which are creditable to him. Certain young men, that had been drinking at a feast, in their return home met the wife of Pisistratus, and grossly insulted her. The next day, however, reflecting upon what they had done, they went in the most humble manner to entreat forgiveness. Pisistratus heard their apology very graciously, and then said, "Gentlemen, I would advise you to behave more modestly for the future; but as for my wife, she was not abroad yesterday." It happened once that Pisistratus, who, as prince of Athens, received the tenth part of every man's rents, and of the fruits of his ground, perceived an old man gathering something amongst the rocks, he inquired of the man what he was doing, and what were the fruits of his labours. "Troubles and a few plants of wild sage, replied he, and of these Pisistratus must have the tenth." Pisistratus said no more, but, when he returned to the city, he exempted him from paying this duty. This prince was eminent also for his love of learning and of the fine arts. He was the first that built a library for public inspection; and by him the poems of Homer were collected and digested into that order, in which we have them at present. Cicero speaks of him as the first model of that eloquence, in which Greece so eminently excelled. He adorned the city with the most splendid buildings. And he continued to direct the government of Athens with wisdom and ability, and died at an advanced age in peace.

B. C. 527. Upon the death of Pisistratus, Hippias and Hipparchus, his sons, succeeded to the government. They appeared to inherit all their father's virtues; and greatly favoured learning and learned men. Anacreon, of Teos, and Simonides, of Cea, were invited to Athens, and maintained there. Hipparchus directed the rhapsodists, or professional bards, to recite the poems of Homer, at the great feast Panathenæa, that the people might be instructed in the sciences, and the moral conduct of life. And so assiduous was this prince in cultivating the minds of the Athenians, that he caused statues of Mercury to be set up in different places, on which were inscribed short moral sentences.

B. C. 512. Hipparchus was slain by a conspiracy. The circumstances that occasioned his death are wrapt in inexplicable mystery. Certain, however, it is, that the motives which impelled to this act were of a private, not a public nature. Aristogiton and Harmodius, two Athenians of middle rank, determined the death of the two brothers. They resolved to put their design in execution at the feast Panathenæa, when, as all the citizens were wont to go armed, their arms would not excite suspicion. Hippias was to have been slain first, but seeing him engaged in discourse with one of the conspirators, they dreaded that all was discovered. Taking courage, therefore, from the supposed desperateness of their condition, they attacked Hipparchus, and dispatched him. Harmodius was killed by the guard of Hipparchus; and Aristogiton, being taken by the people, was delivered into the power of Hippias.

All those whom he suspected of being privy to this design, Hippias caused to be apprehended; and as the supreme power was now lodged in his own hands, he treated the people with a severity unknown before. The effects of this change in his temper naturally fell, in the first place, on those concerned in the conspiracy. He commanded Aristogiton to be put to the torture, that he might extort from him the names of the other conspirators. This man, as soon as he felt the torments prepared for him, mentioned some of Hippias's best friends, who were immediately put to death. He then named more, who received the same fate; and when Hippias asked him, if there were not still others, he replied smiling, " I know of no one now, but yourself, that deserves to suffer death." Leæna, also, a woman that lived with him, behaved with no less intrepidity. Hippias having directed her to be tortured, she bore the pain very patiently for a considerable time; but when she could endure it no longer, she bit off her tongue, that it might not be in her power to declare any thing injurious to the man she loved. The Athenians, who always honoured virtue, would not permit the memory of this action to be forgotten. They erected a statue on which was represented a lioness without a tongue.

This conspiracy being, as Hippias conceived,

completely terminated, he endeavoured to secure himself in the possession of his dignity, by all the measures which human policy and invention could possibly suggest. He contracted friendship and alliances with foreign princes, and married his daughter to the son of the tyrant of Lampascus. After having thus strengthened his power, he increased his revenues by various methods, and obliged the Athenians to bring in their silver and gold at a certain price. These violent and oppressive modes of proceeding rendered Hippias and his government odious and detested.

. In the mean time the Alcmæonids, ejected by Pisistratus, had become numerous and wealthy, and resided at Lipsydrium. This family and their partizans were always contriving means for recovering Athens, and expelling the tyrants from that state. It happened, that the temple at Delphi was burnt. They agreed with the amphictyonic council, to rebuild it: and, being possessed of great riches, they executed their undertaking with more munificence than the contract required, and fronted the temple with Parian marble. This liberality had the desired effect: the pythia was corrupted, and engaged in all her oracles, to conclude her answers to the supplicants from Lacedæmon, with an admonition to the Spartans to procure the liberty of Athens. The Lacedæmonians finding this advice incessantly inculcated, and though the family of Pisistratus was at that time their friends and allies, Athens was invaded. Their first attempt was unsuccessful : but the severities of Hippias drove numbers to join them : and the Lacedæmonians, irritated by their defeat, prepared in earnest for revenge. They sent a larger army, which, being joined by the Alcmæonids, laid siege to Athens. The Athenians attempted to send their children out of the garrison to a place of safety; but the Lacedæmonians made them prisoners. Hippias and his partizans, not being able by any other means to procure them their liberty, consented to surrender Athens, and leave its territory in five days. Hippais retired to Segieum on the Hellespont,

B. C. 509.
which had been conquered by his father Pisistratus, and was under the government of Hegistratus; and Athens once more recovered its liberty. The Alcmæonids were chiefly instrumental in this change; but the Athenians considered themselves under greater obligations to the two friends, who had first conspired against the tyrants. The names of Aristogiton and Harmodius were held in the highest reverence, in all succeeding ages; and statues to their memory were erected in the market-place, an honour never granted to any before; and from them the people caught that innate love of freedom, that deep hatred of tyranny, which neither time nor terrors could ever after efface.

CHAP. IV.

The Transactions of Greece, from the Expulsion of Hippias, to the Death of Darius.

THE Lacedæmonians, were, at this time, at the head of the Grecian states. Obliged by the constitution of their government to submit to a singular kind of monkish poverty, their ambition knew no bounds. The conquest of Messenia, their ancient alliance with Corinth, and their superiority in power over the rest of the neighbouring communities, enabled them, in a great measure, to command the whole of Peloponnesus. Still, however, they permitted no opportunity to pass, which might serve to extend their influence, and increase their dominion. Whenever the Grecian states had war with one another, or internal sedition agitated any of them, the Lacedæmonians were always ready to offer themselves as mediators between the contending parties. The business of their interference was generally conducted with wisdom, and an appearance of moderation. But they never lost sight of the great end for which their services were offered; and always endeavoured to extend their authority, or the influence of their state. To every community, in which their assistance was for any purpose requested, they attempted to give an oligarchical form of government; for in almost every one of the Grecian states, an aristocratical and a democratical faction existed; and the Lacedæmonians were sensible, that a few chiefs, indebted to them for their situation, and which they should be unable to retain without their assistance, would be the most likely to oblige that state to become subject to Sparta, under the more honourable name of alliance.

The same policy it was proposed to pursue with respect to Athens; and the factions that arose there appeared to give a sufficient opportunity for effecting it. By the late revolution in affairs, Clysthenes son of Megacles, and the most eminent of the Alcmæonids, became, of course, the first personage in the commonwealth. Isagoras, however, a man of birth and fortune, and respected by the nobility of Athens, opposed Clysthenes. But the latter, being a favourite of the people, contrived to divide the establishment into ten tribes, instead of four, of which it formerly consisted; and also increased the number of the senate to five hundred persons. Isagoras perceiving the intent of this change in the constitution, applied to Lacedæmon for assistance. Cleomenes, king of Sparta, immediately commanded the Athenians to banish all the Alcmæonids, otherwise war should be declared against Athens. Clysthenes obeyed the decree. Encouraged therefore by this proof of respect, Cleomenes marched an army to Athens, and banished at once seven hundred families. He then proceeded to dissolve the council appointed by Clysthenes, and to commit the commonwealth to the care of three hundred persons, all of them partizans of Isagoras. But the Athenians, being sensible they must either submit to slavery, or resist the Lacedæmonians, flew to arms, and obliged Cleomenes and Isagoras to retire to the citadel, where they were besieged two days, and then surrendered. After Cleomenes and Isagoras had departed from the city, Clysthenes and the banished families were immediately recalled.

The Lacedæmonians repenting the services they had rendered Athens, and perceiving the sinister designs of the Delphic oracle, were desirous of restoring Hippias again to the sovereignty. He was accordingly sent for from Sigeium, and after a long voyage arrived at Lacedæmon, where the Spartan kings, and the deputies of the states in alliance with them, held a consultation. Sosicles, the Corinthian, however, harangued most eloquently against the proposi-

tion for restoring Hippias; and influenced the
deputies of the other states so much, that the Lacedæmonians were constrained to abandon Hippias and his cause for ever.

The Ionians being at war with the Persians,
they sent to Athens to request assistance; whereupon Melanthius, an Athenian nobleman, was
dispatched with a fleet of ships to Ionia. By the
help of these, great exploits were performed,
and the Ionians sacked Sardis. When the Persian king heard of this, he declared himself the
enemy of Athens, and earnestly desired he
might at some time have it in his power to revenge the injury. The Ionians were soon after
reduced to the subjection of Darius.

Hippias, therefore, being disappointed of the
hope held out to him by the Lacedæmonians,
went over into Asia; and applying to Artaphernes, governor of the adjacent provinces belonging to the Persian king, promised him, if he
would restore him to his former authority at
Athens, that he would thenceforth be obedient
and tributary to Darius. The Athenians, in the
meanwhile, not ignorant of the journey or proposals of Hippias, sent embassadors to Artaphernes, entreating him to give no attention to Hippias, but to suffer the people of Athens to remain free and undisturbed in their present situation. This nobleman, however, conceiving that
it would be more advantageous to Darius if
Athens should be under a regal, than a democratical government, answered the embassadors,
that if the Athenians would be safe, they must
receive Hippias as their king. The return of
these embassadors occasioned a ferment in
Athens. Universal indignation, not unaccom-
panied with a fear for the safety and liberty of
their country was immediately excited.

When the news arrived, that the Persian had in view the conquest of Greece, the Athenians and inhabitants of Ægina, with others of the Grecian states, wisely compromised some differences that had arisen amongst them, and which had produced some inconsiderable engagements, that they might exert all their force against the common enemy.

In the mean time, Darius desisted not from his design of undertaking an expedition against Greece, that he might gratify his revenge for the insults and injuries received from the Athenians. Mardonius was accordingly appointed commander of a fleet and army destined to attack Greece; but, being unskilful, he lost many of his ships in a violent tempest, as they were sailing round a point of land, formed by Mount Athos; and his troops, in passing through Thrace, were attacked by the inhabitants of that country in the night, and great numbers of them slain. This expedition having failed by means of these two disasters, Mardonius was compelled to relinquish the enterprise, and to return home.

Darius now, wishing to know which of the Grecian states he might consider as friends or foes, dispatched heralds to the several communities of Greece, to demand of them " earth and water," * as tokens of their submission to his government. To this haughty claim of the Persian monarch many towns on the continent, and most of the islands, acceded. But at Sparta and Athens, a determined refusal was not only given, but the publick indignation was vented against the Persian heralds, one of whom was thrown

---

* An ancient mode of claiming superiority on one side, and acknowledging subjection on the other.

into a pit, the other into a well, and they were told to take their "earth and water" there.

Darius finding that this limited undertaking would have great obstacles to contend with, before Greece could be conquered, increased his armament to five hundred ships, and five hundred thousand men; and gave the command to B. C. 496. Datis and Artaphernes. This expedition accordingly set sail; and Hippias, now an old man, served as guide and conductor. The conquest of Greece being the only and the avowed object, it was resolved to avoid the circuitous rout, which Mardonius pursued. They therefore drew their forces into the plains of Cilicia, and thence passed through the Cyclades to Euboea. As soon however as the Persian fleet was descried by the inhabitants of Eretria, they sent to demand the assistance of Athens. That state immediately ordered four thousand men to their aid. But the Eretrians were divided amongst themselves; and after resisting the enemy six days, the place was betrayed to the Persians, who pillaged and burnt the city, and sold the inhabitants for slaves, according to the command of Darius. Previously to this, Æschines, the son of Nothon, seeing all hopes of defending Eretria useless, advised the commanders of the Athenian troops to return home, and reserve themselves for the defence of their native country. In consequence of this advice, they crossed to Oropus, and arrived safe in Attica.

The Persian generals allowed very little respite to their troops, before they advanced against Athens. In this alarming situation, no measures had been concerted for general security; and the enemy passed into Greece before any common defence had been proposed. The Athenians mustered all their forces, which, when joined by one thousand Platæans, did not amount to more than ten thousand men. These troops were commanded by ten general officers, possessing equal power; amongst whom were Miltiades, Aristides, and Themistocles, men of distinguished valour and abilities. But conceiving that it would be utterly impossible for this small number of forces to withstand the Persian army, they sent to Sparta, to request the immediate assistance of that state. The Lacedæmonians on this emergency readily agreed to the proposal, and ordered their troops to be ready to march; but at the same time declared, that, on account of a law prohibiting the commencement of an expedition, except at the full of the moon, they could not depart within five days. In the mean time, Hippias having informed the Persians, that Marathon was an extensive plain, where their horse might be able to act with the greatest advantage, they marched thither. And the Athenians, being apprised of the enemy's motions, commanded their troops to the same place.

As soon as the Greeks came within sight of the Persian army and the plains of Marathon, Miltiades determined on an immediate attack. In this he was joined by Callimachus, the polemarch; who, according to the laws of the Athenians, had the supreme power over the forces and generals. Each of the generals commanded by turns; but Aristides permitting Miltiades to command in his place, the rest followed his example. Miltiades accepted this compliment for the good of his country, but would not engage till it was his proper turn to take the com-

mand. When that day arrived, without waiting
for more assistance, he disposed his troops in
order of battle, and placed his forces principally
in the wings. Finding the Athenians extremely
animated, he commanded them to lay aside their
missile weapons, to advance down the hill with
great rapidity, and to engage the enemy in close
fight. This order was instantly and cheerfully
obeyed. The Persians, who had not been accustomed to receive the onset of the enemy, imputed this attack to the folly of the Athenians,
and their ignorance of military discipline; and
what served to corroborate this opinion was,
that neither horse, nor pikemen, appeared a-
mongst them. The effect of the shock, however, proved the wisdom of the plan. For,
though the Asiatic horse was reckoned formidable in champaign countries, yet in this confined plain, and encumbered with a numerous
infantry, it was unable to act with advantage.
The battle was a long time contested; but at
length the Persians perceiving the centre of the
Athenian army weak, attacked it with great
force, and broke through the line. This disaster those on the right and left were sensible of,
but did not attempt to remedy, until they had put
the enemies to flight. Then joining their divided forces, they met the conquering centre of
the Persian army, defeated it, and following to
the shore the fleeing enemy, made a very dreadful slaughter. The Persians hurried on board
their fleet; but the Athenians took seven galleys, and destroyed several others. The Persians lost, according to Herodotus, six thousand
three hundred men, and the Athenians one hundred and ninety-two; but amongst the latter
were some of the most eminent men in the com-

monwealth. Every one indeed seemed emulous to save their country, and to share the glory of the battle; and the highest praise is due to the valour of the Athenian troops. "The Athenians who fought at Marathon," says the Greek historian, "were the first among the Greeks known to have used running, for the purpose of coming at once to close fight; and they were the first who withstood (in the field) even the sight of the Median dress, and of the men who wore it; for hitherto the very name of the Medes and Persians had been a terror to the Greeks." Justin says, that Cynegyrus, the brother of the poet Æschylus, having performed prodigies of valour in the battle, pursued the Persians to the shore, and laid hold of a ship which was ready to sail with his right hand. Some of the enemy seeing this, cut it off, on which he seized it with his left; and being deprived of that also, he fastened his teeth in it, and thus expired. The same author tells us, that Hippias, who expected to have been restored to the kingdom of Athens by the power of the Persians, perished in this engagement; but others relate, that he escaped, and died miserably at Lemnos.

· The collective accounts that are given of this battle seem sufficiently consistent, to engage us to confide in the general veracity of the historians. The greatest inconsistency would seem in the small number of the Athenians, that are reported to have been slain, contrasted with the slaughter of the Persians. But this is not improbable; and in authentick accounts of battles in different ages, as great a disparity of numbers has appeared.

· After the battle of Marathon, however, the Persian armament was still formidable; nor

was Athens, by the effects of this glorious victory, immediately delivered from the danger with
which it was menaced. The Persian commander,
in hopes of carrying the city by a sudden assault,
doubled Cape Sunium, and bore away for Athens.
But Miltiades, seeing the danger of his countrymen, and leaving Aristides with a thousand
troops to guard the prisoners and spoils, marched, in all haste, the rest of the forces, and arrived at a small distance from the city before
the enemy was in a condition to attack it. As
soon as the Persian admiral had notice, that
Miltiades and the Athenians were so near, he
weighed anchor from Phalerum, and steered
for Asia, without attempting any thing farther.
The Eretrians, who had been made prisoners,
Darius settled on an estate, about twenty-four
miles from his capital.

No sooner was Athens delivered by the victory of Marathon from impending destruction,
than the Athenians meditated revenge on those
islands, which had exerted themselves in the
cause of Persia. For this purpose, they fitted
out a fleet of seventy ships, to exact fines from
them for their delinquency, or to punish them in
a different manner according to circumstances.
Of this fleet Miltiades was appointed commander. He first sailed to the island of Paros, demanded a hundred talents to be paid him ; and,
in case of refusal, threatened to besiege and plunder the city. The Parians, however, were not
to be terrified. They even refused to deliberate
on what he proposed, and prepared for an obstinate and vigorous defence. Miltiades accordingly invested the city ; but, after encamping before it for twenty-six days, he accidentally re-

ceived a wound, and was obliged to raise the siege.

On his return, the whole city began to murmur. Xanthippus, one of the principal men in Athens, and father of the famous Pericles, accused him of having deceived the Athenians; and demanded that the general assembly of the people should pass sentence of death upon him. Miltiades could not appear in the assembly on account of his wound; and, therefore, his brother pleaded for him. He was acquitted of any capital offence, but condemned in a fine of fifty thousand talents, the expense of the Parian expedition. Not able immediately to discharge so large a sum, he was cast into prison; and, his wound mortifying, he died there. The glory of Miltiades, however, survived the life of that hero; and though the Athenians were unjust to his person, they were not unmindful of his fame. At the distance of half a century, the battle of Marathon was painted by order of the state, and the figure of Miltiades was placed in the foreground, animating the troops to victory.

After the Athenians were freed from all apprehensions of foreign invasion, they became, as is too frequently seen in the annals of nations, disunited amongst themselves; and were divided in opinion, whether Athens should be under an aristocratical or democratical form of government. Aristides espoused the sentiments of the one party, and Themistocles those of the opposite faction. They were nearly of the same age, and equally noble; and though not of royal descent, were in the first rank of citizens. They had likewise both been named among the generals that commanded at the battle of Marathon. The disinterestedness of Aristides, on this me-

morable occasion, has been already noticed ; and
it afforded a promise of his future fame. Formed
in the celebrated schools of moral and political
knowledge, which at that time existed in Athens,
he had been taught to prefer glory to pleasure ;
the interest of his country to his own personal
safety and reputation ; and the dictates of justice
and humanity to every other consideration. His
ambition seemed more desirous of deserving,
than acquiring the esteem and applause of his
fellow-citizens ; and while he enjoyed the in-
ward satisfaction of a pure and upright intention,
he was little solicitous to obtain the external rewards of virtuous exertions. The character of
Themistocles was more dubious. The glory and
fame which Miltiades acquired in the battle of
Marathon, disturbed his quiet, and excited his
jealousy. He was inflamed with ambitious designs ; and was desirous of performing great and
martial exploits. He was eloquent, active, and
enterprising, and had strengthened his natural
endowments by the acquisition of science. The
laws, government, revenue, and military discipline of his country, were the great objects of
his study. In defending his friends, or accusing
his enemies, the courts of justice afforded him
opportunities of displaying his abilities, and he
was generally successful. Whatever matter
came before the publick assembly, he was the
first to discuss and deliberate upon it ; and his
advice, founded on a just knowledge of men and
of things, and assisted by all the arts of eloquence,
commonly prevailed. Nevertheless, with all
these great and shining qualities, his mind was
less smitten with the native charms of virtue,
than captivated with her splendid and external

attractions. Glory was the idol of his heart ; the divinity to which he paid unceasing homage.

Such were the two men, who were then at the head of affairs in the Athenian commonwealth. Aristides saw the danger of allowing to Themistocles, whose virtue was equivocal, the sole management of the republick. He therefore opposed every measure that could contribute to the elevation of a man, who, by means of his abilities and thirst of glory, might possibly subvert the government of his country. But the interest of Themistocles prevailed over that of his rival; and he had the address to procure a nomination to the command of a fleet, destined to act against those islands in the Ægean sea, that had put themselves under the protection of Persia, and to chastise which Miltiades had before attempted, but was unsuccessful. Whilst Themistocles gained honour and fortune abroad, Aristides increased his popularity at home. The splendid eloquence and engaging manners of his rival were not now opposed against the stern but inflexible integrity of Aristides, and he, therefore, became the chief leader of the people. His conduct was so exemplary and upright, that he acquired the surname of Just, and was considered by the Athenians as the most worthy and virtuous citizen in the state.

Such was the situation of Aristides, when Themistolces returned triumphant from his naval expedition. Fully sensible of the caprice and inconstancy of the people, he conceived it would be no difficult task to destroy a rival, who had attained so great a reputation as Aristides now possessed. Insinuating, therefore, that Aristides had acquired an undue influence in the state, which was inconsistent with the liberty of the

Athenians; and that, by assuming to himself the
arbitration of all differences and disputes, he had
silently and imperceptibly established a monarchy, without pomp or guards, Themistocles
irritated the people against his rival. Suddenly,
and when it was least expected, the multitude
flocked to the forum, and demanded the ostracism. Aristides, trusting to the innocence and
integrity of his heart, disdained to employ any
unworthy means for gaining the favour, or
averting the resentment, of his fellow-citizens.
One of the countrymen, who could neither read
nor write, brought his shell to Aristides, and
said, " Write me Aristides upon this." Aristides, astonished at the request of the man, asked
him if he knew any injustice done by that Athenian; or, if he had ever received any injury
from him. " No," replied the countryman, " I
do not even know him ; but I am grieved to hear
him so much praised. " Aristides, without saying any thing more, took the shell, and wrote his
own name upon it. He gave, however, a still
stronger proof than this of the firmness of his
mind. When he was informed by the magistrates,
that the ostracism had fallen upon him, he modestly retired from the forum; and, lifting up
his eyes to heaven, said, " I beseech the gods,
that the Athenians may never be obliged to remember Aristides."

After the banishment of Aristides, the Athenians were still more exposed to the danger,
which this severe measure was intended to remove. Themistocles, however, was called to
the task of fighting the enemies of his country,
which, in all probability, tended to preserve the
liberty of the state. Ægina, an island in the Ægean, which was in alliance with Persia, covered

the sea with her fleets, and bid defiance to Athens.
Themistocles, therefore, advised his countrymen
to augment their navy, and endeavour to destroy
the fleet of Ægina. The proposal was approved, and adopted immediately; a hundred galleys were equipped; and the naval strength of
Ægina was broken. Success animating the
Athenians, they engaged the Corcyreans in a
naval battle, and proving victorious obtained the
empire of the seas. Thus, by the prudence of
her commanders and the valour of her troops,
Athens obtained a superiority over her foes on
both elements, notwithstanding her intestine
broils.

CHAP. V.

*The Grecian Affairs, from the Accession of Xerxes
to the Throne of Persia, to the Return of that
Monarch into Asia, after his Expedition against
Greece.*

THE Spartans had now for a long time
maintained an unrivalled superiority in
Peloponnesus; and the unequal and unfortunate
opposition of the Argives had no other effect,
but to confirm the preeminence of the Laceda-
monians, and to depress themselves. The Corinthians and Achæans, the inhabitants of Elis
and Arcadia, had occasional hostilities with the
Spartan state, and with one another; but their
contests were not attended with any considerable or permanent effects. Cleomenes and Demaratus, kings of Sparta, had disagreed, and, by
the intrigues of the former, the latter was un-

justly deposed from the royal dignity. Leoty-
chidas, his kinsman and successor, insulted his
misfortunes ; and Demaratus, unable to endure
contempt in a country where he had possessed
a crown, sought for that protection, which the
Greeks denied him, from the power and resentment of the Persian monarch. Of the republicks beyond the isthmus, the Phocians had no
other aim than to enjoy in tranquillity the splendour and riches derived to them from the celebrated temple at Delphos. The Thessalians,
however, a numerous and warlike people, frequently invaded their territory. The Thebans
maintained and extended their usurpations over
the smaller cities of Bœotia ; and seemed to rejoice that the command of the sea, and the recovery of distant islands, engrossed the attention
of the Athenians so much, that they had not
time minutely to consider the affairs of the continent. The smaller and more inconsiderable
republicks followed the fortunes of their powerful neighbours. Persia had reduced the Asiatic Greeks, and Macedon paid tribute to
Xerxes. But the African colonies maintained
their independence.

Themistocles, who, according to Thucydides,
was not less sagacious in foreseeing the future,
than skilful in managing the present, declared
it to be his opinion, that the battle of Marathon
was not the end of the war, but only the prelude to new and more glorious contests. This
was subsequently verified. The Persian arms,
after the expedition against Greece, had been
employed in reducing the revolted colonies.
The three last years of Darius were spent in
making preparations for a new and formidable
expedition against Greece. For the Persians,

we are told, had not often experienced such insults as the burning of Sardis, or such defeats as the battle of Marathon. Nine years had elapsed since this famous battle, and Xerxes, the successor of Darius, was in the fourth year of his reign, when he found himself complete master of the east, and possessed of a fleet and army that flattered him with universal empire. After his accession to the throne, inheriting with the sceptre his father's thirst of revenge against Greece, he had dedicated the early years of his reign to the purpose of continuing and augmenting the preparations against that country; and, amidst his various wars and pleasures, he employed all the artisans he could procure, in fitting out an armament adequate to the extent of his ambition. Twelve hundred ships of war, and three thousand ships of burden, were at length completed. The former were stronger and larger than any before seen in the ancient world. They carried on board, at a medium, two hundred seamen, and thirty Persians, who served as marines. The ships of burden contained eighty men. And the whole, amounting to four thousand two hundred ships, and about five hundred thousand men, were ordered to rendezvous in the most secure roads and harbours of Ionia, whither B.C. 481. they proceeded. We are not informed of the exact number of the land forces; but it is certain, that they were extremely numerous, and probably increased on the march between Susa and Sardis, by the confluence of tributary nations to the imperial standard of Xerxes.

It is said, indeed, that, when the army had attained its full complement of men, it consisted of seventeen hundred thousand infantry, and four hundred thousand cavalry, which, with the fleet, made the whole forces amount to near two millions of fighting men. Besides these, an immense crowd of women and eunuchs followed the camp of this effeminate people, which, with the slaves, equalled, perhaps exceeded, the number of the soldiers; and therefore, according to the universal opinion of ancient historians, the army of Xerxes was the greatest ever collected.

B.C. 480. Xerxes having wintered his forces at Sardis, sent messengers early in the spring, with a Greek interpreter, to the several republicks of Greece, to demand "earth "and water," as tokens of their submission. The Athenians seized the interpreter, and caused him to be put to death, for presuming to publish the decrees of the Persian king in the Greek language. Arthemius also, having received large sums of money from Xerxes, and endeavouring to corrupt some of the principal persons of Athens, was banished from the republick by sound of trumpet, and his family degraded. When it was evident, however, that the king of Persia was about to enter Greece in person, with a prodigious army, a general assembly of the Grecian states was held at the isthmus, and the following resolutions were unanimously agreed to : " That the states of Greece would unite to " defend their liberty against the Persians; that " all quarrels among themselves should at pre- " sent be suspended; and that of those, who " deserted the common cause, a tenth part " should suffer death without mercy."

When the news arrived at Athens, that the Persians were about to invade Greece by the straits of Thermopylæ; and that, for this purpose, they were transporting their forces by sea; Themistocles advised his countrymen to leave their city, and embark on board the gallies, and meet the enemies at a distance from the Grecian coast. To this expedient the Athenians would not consent. He therefore put himself at the head of the Athenian forces, and joining the army of the Lacedæmonians, marched towards Tempe. In the mean while, the Thessalians, who would first be encountered by the forces of Xerxes, had sent to request the assistance of the Greeks, and to beg of them to hasten their preparations. This they accordingly did: but Thessaly being a plain country, there could be no hopes of opposing such multitudes of men with a handful of troops, especially as the princes of Thessaly were not to be depended on, and many of the passes into that country were in the hands of the king of Macedon. But, as the allied states were acquainted with only one pass, by which the Persians could penetrate into Greece, they were of opinion, that a body of eight thousand pikemen might be equally as capable as a larger proportion of troops, to defend it against every invader. This narrow defile had the appellation of the straits of Thermopylæ, from the warm springs in that neighbourhood, and was considered as the gate or entrance into Greece. It was bounded on the west by high and inaccessible precipices, which join the lofty ridge of mount Oeta; and on the east terminated by an impracticable morass that was bordered by the sea. Near the plain of Trachis, a Thessalian city, the passage was fifty feet in breadth; but at Alpene, one chariot could not pass another. These passages were defended by walls, formerly built by the Phocians to protect them against their Thessalian enemies: and the Greeks had strengthened them on the present occasion, with as much care as the time and other circumstances would permit. The troops sent to defend the straits of Thermopylæ, not far distant from the Grecian fleet stationed at Artemisium, consisted chiefly of Peloponesians, under the command of Leonidas, the Spartan king; who, in obedience to the demands of the oracle, was prepared to devote his life for the safety of his country. Leonidas being asked by some of the principal persons, if he had not some secret design, frankly answered, " I pre-" tend to defend the straits of Thermopylæ; but " in truth I go to die for my country." And when they still wondered, that he took only three hundred Spartans with him, he turned to those to whom he had communicated his secret, and said, " Considering the design on which we go, " this number is sufficient."

Before, however, these vigorous measures of the Grecian confederates had been adopted and put in execution, Xerxes had marched his army from Thrace, in three divisions; but did not arrive on the extensive plains of Trachis, which, stretching along the shore of Thessaly, forty miles in circumference, were opposite to the station of the Persian fleet, and adjacent to Thermopylæ, before the Greeks had reached these straits. The Persian monarch, understanding that an army of Greeks, headed by the king of Sparta, had taken post at these straits, in order to dispute his passage, assembled his troops, and encamped on the plains of Trachis. But as Xerxes had no particular quarrel with the Spartans, whose opposition, though it could not prevent, might probably retard the punishment

of the Athenians, he sent messengers in his
name to desire them to lay down their arms; to
which the Lacedæmonians boldly replied, " Let
" Xerxes come, and take them." The messengers then, according to the directions they had
received, offered them lands, on condition that
they would become allies to the Persian monarch. This proposal they treated with contempt; and answered, " that the custom of their
" republick was, to conquer lands by valour, not
" to acquire them by treachery." The messengers returned to Xerxes equally astonished at
what they had seen and what they had heard,
and declared to him the unexpected event of their
commission, and the extraordinary behaviour of
the Spartans. Upon which the Persian monarch
demanded Demeratus, their countryman, whom
he had obliged to accompany him in this expedition, to explain the intention of the Spartans.
He replied, that their whole carriage and de-
meanour implied a determined resolution, to
fight to the last extremity.

On the evening of the seventh day after
Xerxes had arrived at the straits of Thermo-
pylœ, twenty thousand chosen men, commanded
by Hydarnes, and conducted by the traitor Epialtes, who had offered to lead them through another passage in the mountains, left the Persian
camp. The next morning, however, they beheld the glittering surfaces of spears and hel-
mets, and soon after perceived a thousand Phocians, whom the foresight and vigilance of
Leonidas had sent to defend this important, but
generally unknown pass. The immense shower
of darts from the Persians compelled the Phocians to abandon the passage they had been
sent to guard; and they retired to the highest

part of the mountain. This gave the Persians an opportunity to seize the pass, through which they marched with the greatest expedition.

In the mean time, by means of a deserter from the Persian camp, the Greeks under Leonidas had been informed of the treachery of Epialtes and the march across the mountain. Leonidas, therefore, immediately called an assembly, to deliberate on the measures to be pursued in consequence of this important and alarming information. All the confederates of Peloponnessus, the Spartans alone excepted, declared it was necessary to abandon a post, which, on account of the double attack intended against it, could not be maintained with any probable hopes of success. They considered it the most prudent measure they could adopt, in the present crisis of affairs, to return to the isthmus of Corinth, and join their confederates to defend the Grecian peninsula from the fury of the barbarians. Leonidas explained the sentiments of the Spartans, and said, that as glory was the only voice they had learned to obey, they were determined at the price of their lives to purchase immortal renown to their country. The Thespians declared they would never forsake Leonidas, and the Thebans were obliged to follow their example.

It was now the dead of night, when the Spartans with unanimous consent, headed by Leonidas, and full of resentment and despair, marched in close battalion to surprise the Persian camp. Dreadful was the fury of the Greeks; and on account of the want of discipline, in having no advanced guard, or watch, greatly destructive to the Persians. Numbers fell by the Grecian spears, but far more perished by the mistakes of their own troops; who in the confusion that

now prevailed, could not distinguish friends
from foes. Wearied with slaughter, the Greeks
penetrated to the royal tent; but Xerxes, with
his favourites, had fled to the farther extremity
of the encampment.

The dawn of day discovered to the Persians
a dreadful scene of carnage, and the handful of
Greeks by whom this terrible slaughter had been
made. The Spartans now retreated to the straits
of Thermopylæ; and the Persians by menaces,
stripes and blows, could scarcely be compelled
to advance against them. The Greeks halted
where the pass was widest, to receive the charge
of the enemy. The shock was dreadful. After
the Greeks had blunted or broken their spears,
they attacked with sword in hand, and made an
incredible havock. Four times they dispelled
the thickest ranks of the enemy, in order to obtain the sacred remains of their king Leonidas,
who had fallen in the engagement. At this crisis, when their unexampled valour was about to
carry off the inestimable prize, the hostile battalions, under the conduct of Epialtes, were seen
descending the hill. All hopes were now dispersed; and nothing remained to be attempted,
but the last effort of a generous despair. Collecting themselves into a phalanx, with minds
resolute and undaunted, the Greeks retired to
the narrowest part of the strait; and, on a rising
ground, took post behind the Phocian wall. As
they made this movement, the Thebans, whom
fear had hitherto hindered from defection, revolted to the Persians; declaring that their republick had sent earth and water, in token of their
submission to Xerxes; and that they had been
reluctantly compelled to resist the progress of
his arms. In the mean time, the Lacedæmoni-

ans and Thespians were assaulted on every side; the wall was beaten down; and the enemy entered the breaches. But instant death befel the Persians that entered. In this last struggle, the most heroick and determined courage was displayed by every Grecian. It being observed to Dioneces, the Spartan, that the Persian arrows were so numerous as to intercept the light of the sun, he replied, this was a favourable circumstance, because the Greeks thereby fought in the shade. What however the Greeks were able to do, they had already performed, collectively and individually; and it became impossible for them longer to resist the impetuosity and weight of the darts and other missile weapons, continually poured upon them. They therefore fell, not conquered, not destroyed, but buried under a trophy of Persian arms. In this dreadful conflict, the Persians lost 20,000 men.

To the memory of these brave defenders of their country, two monuments were afterward erected, near the spot where they fell. The inscription of the one announced, that four thousand Peloponnesian Greeks had arrested, in that place, the progress of the whole Persian force; the other, in honour of Leonidas and his three hundred followers, was characteristick of the Spartans, and contained these memorable words, " Go, stranger, and declare to the Lacedæmonians, that we died here in obedience to their divine laws." This famous action of the Greeks at Thermopylæ contributed not a little, according to the opinion of Diodorus Siculus, to the advantages which the Greeks afterward obtained. For the Persians, astonished at the desperate valour of the Spartans, concluded it was scarcely possible to subdue a nation of so undaunted a resolution; nor did it less inspire the minds of the Greeks with courage, who from that time became sensible, that valour and discipline are capable of vanquishing the greatest tumultuary force.

While the military operations at Thermopylæ were carrying on, the Grecian fleet had united under the command of Eurybiades, a Spartan, and had proceeded to Artemisium, the northern promontory of Euboea, where it was stationed. The fleets of Persia, too numerous to be contained in any harbour on the Grecian coast, had anchored in the road that extends between Castanæa and Sepias, on the shores of Thessaly. The first lines of their fleet were sheltered by the Thessalian coast; but the others, amounting to seven in number, rode at anchor, with their prows to the sea. The vessels had been thus arranged when the waters were still, the sky serene, and the weather calm and favourable. On the second morning, however, after their arrival on the Thessalian coast, a dreadful storm of thunder and rain commenced; and the Hellespontin, a north-east wind that blows in those seas for several days together, raised the waves to a tremendous height. The nearest vessels were saved by hauling towards the shore; but the more remote, being driven from their anchors, foundered at sea, split upon the promontory of Sepias, or were lost in the shallows of Meliboea; and thus four hundred of the Persian gallies were destroyed. In a few days, therefore, they quitted the dangerous station at Sepias, and with eight hundred ships of war that had escaped the storm, beside innumerable vessels of burden, sailed into the Pagasæan bay, and anchored in the road of Aphetæ, opposite to Artemisium.

As soon as the Greeks perceived the dreadful effects of the storm upon the fleets of their enemies, they poured out libations to "Neptune the deliverer." The near approach, however, of such a superior force, damped the transports of their religious festivity; and they determined immediately to retire southward. But the defence of Euboea depending entirely on their continuance at Artemisium, they were with much importunity prevailed on to remain there.

In the mean time the Persians, having recovered from the terrors of the storm, prepared to engage the Grecian fleet: and as they doubted not of success, they sent out two hundred of their swift sailing vessels to intercept them. These vessels, shaping their course by the promontories of Cephaneus and Gerestus, escaped the observation of the Greeks. But this stratagem of the Persians was discovered to them by Scyllias, a native of Sicyon, who deserted to his countrymen. The Greeks, therefore, determined to continue in the harbour until midnight, and then sail in quest of the fleet sent out to prevent their escape. This project, however, was not put in execution; for the boats that had been immediately dispatched to observe the progress of the Persians, returned before evening, without having seen any of the enemy.

The strength of the adverse parties being thus reduced nearer to an equality, the weaker seized this opportunity to display their courage in battle, and their superior knowledge of naval affairs. About sunset, the Greeks approached the Persian fleet that remained in the Pagasæan bay, and offered them battle. And as their numbers were, in their own opinion, very sufficient for still enclosing and conquering the Grecian fleet, the Persians did not decline the engagement. The Greeks formed their ships into a circle, as they expected the Persians would surround them ; and then commenced the action. Though cooped into a very narrow compass, and hemmed in on all sides by the enemy, the Greeks in a little time routed the Persians, took thirty of their ships, and sunk many more ; and had not the night come on, few would have escaped. Immediately after, a storm of thunder and rain succeeded; and the Greeks entered the harbour of Artemisium; but the Persians were driven to the coast of Thessaly. The dead bodies and wrecks were driven against the sides of their vessels; and the barbarians were struck with consternation and dismay. The greatest part of their fleet, however, again reached the Pagasæan bay. The ships that had been sent round the island of Euboea, to intercept the Grecian fleet, encountered the storm, and after having been driven they knew not whither, either by the force of the winds, or the impetuosity of the currents, perished miserably amidst the shoals and rocks of an unknown coast.

The morning arose with different hopes and different prospects to the contending parties. The Persians became sensible of the extent of their misfortunes ; and the Greeks received a reinforcement of fifty-three ships from Athens. They determined, therefore, to attack the enemy again at sunset. They sailed at the appointed time, and having separated the squadron of the Cilicians from the rest, totally destroyed it, and returned again to Artemisium.

These several disasters and disgraces, which would in all probability excite the indignation and vengeance of the Persian monarch against the commanders of his fleet, deeply affected

them. The advantages gained by the Greeks
appeared to have been occasioned by art, stratagem, or favour of the night. They, therefore, resolved to choose a more proper time for
engaging. They sailed forth on the third day
at noon, formed in the shape of a crescent.
Animated by their former successes, the Greeks,
though they probably would have chosen a more
favourable opportunity, determined to hazard
an engagement. The battle continued for a
longer time, and was more dubious than on any
former occasion. The Egyptians particularly
signalized themselves, took five Grecian vessels,
and many others were destroyed. At length,
however, the valour of the Greeks triumphed,
and the Persians acknowledging their superiority, left them in possession of the sea. But
this victory cost the Greeks very dear. Soon
afterward they received an account of the battle
of Thermopylæ, and of the glorious death of
Leonidas; and, by comparing the dates, found
that the sea and land engagements had both
taken place the same day. Several reasons now
conspired to induce the Greeks to sail southward. Having therefore passed along the shore
of Attica, they entered the strait of the Saronic
gulf, which divides the island of Salamis from
the harbours of Athens, where they cast anchor.
· Xerxes considered the departure of the Grecian fleet from Artemisium as equivalent to a victory: he therefore commanded his naval forces
to ravage the coasts of Eubœa, and afterward
possess themselves of the harbours of Athens;
while, at the head of his numerous and irresistible army, he marched into the Attic territory.
Many of the states of Greece now submitted to
the authority and power of the Persian king;

and the defence of liberty was left chiefly to Athens and Sparta. After ravaging and plundering the cities and countries through which they passed, the united army of Xerxes arrived in the Attic territory, three months after their passage over the Hellespont. They proceeded to lay waste the country, burned the cities, and levelled the temples with the ground.

After all the prodigies of valour which had been achieved, the Athenians found it impossible to oppose the army of Persia, and to defend the coasts of Greece against the ravages of the fleet. The inhabitants of Peloponnesus despairing likewise of being able to contend with the enemy in the open field, had begun to erect a wall across the isthmus of Corinth. Under these difficulties, the Athenians, by the advice of Themistocles, embraced a resolution worthy of a generous and free people; they abandoned to the Persian fury their villages, their territory, their walls, their city, their temples, with the revered tombs of their ancestors. Their wives, children, and aged parents were transported to places of security; and all the Athenians, capable of using arms, or that might be in any manner serviceable, embarked on board the fleet stationed at Salamis. The Grecian armament, greatly increased since its engagements with the Persian force, amounted to three hundred and eighty vessels; and the fleet of Xerxes, which now took possession of the Athenian harbours southward of the strait occupied by the Greeks, having also received a powerful reinforcement, was restored to its original complement of twelve hundred sail.

Xerxes, notwithstanding the disasters and disgraces which had hitherto attended his naval armament, was still desirous of making another trial of his fortune by sea. Against this, however, some of his party advised, but were over-ruled. When the Grecian commanders perceived that the enemy were preparing to hazard another naval engagement, they deliberated whether they should remain in their present situation, or proceed further up the gulf toward the isthmus of Corinth. This latter opinion most of the confederates embraced, as by that means they would be more able to defend, in any emergency, their respective cities. But Themistocles, the Athenian admiral, sensible of the fatal effects that would thence ensue, and how impossible it would be to prevent the dispersion of the Grecian armament, if they sailed from Salamis, opposed this measure with all his might. Eurybiades, however, the Spartan admiral, who was chief in command, dissented from the opinion of Themistocles; and being provoked at an expression which the latter had made use of against him, endeavoured to strike the Athenian with his batoon. Upon this, Themistocles cried out, " Ay, strike if you will, but hear what I have to say." Another of the Lacedæmonians observing, that the Athenians, who had no city to defend, ought to have no voice in the council: Themistocles replied, " the Athenians have indeed abandoned all their private estates and possessions for the general safety of Greece; but nevertheless they have two hundred ships of war, which no Grecian state can resist: and should the confederates persist in their present dangerous resolution, the Athenians will seek for themselves as fair a country, and as large and free a city, as that they have left." The firmness of this discourse at once shook the intention of the Greeks, and they resolved to remain at Salamis.

But the Peloponnesians, nevertheless, were still ready to return to their first determination. Themistocles, by a master-stroke of policy, therefore, sent privately to Xerxes to inform him, that the Greeks, seized with consternation and dismay at the approach of danger, had determined to make their escape under cover of the night; and that this was the time for the Persians to achieve the most glorious of their exploits, and by intercepting the flight of their enemies accomplish their destruction at once. Xerxes believed the report, and the several passages were immediately secured. Aristides, who seems not to have availed himself of a general act of indemnity that had passed, was the first that brought intelligence of the blockade made by the Persians. A battle was thereupon instantly resolved.

Confiding in their strength, and under the necessity of using vigorous efforts, the Persians were eager to engage. Accident, however, seems to have made the Greeks the assailants. At daybreak, their order of battle was arranged. The Athenians were placed on the right, opposite the Phenicians; the Lacedæmonians on the left, opposite the Ionians. As soon as the morning arose, sacred hymns and pæans began; the trumpets sounded; and triumphant songs of war were echoed through the fleet. The two armaments moved to engage. A Phenician galley decorated more than the rest, and eager to meet the Grecian fleet, outstripped her companions; but being met by an Athenian galley, at the first shock her sculptured prow was shattered, and at the second she was

buried in the waves. The battle soon became
general, and was vigorous on both sides.—
Xerxes, seated upon a lofty throne, beheld from
the shore this bloody and destructive scene. But
neither the hope of acquiring the favour, nor
the fear of incurring the displeasure of the des-
pot, could impel the Persians to the performance of actions, worthy of those which the love
of liberty and of their country excited in the
Greeks. The foremost of the Phœnician ships
were soon dispersed or sunk; and the rest of
the enemy's vessels being thrown into confusion, the Athenians surrounded them, com-
pressed them into a narrower space, and increased their disorder. They were at length
entangled in each other, rendered incapable of
acting, and to use the expression of the poet
Æschylus, who was present in the battle, "were
caught and destroyed like fish in a net." In
the mean time the Lacedæmonians, who opposed the Ionians on the left, rendered the victory complete. Many of the Asiatic Greeks
deserted the Persians and joined the Lacedæmonians; others declined to engage; and the
rest were sunk or put to flight. The sea is
said to have been scarcely visible, for the quantity of the wreck and the floating carcases.
Forty Grecian galleys were sunk in the engagement, but the crews were mostly saved
aboard other ships, or by swimming to the
friendly shores of Salamis. When the rout
was become total, Aristides, with a body of A-
thenians, landed on the rocky isle of Psytalia,
where the flower of the Persian infantry had
been stationed, in order to destroy the shattered remains of the Grecian armament, and put
all the Persians to the sword. As Xerxes be-

held this dreadful havock, he started from his throne in wild agitation, rent his royal robes, and, in the first moments of returning tranquillity, commanded his forces to their respective camps.

An anecdote is related of the queen of Halicarnassus, which is too remarkable and too celebrated to be omitted here. This woman had accompanied Xerxes as an ally in the expedition against Greece, and being pursued in this battle by an Athenian galley, met a Persian vessel commanded by a tributary prince of Calydna in Lycia, with whom she was at variance. She darted the beak of her galley against the Lycian vessel, with great dexterity, and buried it in the waves. The Athenian galley, deceived by this measure, equally artful and audacious, believed the vessel of the queen of Halicarnassus to be one of those that had deserted the Persian interest, and therefore quitted the pursuit. Xerxes, who was a spectator of her conduct, is said to have been so well pleased with it, that he cried out, the soldiers behaved like women in the conflict, and the women like soldiers.

In the mean time, the confederates pursued the Persian fleet on every side; many were sunk, and more taken. Two hundred of the Persian vessels were burnt, and the rest dispersed; and those who had allied themselves to the Persian monarch fearing the indignation and vengeance of the Greeks, made the best of their way to their own country. To hinder any of the barbarians from escaping, the Greeks, in the first emotions of triumph, determined immediately to sail northward, to break down the bridge raised over the Hellespont, and to intercept them on their return. This advice was re-

commended by Themistocles. Upon mature
consideration, however, it appeared, that the
Persians were still sufficiently numerous to afford just grounds of terror. To the cowardice
and inexperience of the Persians, and not to their
want of strength, the Greeks were indebted for
the several advantages obtained over them. But.
if the Persians should be driven to despair, and
to their former calamities were added the impossibility of a retreat, they might probably exert
themselves more than they had hitherto done,
and retrieve their past errors and misfortunes.
These weighty considerations suggested themselves to Eurybiades the Spartan, and were immediately adopted by Themistocles and the Athenians. When Themistocles perceived that the
Grecian chiefs were about to acquiesce in this
reasoning, he formed another scheme, which was
put in execution. He sent one of his confidants
to inform Xerxes, that the Greeks intended to
break down the bridge over the Hellespont; and
promising to delay, as much as he could this project of his countrymen, advised the Persian
monarch to return into Asia, with the utmost
speed. Herodotus insinuates, that in acting
thus, Themistocles had in view the safety of the
Persians, rather than the interest of Greece. But
it seems plain from the nature of the action, that
this scheme was intended to oblige Xerxes to
abandon the war of his own accord.

The situation of the Persian monarch now was
such, that the least repulse might be sufficient
to make him return from the Grecian expedition.
Mardonius was too well acquainted with the disposition of his master, to suppose that he would
continue much longer in a country, that had been
the scene of so many and great calamities, and

which might probably be the destruction of himself and all his forces. This artful courtier, therefore, represented to Xerxes, that he had come to fight against the Greeks, not with rafts of timber, but with soldiers and horses; that the Persian valour had surmounted all difficulties, and their invincible sovereign was now master of Athens, the main object of this expedition; that having accomplished the principal design of the enterprise, it was time that the king should return from the fatigues of war to the cares of government; and that with three hundred thousand chosen men, he would undertake to prosecute the designs of Xerxes, and to complete the conquest. An assembly was held the same night, in which the rest of the courtiers coincided with Mardonius, and urged Xerxes to return into Asia. The Persian monarch, therefore, while he followed the dictates of his own pusillanimity, pretended to leave Greece with reluctance, and to obey the anxious solicitude of his subjects.

The remains of the Persian fleet, driven from the coast of Greece, returned to the harbours of Asia minor; and afterward assembled and rendezvoused during the winter at Cumæ. Xerxes and his troops arrived in forty-five days at the Hellespont, whither the transports had been ordered. This journey was performed with extreme hardship and fatigue. The rapidity of the march occasioned the deaths of many of his followers; and, to fill up the measure of their calamities, famine and pestilence prevailed amongst them. Excepting, therefore, the three hundred thousand chosen men committed to Mardonius, a detachment of whom guarded the Persian monarch to the coast, a remnant of so

many millions scarcely survived. The bridge
erected over the Hellespont with so much ostentation, had it remained entire, might have exhibited a mortifying monument of folly, vanity,
and lost greatness; but this magnificent and
stupendous fabrick had been destroyed by a tempest. And such is the obscurity and inquietude
with which this mighty monarch quitted the
Grecian territory, compared with the grandeur
and triumphal entry displayed on his arrival,
that it is not certainly known whether he crossed
the channel in a Phenician ship of war, or only
in a fishing boat. Xerxes travelled thence to
Sardis, where, in endeavouring to compensate
for the disappointments of ambition, he buried
himself in pleasures more infamous and degrading, than all the disgraces which he had incurred
in Greece, and all the calamities that his subjects
inflicted on others, or suffered themselves. It
must, however, be observed, that all these relations are of necessity borrowed from the Greek
historians, who would doubtless in some respects
be partial to their country, and prejudiced
against their foes.

CHAP. VI.

From the Retreat of Xerxes into Asia, to the final
Event of the Persian Invasion.

THE different affections of Grecian minds
after the victory of Salamis, so glorious, so
important, and so unexpected, and that occasioned the hasty retreat of such an immense
army, to resist which seemed wholly impossible,

may in some measure be conceived, but cannot be described. The Greeks, however, soon understood, that notwithstanding the return of Xerxes, Mardonius, with three hundred thousand men, whom he had cantoned in Thrace, Macedon, and Thessaly, for the winter, intended to take the field early in the spring, and try again the fortune of war. This intelligence deterred the Athenians from bringing their wives and children home, as they intended, from Trœzene, Salamis, and Ægina; because their country might probably be again exposed to the fury and resentment of the barbarians. But a few families returned while the rest remained on board the fleet, or went to reside with their friends in Peloponnesus.

It would naturally be expected that the Greeks, under the apprehensions of another formidable campaign, would have employed themselves during the winter months in raising contributions, levying and disciplining soldiers, and concerting proper and judicious measures for opposing the troops of Mardonius. They, however, did none of these. The winter was spent by them in dividing the spoil; assigning to the different commanders the prizes of conduct and valour; performing the last offices to those who had fallen in the defence of their country; celebrating their games and festivals; and in offering to the gods their thanksgivings and presents, for protecting them from the myriads of Xerxes. Their offerings to the gods consisted of vases, statues, and other ornaments of silver and gold. The rewards bestowed on the generals were only wreaths of pine, laurel, or olive; which made Tigranes, the Persian, exclaim, "Heavens! against whom have we come to fight? insensible to interest, they fight only for glory!" The states of Greece being assembled in the temple of Neptune, in order to confer the customary honours on him, who by the free votes of their leaders had deserved best, each chief was directed to write the name of the man he supposed most worthy, and also of him whom he thought deserving the second reward. Each commander put his own name in the first place, and that of Themistocles in the second, a circumstance which evinced the superiour worth and conduct of the Athenian admiral. Thence he went to Lacedæmon, where he was received with the greatest honour and respect. The Spartans, partial as they were to their own leaders, after having decreed the prize of valour to Eurybiades, assigned that of prudence to Themistocles, and crowned him with a wreath of olive. They also presented him with the most magnificent chariot in Sparta; and when he returned to Athens, he was escorted by five hundred horse, an honour never before paid to any stranger.

As many of the islanders had again become obnoxious for their forwardness and zeal in the cause of Persia, the Athenian commander sailed with a small squadron to the Cyclades, laid them under heavy contributions, and, as it is said, without the participation or knowledge of his colleagues in command, enriched himself with the spoil. The Parians avoided all publick payment, by bribing Themistocles. The Andrians alone, of the islanders on the European side of the Ægean, refused to pay any thing. *I come,* said the Athenian, *to you, accompanied by two very powerful divinities, Persuasion and Necessity. Alas!* replied they, *we also have divinities on*

our side, Poverty and Impossibility. In consequence of this reply, siege was laid to their principal town, but without effect; and the fleet
was compelled to return.

On the approach of spring, Mardonius prepared to take the field. His army con-
B. C. sisted of Medes, Persians, Scythians, and
479. Indians; and though greatly inferiour in
numbers to the myriads, which Xerxes had
brought from Persia, it was not, on that account
the less formidable. But before the Persian
general left Thessaly, he determined to try
what he could effect by negociation. He sent
therefore Alexander, king of Macedon, tributary and ally of Xerxes, to treat with those Athenians that had returned to their city, and in the
name of the Persian monarch, to offer them
proposals of peace. Upon his arrival, the
Athenians received him in the most friendly
manner, but delayed to call an assembly to hear
and answer his discourse, until the Spartans,
who had been apprised of the intentions of
Mardonius, should send embassadors to assist
at the consultations. When the parties were
all convened, Alexander opened his commission, and informed the Athenians, that Mardonius had received a message from the Persian
monarch, intimating his will to leave them in
possession of their territories, their liberties,
and laws, provided they would desert the general cause of Greece, and enter into an alliance
with him. And to induce them to embrace
this flattering though fallacious offer, Mardonius endeavoured to add weight to these considerations by observing, how impossible it
would be for the Athenians *ever* to conquer, or

VOL. III. K

always to resist, a monarch possessed of so
much power and such unbounded resources.

The Lacedæmonian embassadors spoke next.
They said that Sparta, having engaged in a
bloody and destructive conflict, to avenge the
quarrel of her Athenian allies, it would be unjust and dishonourable in the Athenians, to
abandon their friends and confederates; when
hostilities had been extended over all Greece
on their account. They urged the regret which
the Spartans felt for the misfortunes of the
Athenians, who had been deprived of their
houses and their harvests; and as a mark of
their regard, would, in conjunction with the
allies, maintain their wives and children during
the continuance of the war; and afford them
every assistance in their power. The Athenians having deliberated on these propositions,
answered both parties by the voice of Aristides,
who, as archon, or chief magistrate, presided
over the assembly. To the Macedonian they
said, " That as they were well acquainted with
the strength of Xerxes, he might have omitted
to insult them by describing its great superiority; but that in the defence of liberty, no power was too great to oppose. Return then and
tell Mardonius, that the Athenians, as long as
the sun and moon endure, will never make
peace with Xerxes, desert the cause of Greece,
or forget the injuries which the Persians have
done them; but that trusting to the protection
and assistance of those gods, whose temples
and altars the impious tyrant has polluted and
destroyed, we will resist him to the last extremity. And you, Alexander, be not again the
bearer of such messages as these, lest we forget the respect we owe you as our friend, and

consider not the sacred ties of hospitality, by which we are reciprocally connected." To the Lacedæmonians they replied, "That they were surprised the Spartans should entertain so mean an opinion of them; that neither the richest possessions on earth, nor all the wealth of the Persian king, should seduce them from the common defence of Greece; that without being troublesome to the allies, they hoped to provide for their families; but requested, that the army of the Lacedæmonians might march with all expedition towards Bœotia, and being joined by that of the Athenians, endeavour to stop the progress of Mardonius, who would immediately proceed southward, and invade Attica.

Mardonius did not deceive the expectations of the Athenians. According to the orders of his master, he marched directly towards Attica by the same road that Xerxes had before taken. In the mean time, the habitual hesitation and tardiness prevailed in the councils of the Spartans. Mardonius was advanced into Bœotia, and the Athenians in vain expected the Lacedæmonian army. The Athenians were therefore once more compelled to desert their country, and to retire with their effects to Salamis. This measure, however, was probably not so grievous on the present, as on the former occasion. The Grecian fleet now commanded the seas. In the island of Salamis, the Persian army could not annoy them. Thither all their families and effects were removed; and Mardonius, in the tenth month after the departure of Xerxes from the Grecian territory, retook Athens.

The conduct of the Peloponnesians, and especially that of the Lacedæmonians, was mean,

ungrateful, and dastardly. They had fortified
the isthmus with additional walls and ramparts;
and believed themselves secure behind the bulwarks they had raised; and therefore equally
disregarded the distresses, or resentment, of
their northern allies. But the Athenians exhibited the greatest magnanimity and heroism.
Fugitives in the island of Salamis, and deprived
of their allies, the Persian general thought the
opportunity favourable for attempting another
negociation, and drawing the Athenians from
the general confederacy of Greece. The same
terms which the Macedonian king had before
brought, were again offered. The minister, a
Hellespontian Greek, named Múrichides, was
admitted to an audience by the council of five
hundred. Lycidas, who promoted the referring
of this proposal to the people, was stoned to
death with his wife and family, by a tumultuous
crowd. Such was the popular zeal against tyranny, and their persevering enmity against
Persia. The law of nations, however, was observed as to the person of Murichides, and he
was permitted to depart, without receiving injury or insult. Mardonius after having laid
waste and plundered, a second time, the Athenian territories, cities, villas, and temples, returned into Bœotia.

Ministers had now been sent from Salamis
to Sparta, in behalf of Athens, Platæa, and Megara. These embassadors remonstrated warmly with the Lacedæmonians, on the shameful
neglect of their engagements. The Spartans
were, at that time, celebrating the solemn feast
of Hyacinthía, which furnished them with a
pretext for delaying any answer for several
days. The Athenian embassadors, thinking

themselves insulted and their country betrayed, determined to depart the next day. But having expressed to the Spartans their sense of such treatment, declared that the Athenians would join the Persians, and then the Peloponnesians must become sensible, when it was too late, that the wall across the isthmus would only afford a partial and feeble defence; and that, though it might secure them on the side of the land, it could not protect their coasts from the Persian armament, reinforced by the Athenian fleet.

This threat, or the returning sense of publick utility, urged the Lacedæmonians, at length, to take the field. Five thousand Spartans, each attended by seven Helotes, and composing an army of forty thousand fighting men, left the city silently in the evening, under the command of Pausanias, the guardian and kinsman of Pleistarchus, son of Leonidas. Having marched beyond the isthmus, they joined the army of the Athenians and their allies; and the whole heavy armed troops amounted to nearly forty thousand; while the light armed were the thirty-five thousand Helotes attendants on the Spartans, and about as many more, one to each soldier, attended the other divisions.

The Greeks having marched into Bœotia, took post at the foot of mount Cithæron, directly opposite to the enemy. Here the hostile armies remained eleven days encamped, before they attempted any thing of moment against each other. Mardonius had judiciously left the passage of the mountains open to the Grecian troops, to draw them if possible into the champaign country; where the Asiatic horse would be able to act with most advantage, and make the victory more easy. But Pausanias would not quit his situation, and the Persian general durst not attempt to force his position. He therefore gave orders to Masistius, the commander of the Persian cavalry, to advance with all the horse, to harrass the Greeks, and endeavour to make some impression upon them. The Persian cavalry used missile weapons, darts or arrows, or both. They generally attacked or harrassed by small bodies in succession. They were vehement in onset, never continued the contest long; but, if the enemy remained firm and impregnable, retreated to prepare for another charge.

On the side most exposed to the enemy's cavalry, were three thousand soldiers from the rocky district of Megara. These Masistius attacked; and having wearied them by the succession of fresh troops, who approached sufficiently near to throw their darts and use opprobrious language, and then retired, the Megarians were compelled to send to Pausanias for succour. The Spartan general addressed the whole army, to know if any of the troops would exchange situations with the Megarians. The Athenians alone offered their service. They had not long occupied the post, before they were attacked by the enemy's cavalry, whom they repelled, and killed Masistius. Hereupon a terrible conflict took place for the dead body; but, in the end, the Persian cavalry were obliged to retire.

The Greeks finding themselves in want of fresh water, determined to decamp. They proceeded, therefore, in arms along the foot of mount Cithæron, until they came to a plain, in the vicinity of the village of Hysia in Platæa. Near this place were many gentle eminences,

and the copious fountain Gargaphia. This was
a necessary resource to the Greeks, as the enemy, by the great superiority of their cavalry,
commanded both sides of the Æsopus.

It might have been expected, that men ready
to hazard every thing in the defence of their
country would have preserved in the field perfect agreement and unanimity amongst themselves. The Lacedæmonians, as the most considerable people of Greece, were universally allowed to take the right wing of the army. The
Athenians, unquestionably the next in consequence, thought themselves entitled to the left
wing; but the Tegeans, who were acknowledged to be excellent soldiers, and had always
obtained the second honours of the field, disputed this point of honour with them. This
quarrel, ridiculous as it may appear in the eye
of reason, might have been attended with serious and ruinous consequences to the general
safety of Greece, had not the Athenian commanders acted with wisdom and dignity. The
Tegeans, in a studied oration, vindicated their
claim to precedency; and supported it by a
long detail of the great and honourable actions
of their ancestors. Upon which Aristides, the
Athenian commander, replied, " We under-
stand that the Greeks are here assembled to
fight against the enemies of their country, not
to dispute about precedency. But were we inclined to boast of the glorious deeds of our ancestors, we might, perhaps, make mention of
actions equally honourable with those the Tegeans have related. Let the battle of Marathon
efface any suspicions that we are inferiour to
them. In a moment like the present, however, we consider all contests about precedency

as unbecoming and unseasonable. Place us, therefore, O Spartans! wheresoever, and with whomsoever you think proper. And wherever our station shall be, rest assured, that the Athenians will defend the cause of Greece, like brave men and lovers of their country. Command, therefore, and depend upon our obedience." These words were scarcely ended, when the whole Lacedæmonian army cried out, that the Athenians were worthy of the post of honour, in preference to the Arcadians; and accordingly they assumed it without opposition.

The army was then marshalled in the following order: Five thousand Spartans of the city, attended by thirty-five thousand light armed Helotes, held the first place: next to these, were five thousand Lacedæmonians of the other towns of Laconia, accompanied by five thousand Helotes. The Tegeans, in number fifteen hundred, held the next place: then five thousand Corinthians, fourteen thousand two hundred from the inferiour states of Greece, and eight thousand Athenians. The whole number of fighting men, amounted to one hundred and eight thousand two hundred.

As soon as Mardonius was informed that the Greeks had filed off towards Platæa, he moved and encamped over against them; still keeping the Æsopus in his front. Having summoned the principal officers of his army, he informed them of his intention to attack the Greeks the next day; and directed them to prepare accordingly. This news was brought to the camp of the confederates by Alexander, king of Macedon; and the Greeks thereupon held a consultation, in what manner they should resist the attack of the Persian general. Pausanias proposed a change in

the order of the Grecian army, and that the
Athenians, who alone had experienced the onset
of the Persians, should take the right wing, and
the Lacedæmonians the left. Aristides and his
countrymen embraced the offer with joy and
exultation. Day broke; when Mardonius, perceiving the confederates in motion, deferred the
intended attack. Changes were also made in
the order of the Persian army. This day passed in evolutions; and the enemy's infantry never
came into action against the Greeks. Their
cavalry, however, harassed the more accessible
parts of the Grecian line without ceasing. They
only approached to discharge their arrows, and
then hastily retired: but they thereby maintained a constant alarm; and while they inflicted
many wounds, afforded little opportunity for
revenge. The cavalry, however, made a more
serious attack upon that part of the Lacedæmonian line, which guarded the Gargaphian
fountain, and made themselves masters of the
place.

The Grecian army, therefore, being deprived
of water, and provision also beginning to fail
them, a decampment was rendered indispens-
able. It was determined to occupy a narrow
slip of ground towards the source of the Æsopus, and confined between that river and mount
Cithæron. The obscurity of midnight was chos-
en as the most convenient time for effecting
this purpose; but the Greeks were by no means
unanimous in this measure. Anompharetus, the
Spartan, and next in command to Pausanias,
declared, that neither he, nor the division which
he commanded, should ever flee from the enemy. The confederate army was, therefore,
dispersed in so many different directions that

the next morning it presented the appearance rather of a flight, or a rout, than of a regular march.

Mardonius having received intelligence of the departure of the Greeks, doubted not but they had abandoned their camp and made this precipitate retreat, through fear of the Persian arms. He gave orders, therefore, to his soldiers to pursue the fleeing foe, and to complete the conquest. The Lacedæmonians and Athenians were still within his reach, the former at the foot of mount Cithæron, the latter on the plain. Having sent his Grecian auxiliaries against the Athenians, he advanced at the head of the Persian troops to attack the Lacedæmonians. No contrast could be greater, than the two hostile armies afforded. The barbarians, hurried on with all the haste and confusion of an ill disciplined multitude, eager to share in certain victory: the Lacedæmonians, carefully covered with their shields, silently observed the sacrifices. As soon as Pausanias perceived that the admonitions of the gods were favourable and propitious to the Grecian interest, the Lacedæmonians proceeded with intrepidity to close combat. The Persians, who had been reinforced with the Sacæ, a Scythian tribe, sustained the shock with great courage. The Greeks slew immense numbers; but fresh troops still succeeded to the fight, and made a most hideous noise. Mardonius, mounted upon a white steed of great strength and swiftness, signalized himself by his valour and determined bravery. A thousand horsemen, consisting of the flower of the Persian nobility, ambitious of imitating the example of Mardonius, and of emulating his fame, constantly attended him. Had the skill of the Persians been equal to their courage, or had the troops been regularly and properly disciplined, the victory would either have been against the Greeks, or, at least, it must have been obtained with more difficulty, and a greater loss of men. But the Persians acted without union or concert; and, attacking the Lacedæmonians by parties only, were easily defeated. The Athenians, endeavouring to join the Spartan army, engaged the Bœotians and other Greeks, whom Mardonius had sent against them. The number and courage of the Persian troops, however, kept the battle doubtful, until Mardonius was slain. The death of the general was immediately followed by the defeat of the Persians, and by the flight of the barbarian army. The Athenians also routed the Greeks, who were allied with, and fought under the Persian banners. Artabazus, the next in command to Mardonius, and against whose advice these measures were pursued, deeming all lost, retired with forty thousand men, marched with great expedition to Thrace; and arriving at the Hellespont, passed over into Asia.

The rest of the Persian army withdrew into their camp, strengthened the works before thrown up, and defended themselves with great bravery against the Lacedæmonians. The Athenians, however, coming up, vigorous efforts were used on both sides; but an assault at length succeeded. A horrid slaughter ensued. Of three hundred thousand men, whom Mardonius brought into the field, scarcely three thousand escaped, exclusively of those who retreated under Artabazus. The number of the Greeks that fell in this engagement is uncertain, but must have been considerable.

The events of this battle not only completely freed the Grecians from the terrors of servitude, but made them masters of greater wealth than they could ever have hoped to possess. When Xerxes left the army for Asia, he gave most of his riches and valuable furniture to Mardonius his general and brother-in-law. The rest he divided among his inferiour favourites. Couches, magnificently embroidered; tables of gold and silver; golden bowls and goblets; stalls and mangers of brass; chains, bracelets, scymitars, some of solid gold, others set with precious stones; and many chests of Persian money, which began after that time, and continued several years, to be current in Greece; all came into the possession of the conquerors. The tenth of the whole spoil was consecrated to the gods. Peculiar presents were offered to Jupiter at Olympia, to Neptune at the isthmus, and to Apollo at Delphi. A tenth of the remainder was divided amongst the generals. After which, prizes were distributed among the bravest survivors, according to their respective achievements.

Having buried their dead with all the circumstances of funereal pomp, and raised trophies to commemorate their success, the confederates, as had been customary after a victory, determined to punish those who had deserted the cause of Greece, and allied themselves with the Persian monarch. With this view, Pausanias marched immediately to Thebes, and laid waste the country. The Thebans at first attempted to make a defence; but after mature deliberation, capitulated, and surrendered the leaders of the Median faction. These thought to have purchased their ransom with money;

but were disappointed; for Pausanias disdaining their proposals, carried them to Corinth, and caused them to be put to death.

The battle of Platæa, it is said, happened on the twenty-second of September. The same day, another battle, neither less glorious nor less decisive, was fought between the same nations at the promontory of Mycale in Ionia, opposite to the isle of Samos. After the shattered remains of the Persian armament had been driven from the Grecian coast, and obliged to seek protection in the ports of Asia minor, the confederates were encouraged to send their fleet into those parts by the Ionians, who informed them that all the Asiatic Greeks would thereupon revolt from the Persian interest, and espouse the cause of Greece. The Grecian fleet, therefore steered eastward, under the command of Leotychides, the Spartan king, and Xantippus, the Athenian admiral. The commanders of the Persian armament, as soon as they were informed of the arrival of the Grecian fleet in those seas, wishing to avoid another naval engagement stood in for the shore, and sought the protection of an army of sixty thousand men, which had been left for the defence of Ionia. The Greeks perceiving their intent, resolved to attack them on shore; while Leotychides, sailing towards the coast, made a proclamation, and endeavoured to occasion a revolt among the Ionians. After this, the Greeks disembarked their whole force capable of acting by land, which consisted of the greatest part of their crew. The Persians having received information, that the Samians had been intriguing with the Greeks, disarmed them; but confiding very much in the Milesians, they intrusted to them the guarding of the passes through the mountains, by which on an emergency they could retreat. These dispositions being made, they prepared to defend their fortifications. The Grecian forces marched in two columns: the one consisting of the Athenian, Corinthian, Sicyonian, and Trœzenian troops, held the plain along the shore; the other, composed of the Lacedæmonians and their allies, fetched a compass over the hills. The former arrived first, and after an obstinate and bloody conflict, forced the Persian camp; about the same time that the Lacedæmonians attacked them in the rear. The Samians, though unarmed, exerted themselves against the Persians; and the Milesians, who were to have guarded the passes, attacked the Persians as soon as they fled, and killed them, or made them prisoners. Tigranes, the general of the Persian troops, and two of the principal naval commanders, were amongst the slain. When the slaughter had ceased, the Persian ships and camp, and all the valuable treasures contained in them, became the prize of the victors. Ionia regained its freedom, and the Asiatic coast was abandoned by the Persian monarch. When the Greeks had taken every thing of value out of the enemy's camp and fleet, they burned the ships and all their contents.

After this signal blow, which not only completed the ruin of the Persian expedition against Europe, but restored liberty to the fairest portion of Asia, the Grecian fleet returned to Samos. Here they deliberated, whether the Ionians should be transported into Greece, and have those countries bestowed upon them, which had sided with the Persians. But the Athenians dissuaded from this measure; and insisted that, as they were Athenian colonies, no other Grecian state had a right to interfere in their disposal. The Greeks then determined to sail to the Hellespont, and destroy the bridges; but they found them already broken down by the weather and the current. Winter approaching, Leotychides, the Spartan commander, with all the Peloponnesians, returned to Greece; but the Athenians, under the command of Xantippus, determined to make other attempts before they returned home. This resolution being agreed on, they sailed to the Chersonese, and besieged Sestos, where the Persians had collected all their force. This siege continued a long time; but a famine prevailing among the garrison, they endeavoured to make their escape, and the place was given up.

The Persian expedition against Greece was thus concluded after two campaigns which covered the Greeks with glory, and which will ever be recorded among the most memorable in the annals of war.

CHAP. VII.

The Affairs of Greece, from the final Overthrow of the Persians, to the Thirty Years Truce.

THE common fears, which, notwithstanding innumerable sources of dissention, had formed and upheld a partial confederacy of the Grecian states, were dispelled by the decisive victories obtained at Platæa and Mycale. The symptoms of jealousy and discord between the two principal communities of Greece, which had already appeared in the separation of the

Athenian and Spartan fleets, broke out with
more virulence after they returned home. The
Athenians brought back their families to Athens;
and, upon retaking possession of the site of their
city, found the walls destroyed, and only a few
houses remaining, which had been reserved for
the residence of the principal Persian officers.
They therefore determined to rebuild the city
with the greatest expedition, and with some
degree of magnificence. The events of the late
invasion would no doubt impress the Athenians
with the propriety and necessity of providing
for the future security of their country. What
others therefore considered as the means of promoting tranquillity and ease, Themistocles viewed as the certain presage of the political greatness of Athens, to which he probably looked for
the foundation of his own preeminence. According to his suggestions, every thing else was
postponed, until the fortifications, which were
put under his direction, should be completed.
A large space was marked out for the new walls,
and the work was prosecuted with diligence and
vigour.

While the Athenians were thus employed in
repairing the ravages of war, and fortifying their
city against all future attacks, the Lacedæmonians sent an embassy, to remonstrate against a
design peculiarly dangerous and alarming to the
other Grecian states. The ostensible reason,
alleged against this undertaking of the Athenians, was, that if the Greeks had possessed any
town of impregnable strength, they must have
found it impossible to drive Xerxes from their
country. As it was the avowed policy,
B. C.
477.
not of the Lacedæmonians only, but of all
the Peloponnesians, to deter the Athenians from executing their purpose, they might

have appealed to arms, after finding arguments ineffectual, and Athens was not in a situation at present to resist them. It was therefore judged more advisable to temporize; and the conduct of Themistocles on this occasion had been considered as a master-piece of policy. To the Spartan ministers, who brought the remonstrance, it was replied, that the Athenians would send embassadors to Lacedæmon, who would satisfy the Spartans on the subject of their message. With this answer the Lacedæmonians were dismissed, and apparently satisfied.

Themistocles and some other Athenians being accordingly appointed embassadors to Sparta, the former hastened his journey to that city; but intimated to the senate, it would be proper to detain one or both of his colleagues, until the walls of Athens were raised to the height required. When he arrived at Lacedæmon, he delayed to open the business of his embassy, alleging, that he waited for his colleagues, whom he expected daily. In the mean time, the Athenians prosecuted the work with the most diligent application: citizens toiled with slaves; women and children assisted all that they were able; neither night nor day was the business intermitted; and materials were procured from sepulchres and publick buildings. The Lacedæmonians being informed that the building of the wall was still carried on, and that the colleagues of Themistocles were at length arrived, summoned the embassadors before them. Themistocles argued, that it did not become a great state, to regard vague and idle rumours; that his colleagues had assured him of the contrary to what the Lacedæmonians affirmed; and that the Spartans might send deputies with the

Athenian embassadors, to take cognizance of
the real state of things, whilst he himself would
remain as a hostage, and be answerable for the
event. The Spartans, therefore, agreed to dispatch a second embassy to Athens, to consist
of some of their most respectable citizens.
These men had no sooner arrived at their destination, than they were taken into custody as
pledges for the safe return of Themistocles,
who by this time was informed that the walls
were completed. Throwing off the mask, therefore, which he had hitherto used, Themistocles appeared in the Lacedæmonian assembly,
avowed the whole transaction, and declared that
the Athenians were most competent to decide
what their own interest, and the general welfare
of Greece demanded. Athens was now in a condition to repel any foreign or domestick foe, and
if the Spartans entertained any resentment of
this measure, which, whilst it conduced to the
publick interest, was not less calculated to dis-
please private ambition, their anger would be
equally unjust and useless; and concluded with
intimating, that the Athenians would not dismiss their embassadors, until he was set free.

Whatever secret indignation the Lacedæmonians might feel on this occasion, they deemed
it more prudent to suppress their animosity,
than to vent reproaches. The embassadors of
each state were then permitted to return home;
but the conduct of Themistocles, in thus deliv-
ering his country from the imminent danger of
falling under the Spartan yoke, laid the foundation of that unrelenting hatred, with which he
was afterward persecuted by the Lacedæmonians.

The next concern of Themistocles was to en-

large the Athenian harbours. He observed that
the port of Phalericum was small, narrow, and
inconvenient; and advised his fellow-citizens to
render Piraeus the largest and most capacious
haven in Greece, and to unite the city to it by
long walls. His address, eloquence, and bribes,
were seasonably applied in diverting the resentment of the Spartans, who, though less jealous of naval than military power, were scarcely
hindered from entering Attica with an armed
force. But the Athenians persuaded the Lacedæmonians and their allies, the common interest of the Grecian confederacy required, that a
large and capacious harbour should be formed,
in which the combined fleets of Greece might
rendezvous, and observe the designs of the enemy. In the mean time the work was carried
on with great spirit and activity, and in less
B. C. than twelve months the Piraeus, under
476. the care and direction of Themistocles,
became the best and most complete naval arsenal, that the world had hitherto seen.
The new walls were sufficiently broad to admit
two carriages abreast; and formed of large
blocks of marble, squared, and exactly fitted
without cement; and the outer stones were
firmly connected by cramps of iron fixed with
lead. The Athenians also determined, by the
advice of Themistocles, to increase their fleet
yearly, by the addition of twenty ships.

This great politician was not, however, very
scrupulous with regard to the means employed
for augmenting the power of Athens, and less-
ening that of Lacedæmon and the other Grecian states. He declared on a certain day, he
had a design to communicate which was of the
greatest importance; but that, as it would require secrecy and dispatch to carry it into exe-

cution, he could not reveal it to the people. He desired, therefore, that a proper person should be chosen, to whom his proposal might be made known, and who might direct by his advice, and confirm by his authority, what he intended. Aristides, as the best and wisest man, was unanimously appointed to decide, how far the proposal of Themistocles was useful and just. Themistocles informed him, his design was to set fire to the fleet of the other Grecian states, which was at that time in a neighbouring port, and thus procure to Athens the unrivalled sovereignty of the seas. This project Aristides disdained; and returning to the Athenian people, acquainted them that the proposal of Themistocles was highly useful to Athens, but, at the same time, that nothing could be more unjust or dishonourable. The Athenians, therefore, prohibited Themistocles from putting it into execution.

About this time, the Lacedæmonians proposed in the council of the amphictyons, that every city and state of Greece, which had not fought against the Persians, should lose the right of sending deputies to that assembly. This motion was particularly intended against the Argians and Thebans, in hopes that two of the most powerful states being removed, who were greatly inimical to the Spartan interest, the Lacedæmonian influence might thenceforward govern the assembly. Themistocles perceiving the intentions of the Spartans in making this motion, opposed it as much as possible, and obtained a decree, that it would be impolitick and unjust to deprive a Grecian state of its inherent rights, on account of the crimes and misconduct of those, who, at any particular time, directed its councils.

Aristides having nothing more at heart than the honour and advantage of his country, endeavoured to quell faction, and quiet the minds of the Athenians. He proposed that every citizen should have an equal right to the government, and that the archons should be chosen from the body of the people, without preference or distinction. This measure was agreeable to all parties. The states of Greece, finding it requisite to be always upon their guard against the Persian monarch, proposed a general taxation, proportioned to the maintenance of a regular and adequate force, and levied according to the abilities of each community. Aristides was intrusted with this commission, which he executed with so much fidelity and activity, that all the Greeks were satisfied with his conduct, and his taxation was universally styled, " The happy lot of Greece." When this business was finished, he obliged all the Grecian states to swear, that they would observe the articles of their grand alliance.

As many Grecian towns, not only in Asia minor, but also in Europe, were still under the dominion of Persia, a fleet was assembled, to the principal command of which Pausanias, the Spartan admiral, was appointed. Aristides and Cimon, the son of the late Miltiades, commanded the Athenian squadron. This was the first time that Cimon, who was yet very young, was placed in a situation in which he could exhibit the virtues and courage of which he was possessed. He had formerly suffered himself to be imprisoned, until he could pay the fine imposed upon his father; and by this filial act of duty gave presages and promises of his future greatness of mind, and goodness of heart. After he was liberated from prison, he was opposed to Themistocles, and seems to have supplanted him. The fleet sailed first to Cyprus; and the garrison being cut off from all support and assistance from the Persians, by the great superiority which the Greeks had at sea, were more solicitous to obtain for themselves favourable terms of capitulation, than to defend the place for their king. Most of the Grecian cities were also rescued from the Persians, with very little effort. The fleet then proceeded to the Hellespont and the Propontis, and took Byzantium, the key of communication between Europe and Asia, and the grand depot of the Persian arms. The siege of this place was obstinate; but at length the walls were stormed, and an immense booty, with several persons of the royal blood, fell into the hands of the conquerors.

The haughty disposition of the Spartan admiral had been elated with his victory at Platæa; and his late success against Byzantium still farther augmented it. The tenth of the spoil which had been allotted him as general, raised him above the equality required by the institutions of his country; and the wealth and riches found in Byzantium not a little contributed to occasion his ruin. Conceiving himself to be too great to continue a subject, he aimed at the regal power, through the assistance of the Persian monarch, the enemy of his country. An Eretrian of the name of Gongylus, well acquainted with the Persian language and customs, became his principal confidant. To him he intrusted the Persian nobles taken in Byzantium. This man, with his prisoners, escaped across the Bosphorus, and carried a letter to Xerxes, in which Pausanias, after mentioning his restoration of the captive princes as an indubitable mark of his sincerity, offered to Xerxes to assist him in conquering Greece, provided he would give him his daughter in marriage, and allow him to hold that country as a dependent province. As the subjugation of Greece was a great object with the Persian monarch, he is said to have been greatly pleased with these proposals, and to have sent Artabazus, a nobleman of consequence, and in whom he could confide, to treat and cooperate with the traitor Pausanias.

The Spartan admiral, however, acted with the inconsistency and precipitancy of a man under the delusion of ambition, or guided by evil counsels. He was difficult of access to his colleagues in office; disdained to concert measures with them, which they were to execute; the conquered barbarians were his guards; and he punished the slightest offence in the allied army with a rigour hitherto unknown, and therefore insupportable to Grecian troops. He kept the fierce spirits of the Spartans indeed in subjection, but without any degree of moderation; for the distinctions exacted for them served only to exasperate and inflame the minds of the confederates, whom he would not permit to forage, to draw water, or cut straw for their beds, until his countrymen had been supplied with these articles.

The intolerable pride and insolence of Pausanias disgusted and provoked all the Greeks, but more especially the Ionians, who complained, that they had no sooner been delivered from the yoke of Persia, than they were made to suffer under the more galling tyranny of Sparta. On the contrary, the justice of Aristides, and the

candour and generosity of Cimon, won the
affections both of officers and men. The allies
saw that the Athenians were far more powerful
at sea than the Lacedæmonians; and therefore
applied themselves to the Athenian commanders
for redress and protection, and promised for the
future, to acknowledge Athens as the first city
of Greece. Upon this Aristides told them, that
he was convinced not only of the reasonableness
but the necessity of their proposal; yet, as he
wished not to hazard the safety or honour of his
country, by attempting to perform what might
not succeed, he would not comply with their
request, until by some publick action they had
proved their sincerity, and fixed the concurrence
of all the troops beyond the power of retracting.
After this declaration, Uliades and Antagoras,
the commanders of the fleets of Samos and
Chios, the bravest of all the maritime allies, insulted the galley of Pausanias, at the head of
the Grecian fleet; and when the Spartan admiral reproached and threatened them, they desired him to thank Fortune for her favours at
Platæa, the memory of which victory alone restrained the Greeks from punishing his arrogance and cruelty. These words reechoed
through the fleet, and were the signal of general
revolt. The different squadrons of Asia and
the Hellespont sailed from their stations, joined
the ships of Uliades and Antagoras, abjured
the tyranny of Sparta, and the insolence of Pausanias; and ranged themselves under the banners of Athens. Thus by the domineering conduct of Pausanias did the Lacedæmonians lose
that preeminence that they had hitherto maintained, while Athens obtained the supremacy
by the prudence and virtue of Aristides.

Apprized of the conduct and treachery of Pausanias, the Spartans recalled him to be tried for his life; but his immense wealth corrupted the judges of his country, and the ephori pretending there was not sufficient evidence against him, he was only degraded from his office. This censure, however, did not deter him from the treacherous designs in which he was engaged. He still continued to negociate and correspond with Artabazus; and at length began to tamper with the Helotes and Messenians, those oppressed slaves, who were ever ready to rebel against the caprice and tyranny of their unrelenting masters. But as it exceeded even the opulence and effrontery of Pausanias, to corrupt and influence the whole republick, he was again impeached of treason to Greece, and his accusers, in consequence of an event that took place, had it in their power to make good their charge against him. An unhappy youth, named Argilius, who lived with Pausanias as the minister of his pleasures, was intended to be the victim of that monster's ambition. Pausanias appointed this man to be the messenger of a letter to Artabazus, in which, as usual, after having explained the state of his affairs, he hinted to him to put the bearer to death. The youth having observed, that none of the messengers of Pausanias ever returned, determined to open the letter. Finding by the contents the fate he was to have met with, he was fired with resentment, and carried the letter directly to the enemies of Pausanias, who prudently advised him to take refuge in the temple of Neptune, expecting that his master would soon follow him. In the mean time, a double tent was set up, in one part of which certain Spartans were concealed, and in the other Argilius received his master, who came to expostulate with him. By their mutual reproaches, the Spartans, who heard them, became direct witnesses against Pausanias, so that when he returned to Sparta, the ephori resolved to imprison him; but some of his friends giving him intelligence of their design, he fled for protection to the temple of Minerva. It being unlawful to take a person from that asylum, the Lacedæmonians were at a loss how to act. The mother of Pausanias, however, taking a tile in her hand, came to the temple, and placed it at the door. The Spartans considering her conduct, followed the example, and blocked up the entrance; and in this manner starved him to death.

The fate of Pausanias, in a little time, involved that of Themistocles. He was fast advancing to the attainment of the same authority at home, which the integrity and merit of Aristides had procured abroad for his country and himself; when complaints arrived from Sparta, that he had conspired with Pausanias against the liberties of Greece. The known resentment of the Lacedæmonians against Themistocles, sufficiently explains the reason, why they who had been so dilatory in convicting Pausanias, should be ready to bring to justice his supposed accomplice. But when we reflect upon the abilities and courage displayed by Themistocles in the decisive victory at Salamis; his councils and address in fortifying the city with impregnable strength; his foresight and activity in procuring the Athenians a fleet against which no nation could contend; and his patriotism and merit in saving Athens from the most formidable invasion recorded in history; we cannot conceive how his countrymen could admit an accusation of this nature against him. He had not the integrity and virtue of Aristides, but he was not, perhaps, the guilty person that the Lacedæmonians represented him. In fact, Pausanias had communicated his designs to Themistocles; but the Athenian rejected his proposals with the utmost indignation. Themistocles, however, concealed the design, either because he considered it base and dishonourable to divulge the secrets of his friends, or because he imagined it was impossible for such ill-concerted schemes to produce any effect. Be that as it may, the Athenians, upon the accusation of the Spartans, banished Themistocles by the ostracism. He retired to Argos; and it is not improbable but he might have been recalled to Athens before the expiration of the time, had the Lacedæmonians given his countrymen leisure to reconsider what they had done.

Pausanias having suffered, the Spartans informed the Athenians, that, from the papers found in the possession of that traitor, the guilt of Themistocles was fully authenticated; that it was not sufficient, therefore, to have driven him from Athens, by a decree which might at any time be repealed; that crimes against the general confederacy of Greece ought to be brought before the amphictyonic council; and that the punishment should be death, or perpetual banishment. The Athenians shamefully complied with this demand of the Spartans; and Themistocles being informed of his condemnation, sailed to Corcyra. His enemies still continuing to pursue him, he fled to the opposite coast of Epirus, and took refuge amongst the barbarous Molossians. Admetus, king of that country, had, on a former occasion, sought the assistance of the Athenians, when Themistocles was in the plenitude of his power, but had been rejected. Admetus was from home, at the time that Themistocles came to implore his protection; and on his arrival, was surprised to see his adversary a suppliant to him for an asylum. When the king appeared, Themistocles took the young son of the monarch in his arms, sat down among the household gods, and besought the clemency and protection of Admetus. The king, moved with sorrow and compassion to see the greatest man of Greece in this humiliating condition, raised him immediately from the ground, and promised to afford him every thing in his power. When the Lacedæmonians and Athenians, therefore, sent to demand Themistocles, he refused to deliver him up, because he had made his palace an asylum, in the confidence that it would afford him safety and protection. Thus did the Athenian exile continue to spend the close of life in indolence and retirement; and having learned to pardon and despise the ingratitude of his country, he expected that he should have been forgotten and forgiven. But the Athenians and Lacedæmonians would not permit him to remain in quiet; and still required Admetus to surrender him, under pain of their highest displeasure. This prince informing him of the dilemma to which he was reduced, Themistocles resolved, without hesitation, to retire to a still greater distance from his cruel and ungrateful countrymen. He accordingly went on board a vessel for Ionia, and with the utmost precaution concealed his rank. But a storm arising, the ship was driven

near the island of Naxos, at that time besieged
by the Athenians. The imminent danger he
was in of falling into the hands of his enemies,
obliged him to make himself known to the pi-
lot, who was prevailed on to steer for Asia. The
Persian monarch, having heard that the Greeks
had proscribed him their country, set a price
upon his head; and commanded that every
person, who should arrive in any part of the
coast of his dominions, should be strictly examined. Themistocles, however, found means to
reach Cuma in Æolia undiscovered; and by
the assistance and friendship of his host, a man
of considerable property, he was conducted in a
covered waggon to Susa. The ladies in Persia
being kept always from public view, the conductor of the waggon reported that Themistocles was an Ionian lady, whom he was carrying
to a nobleman at the Persian court. He was,
therefore, permitted to pass without farther inquiry.

When the unfortunate exile arrived at the vo-
luptuous palace of Artaxerxes, who had succeeded his father in the kingdom, he informed
the guards that he was a Grecian stranger, and
requested an audience of the monarch. The
officers informed him of a ceremony, that they
knew was insupportable to some Greeks, but
without which it would be impossible to have an
interview with Artaxerxes: this was no less than
to fall prostrate before the Persian monarch, and
to worship him as the living image of the gods
on earth. Themistocles being admitted into
the royal presence, prostrated himself accordingly, made a most moving speech, and informed the king of his name, his country, and
misfortunes. " You see at your feet," says he,

" Themistocles, a man that has indeed injured
the Persians much, but who has it in his power to
render them very important services.   My life
is at your disposal.   If you save it, you will
eternally oblige a man that begs it at your hands;
if you take it away, you will destroy the greatest enemy the Greeks have."   The king was
struck at his intrepidity and eloquence ; but
made him no answer.   He soon, however,
gave a loose to his joy, and told his courtiers,
that he considered the arrival of Themistocles
as the happiest of incidents, and wished his enemies would always pursue the same destructive
methods, and banish from among them all that
were good and wise.   Plutarch says, that Artaxerxes was so well pleased with him, that in
the night after the audience, he cried out three
times in his sleep, " I have got Themistocles,
the Athenian."   The next morning the king
sent for him ; and as soon as the first compliments were over, said, " I am two hundred
talents in your debt, for so much I promised to
him that should bring Themistocles."   Artaxerxes bestowed upon him three cities for his
support, and he lived in all the splendour and
magnificence of a Persian grandee.   It is said,
that such was the favour he possessed at court,
and so great the consideration in which he was
held by all ranks and degrees of people, that he
cried out to his wife and children one day at
table, " Children, we should have been certainly ruined, had we not been formerly undone."
  In this manner he lived in affluence and contented dependence, until the Persian monarch
pressed him to undertake an expedition against
Greece. Although Themistocles professed himself an enemy to his country, yet he was not so

void of patriotick feelings, but that he nourished a latent spark of affection for Athens, which no resentment nor injuries could wholly efface. He felt inexpressible pain at the thoughts of being instrumental in the ruin and destruction of a city which had flourished by his counsels and exertions. He found himself unable to perform that duty and gratitude he owed to the king, or to erase from his heart the love of his country. The only means left to ease him of this perplexity, was death. Having, therefore, made a solemn sacrifice, at which he entertained all his friends, he swallowed poison, and thus put an end to his life. He died at Magnesia, aged threescore and six years, and was honoured with a stately tomb; but his ashes, according to his particular request, were privately carried into Attica, and buried there. Themistocles united in himself all the great and prominent features of the Greek character. He was sagacious, eloquent, and brave; but unprincipled, artful, and mercenary. The means employed to attain his object gave him little or no concern, provided he thereby obtained what he sought. It was a usual saying with him, that every thing, which contributes to the advantage or glory of the commonwealth, is lawful and laudable. In short, he was possessed of too many virtues, to be considered as a despicable character, and too many defects ever to be regarded as a good one.

It is worthy of observation, that the three great commanders of Greece, who had B. C. 471. resisted and disgraced the arms of Xerxes, quitted the scene almost at the same time. While Pausanias and Themistocles suffered punishment for their real or pretended crimes, the good Aristides died of old age, uni-

versally regretted and lamented by his affection-
ate fellow-citizens. He who had for a long time
managed the treasury of Greece, left not a sum
sufficient to defray his own funeral expenses.
The publick gave his son three hundred pounds,
to enable him to pursue and finish his education;
and his daughters were maintained and portion-
ed by the state. This honourable poverty well
corresponded with the manly and dignified
gravity of his character, whose pure and unsul-
lied splendour far outshines the doubtful fame
of his great and daring, but unfortunate rival.

Upon the death of Aristides, Cimon, who is
said to have united in his own person the courage of Miltiades, and the prudence of Themistocles, with more integrity than both, was left
without an equal in favour and authority with
the Athenian people, and the conduct of the
Persian war immediately devolved on him. He
first led the Grecian armament against the coasts
of Thrace, and attacked the towns of Amphipolis and Eion, situated on the river Strymon.
The former was soon taken; but the latter opposed an obstinate and vigorous resistance. Cimon having reduced the garrison to extremities,
offered terms of capitulation. But Butes, the
Persian governour, with a ferocious heroism, refused to surrender the place; and, when hunger
pressed upon them, throwing the gold and silver, and other things of value, into the river
Strymon, caused a large pile of wood to be raised, killed his wife, concubines, children, and
slaves, and, setting fire to the pile, precipitated
himself into the midst of the flames, and thus
perished. His companions and attendants,
equally desperate, followed the example of their
intrepid leader. Cimon having punished the

Thracians, who had assisted the Persians in Ionia with provision, settled colonies in that neighbourhood.

. The inhabitants of the little isle of Scyros, a Thessalian tribe, had been guilty of many enormities and depredations in the Ægean sea. The amphictyonic council now interfering, commanded Cimon to put an end to those piracies, and to free the Greeks from domestick, as well B. C. 470. as foreign enemies. Cimon immediately obeyed, and reduced the place; and the inhabitants being sold for slaves, the island was repeopled from Athens.

Those great reasons and urgent necessities, which had given birth to the Grecian confederacy against Persia, now ceased to exist. In Europe, the only place which was under the government of the Persian monarch was Doriscus. Every other garrison in Thrace, and on the Hellespont, a name under which the early Greek writers often included the whole tract of water from the Ægean to the Euxine sea, had yielded to the Grecian arms. It could not, therefore, be supposed, that Greece was any longer in imminent danger from the ambition and resentment of the Persian monarch; but it was nevertheless highly necessary, that a navy should be maintained, sufficiently powerful to deter, or repel, any future attacks of an enemy still formidable if put in motion. Many, however, of the inferior states of Greece, when danger no longer pressed, first became lukewarm in the cause, and then averse to the continuance of a war which burthened them with expenses. The citizens grew weary of serving in the fleet, under what they considered, in some measure, a foreign command; and which seemed to promote in no shape the

interest and advantage of their own commonwealths. The several administrations, accustomed always to a perfect independency, would
still determine, each for itself, when it could not
exert the irksome and invidious office of taxing
the people, for the support of the navy, or enforce the still more invidious office of compelling
personal service. The Athenian government,
on the other hand, at first modest, and, under
the administration of Aristides, scrupulously
just in the exercise of supremacy, grew afterward rigid and imperious. Some of the subordinate commonwealths, influenced by views of a
publick or private nature, concurred in the measures of Athens, became jealous of the defection
of others, and ready to join in compelling ad-
herence to the confederacy.

The inhabitants of Naxos a rich and populous
island, and one of the Cyclades, were the first
to venture opposition against the grand alliance.
Confiding in that strength with which they had
formerly baffled the force of the Persians under
the command of Datis and Artaphernes, they
sustained the war for a considerable time against
the arms of the confederates. But, being at
length compelled to capitulate, they surrendered
upon terms that deprived them of their liberty
and independency. Thus was Naxos, contrary
to the express articles of the covenant agreed on
by the Grecian states, reduced to the subjection
of Athens. This example being made of the
Naxians, it became necessary to exert themselves against the common enemy, that clamour
and faction might cease, and vigour and courage
once more animate the confederates. In the
Grecian communities that bordered on the Persian empire, all who aspired to be tyrants, whom

faction had banished, or who were discontented
with the government under which they lived,
still looked to Persia for patronage and protection. The prospect of revived vigour in the councils of a new king gave hope and encouragement
to such views; and most of the Cyprian towns
had already deserted the cause of Greece. Some
Grecian cities also in Asia minor were still under the subjection of the Persian government;
and in Caria the arms of the confederates had
never yet been seen; while the people of Phaselis, a Grecian settlement in the adjoining province of Pamphylia, made no scruple of professing their preference of the Persian to the Grecian
alliance.

With the formidable and numerous armament
which Cimon had now under his command, he
stretched towards the coasts of Caria; and such
was the terrour which the fame of his troops inspired, that many of the Greek cities in that
valuable province were deserted by their garrisons, before any enemy appeared. Seconded
by the ardour of the natives, Cimon successively
besieged and reduced all the walled towns and
fortresses, in many of which were numerous and
powerful garrisons; and the Persians were expelled from Caria. He then entered Pamphylia, the whole coast of which submitted to him.
Phaselis alone refused to admit the Grecian fleet,
or to desert the Persian monarch. The place
was immediately besieged; but such had been
their ancient connection with the Chians, who
served under Cimon, that a treacherous correspondence was held with the enemy. After other
means of intercourse had been cut off, the Chians shot arrows into the place, and informed the
besieged of every measure adopted by the as-

sailants. Wherever the confederates made an attack, the garrison and townsmen, having previous notice, were prepared to resist. At length, however, by the perseverance of Cimon, Phaselis was compelled to capitulate. The vigorous resistance of the garrison was not followed by any particular punishment. The Chians, who were universally allowed to be the best sailors in the Athenian fleet, prevailed on the lenity of Cimon to allow them a capitulation, provided they paid ten talents, and added the whole of their naval strength to the Grecian armament.

The distracted state of Persia, at this time, hindered Artaxerxes from making any vigorous efforts to resist the European invasion. But as soon as that prince had crushed the ambition of his competitors, and quieted domestick faction, he assembled an army on the banks of the Eurymedon in Pamphylia, and sent a fleet to cooperate with it. A reinforcement of eighty triremes from Phenicia was also expected, upon the arrival of which he proposed to begin his operations.

Cimon, having notice of these circumstances, resolved to quit the objects he had in view on the continent, and to attack the hostile fleet before the expected squadron should arrive. Among the ancients, naval operations were almost always connected with those by land. Cimon, therefore, embarked a considerable part of his forces, and sailed for the Eurymedon. On his arrival, the Persian fleet, already much more numerous than that of the Greeks, advanced to meet him. An engagement immediately ensued; but, after an obstinate and bloody battle, many of the Persian ships were sunk; a hundred were taken; and the rest fled in disorder toward the shores of Cyprus. A powerful detachment of the Grecian fleet pursued the Persian vessels, which the terrour of their crews abandoned to the victors. Thus did the mighty preparations of Artaxerxes, instead of weakening, strengthen, in one day, the hostile navy of Greece with three hundred sail.

Far from being intoxicated with this flow of prosperity, the great and vigorous mind of Cimon considered only how the advantages already obtained might be improved. As the soldiers encamped on the Eurymedon were entirely ignorant of the battle, Cimon resolved to put in execution a plan for surprising the Persian camp. On the evening, therefore, of the same glórious day, he stripped the prisoners, amounting to twenty thousand men, of their Persian habiliments, with which he dressed his own soldiers. The bravest of the Greeks condescended to assume the tiara and the scymitar, and thus disguised sailed up the river Eurymedon. As soon as the Persians beheld the Greeks in this attire, supposing them to be their expected companions, they received them with open arms into their camp. But the confederates were no sooner admitted, than, on a signal being given, they drew their swords, and attacked, with the concert of disciplined valour, their defenceless and astonished adversaries. Consternation and dismay seized this numerous and unwarlike host; nor did they recover from their surprise, until Cimon had advanced to the camp of their general. The few that had more presence of mind betook themselves to flight; but the rest remained without power, and fell an easy prey to the conquerors. Thus did Cimon erect in one day two trophies for two victories, gained on different elements by the same armament. After this, receiving intelligence that the Phenician gallies, which had been intended to reinforce the fleet, lay in the port of Hydrus, in Cyprus, he sent a squadron of his best ships thither, and every trireme was destroyed or taken.

By these great successes, the naval strength of Persia was so broken, the land-forces so much disheartened, and the spirit of enterprise, which had formerly animated its councils, and excited its commanders, was so weakened and depressed, that offensive operations against Greece were immediately intermitted. It became the boast of the Greeks, that no Persian ship of war appeared westward of the Chelidonian isles on the coast of Pamphylia, or of the Cyanean rocks at the entrance of the Euxine ; and that no Persian troops approached within three days journey of the Grecian seas.

B. C. 468.
Cimon returned in triumph to his country, with such trophies as Greece had never before won, in a field so distant. Of the wealth that was the fruit of these victories, and which had been taken from the Persians, part was deposited in the publick treasury, part rewarded the individuals who had accompanied Cimon, and a large proportion became the property of the commander. In order to obtain and ensure the affections of the people, Cimon spent with liberality and profusion what he had acquired. He threw down the fences of his gardens, and permitted all to partake of their produce ; a table was daily spread at his house for the poorer citizens ; and he assisted with his wealth not only his own particular friends, but the greatest part of the Athenians. In going about the city, he was generally accompanied by a

large retinue handsomely dressed; and when he met an elderly citizen ill clad, he directed one of his attendants to change clothes with him. In his youth, Cimon had affected a roughness of manners, and a contempt for the elegancies of life; but in his riper age he discovered that no natural connection subsisted between grossness and virtue. He raised the first of the Athenian porticoes, where the people were wont to assemble, and to hold promiscuous discourse. He founded the fame of the celebrated groves of Academus, by forming commodious and elegant walks in the wood, and adorning them with running water. He planted palm trees in the forum, which afforded an agreeable and salutary shade to those who exposed their wares there, and to those who came to purchase them. The stores, with which his victories enriched the treasury, furnished the sums employed upon the works executed under his direction, and especially the completion of the fortifications of the citadel. The riches which these conquests had produced to Athens brought with them their constant attendant, corruption; but, though venality prevailed much, Aristides, in the midst of a voluntary poverty, and Cimon, who lived with the greatest splendour and magnificence, escaped it, and were never charged with partiality or avarice.

While Cimon, by a splendid and princely liberality, endeavoured to confirm his interest with the people, he was not unmindful of the general welfare. The citizens of the Grecian confederacy grew still more impatient of the requisitions made upon them for publick service, and longed to return home that they might enjoy peace and domestick happiness. But that the main-

tenance of a navy was necessary, so long as the
Persian army existed, or the Grecian seas offered a temptation for piracy, could not be denied.   Most of the allies, therefore, agreed to
compound for the personal service of their citizens, by furnishing ships, and paying a sum of
money to the common treasury ; and the Athenians were to man the fleet.   While by the consequences of this agreement, Athens greatly
strengthened herself, and reduced to impotence
many of the allied states, she became less scrupulous of using force against those who disputed
her sovereign authority.

The reduction of Eion by the confederate
arms under Cimon had made her better acquainted with the value of the adjacent country.   It
abounded with mines of silver and gold, and a
lucrative commerce was carried on with the
Thracian hordes.   These excited the avidity of
the conquerors ; but the inhabitants of the neighbouring island of Thasus had anciently possessed the mines and commerce of that country.
When, therefore, the Persians were overcome
by the arms of Greece, the Thasians asserted
their rights, and insisted that they should again
revert to them entire.   The Athenians, on the
contrary, claimed the principal share in right
B. C. of conquest.   The Thasians, irritated at
465. the conduct of their allies, renounced the
confederacy ; and Cimon was ordered by
the Athenian government to proceed against
them.   The Thasians, venturing a naval engagement, were defeated ; and Cimon, debarking his
forces, reduced all but the principal town, to
which he laid siege.   In the mean time, the
Athenian government sent a colony of ten thousand men to inhabit the country around Eion.

But the Thracian tribes attacking the Greeks, overpowered, and cut them in pieces, and annihilated the colony.

During these trânsactions, Cimon carried on the siege of Thasus with great vigour, but met with an obstinate resistance from the besieged. The Thasians, however, not depending upon their own strength for success, requested the assistance of the Lacedæmonians. The Spartans, sensible of the necessity of interfering in this dispute, and thereby giving a check to the growing, and already formidable power of Athens, determined to send troops to invade Attica. But a sudden and destructive earthquake overturning the city of Sparta at this crisis, and in its consequences threatening ruin to the state, the Lacedæmonians were compelled to abandon the enterprise. The Thasians, therefore, having withstood the confederate arms for three years, were obliged to capitulate, upon terms, indeed, sufficiently severe, but by which they avoided the wretched condition of slavery.

B. C. 462. Cimon, thus successful, did not meet, on his return home, with that reception which his merits and victories entitled him to expect. Like other great men, his predecessors, his glory excited envy. Through the prevalence of faction, he was prosecuted for having received bribes from Alexander, king of Macedonia, to stop the progress of the Grecian arms against that country. Cimon, indignant at the ungrateful return for the services he had performed, only told the people that he had never sought any connexion with the Macedonians, but confessed he considered them as a brave and virtuous nation ; nor would he ever prefer wealth to those qualities, though he had enriched Athens with the spoils of its enemies. The popularity of Cimon was yet great; and this defence procured him an honourable acquittal.

In the mean time, Lacedæmon had been in the greatest consternation, and on the brink of ruin. The earthquake came suddenly at midday. Twenty thousand persons lost their lives; and only five houses remained standing in Sparta. The Helotes assembled from all parts, with intent to destroy their severe masters that survived, and to seize the country; but the prudence and foresight of Archidamus saved Lacedæmon. In the midst of the general confusion, while some were endeavouring to preserve their most valuable effects, and others fleeing different ways to avoid destruction, he caused the trumpet to sound to arms, as if an enemy had been at hand. The Lacedæmonians immediately obeyed the signal, and armed themselves; and the Helotes seeing a regular army, instead of a confused and scattered multitude, desisted from their meditated attempt. But quitting the city, the Helotes spread themselves over the country, and excited their comrades to rebellion.

They seized Ithome, and made it their principal post. But they so far outnumbered the Lacedæmonians, that though defficiently armed, they were formidable even in the field. Application was therefore made to the neighbouring allies for succour; and the Æginetans and Platæans immediately went to their assistance.— Thus reinforced, the Spartans obliged the insurgents to retire within the walls of Ithome. But that place being naturally strong, and the Lacedæmonians inexpert in sieges, the assistance of the Athenians was requested, who were esteemed skilful and experienced, beyond the other Greeks, in this kind of warfare.

This measure seems to have been, on many accounts, very imprudent and unseasonable, and led, not indeed immediately, but in its direct issue, to the Peloponnesian war. Cimon, thinking it ungenerous to take advantage of the misfortunes of a rival city, persuaded the Athenians

B. C. 461. to send assistance to Sparta; and a considerable body of troops, under his command, marched into Peloponnesus. Being arrived at the camp of the besiegers, they made an attack upon Ithome, but without success. The Spartans suspecting that the Athenians favoured the interest of the insurgents, dismissed them, on pretence that their help was no longer necessary. But, as they still retained the troops of the other allies, the Athenians were justly incensed against them; and disposed more than ever to endeavour to humble the Spartan greatness. As soon as the Athenians had returned home, they passed a decree, renouncing the confederacy with Lacedæmon, and made an alliance with Argos, the inveterate enemy of Sparta; to which also the Thessalians acceded.

In Athens, as in every free government, there would always be a faction adverse to the party that governed: matters had been for some time ripening to a change; and the renunciation of the alliance with Sparta was the triumph of opposition. Cimon had always professed himself a friend to the Lacedæmonians, and an admirer of their institutions; and he had always acted in the capacity he professed. His eldest son he named Lacedæmonius, as a proof of his partiality to that state. And the more completely to demonstrate his disesteem for the Athenian character, his two other sons were called Thessalus and Eleius. He had also been the chief promoter of sending succours to Sparta, when that city desired the assistance of the Athenian people. All these circumstances were now turned to his disadvantage, with all the violence and acrimony of the spirit of party. The epithet Philolacones, or friends to the Lacedæmonians, was bandied about as the mark and opprobrium of the existing government. Whilst the publick mind was thus in a ferment, a favourable opportunity was seized; the ostracism was proposed and carried; and by the banishment of Cimon, the party in opposition became possessed of the reins of government.

The ostensible head of this party was Ephialtes; but Pericles, the son of Xanthippus, had of late obtained an ascendancy in the popular favour. Pericles possessed many advantages, derived both from nature and fortune. His father, a man of one of the first families in Athens, and of large property, had been instrumental in the prosecution of Miltiades; but had chiefly distinguished himself by his bravery and conduct in the battle of Mycale. He married Agariste, the niece of Cleosthenes, who was principally concerned in expelling the Pisistratids from Athens. Their son, born with uncommon abilities, had studied under the most celebrated masters of Greece. Damon had taught him the policy of his country; and Anaxagoras instructed him in natural philosophy and eloquence. In person, manner, and voice, he remarkably resembled Pisistratus. This circumstance for a long time obliged him to conceal the shining qualifications of which he was possessed. In his youth, therefore, he employed his active hours in arms, and his leisure in studies. But when Aristides was dead, Themistocles in banishment, and Cimon absent in foreign service, Pericles applied himself very diligently to publick business. His eloquence is said to have been so nervous and elevated, that it procured him the surname of Olympus. His family interest and party connexions led him to court the popular favour, and to oppose the aristocratical side; though his natural disposition and private inclinations would have inclined him to pursue a different conduct.

· The disposition of the Athenians appearing now to be extremely favourable to those who inclined to the populace more than to the nobility, Ephialtes proposed to contract the powers, and reduce the dignity, of the court of Areopagus. The proposition, which the people passed into a decree, was, that most of the causes, cognizable by that court should be transferred to the assembly of the people; and this assembly was to direct, without control, issues from the publick treasury.

During the confusion in which the Persian government was involved after the death of Xerxes, Inarus, an African chieftain on the western borders of Egypt, had caused the greatest part of that country to rebel; but fearing the power of Artaxerxes, he requested the assistance of the Greeks. The Athenians accordingly sent a fleet, which, having performed great exploits, enabled the Egyptians to defeat the Persians in the field, and to subdue two districts of the great city of Memphis. The third, which was called the White-wall, could not be reduced, and the Persians who retired thither, having carried great quantities of provision and ammunition with them, sustained a vigorous siege. In the mean time, an ancient dispute between Megara and Corinth, respecting the limits of their territories, had led to hostilities.

B. C. 458. Both states were allied to Sparta; but the Megarians, hopeless of procuring aid from Lacedæmon, put themselves under the protection of the Athenians, and requested assistance from them. The Athenian administration immediately complied, and sent troops to garrison some of their principal towns. In the descent on the Argolic coast, the Corinthians and Epidaurians defeated the forces of Athens; but the Athenian fleet soon after obtained a victory over the Peloponnesians. The Æginetans then joined their fleet with that of Corinth; and the Athenians having assembled all the naval force of their confederacy, a battle was fought, seventy ships of the Peloponnesians and their allies were taken, and siege was laid to the capital of Ægina. The Athenians were finally victorious, and Corinth was so weakened by this war, as to be incapable of any considerable exertions for some time.

Lacedæmon, enfeebled by misfortunes and internal discord, had not been induced by the revolt of Megara, or the sufferings of so near an ally as Corinth, to come to a rupture with Athens; though this republick had evinced great enmity towards Sparta, and styled itself the *Protector of Greece*. Doris, however, the mother-country of the Peloponnesians, having been attacked by the Phocians, and several of its towns taken, the Spartans dispatched an army, under the command of Nicomedes, to its assistance. The Phocians, unable to resist this force, surrendered the

Dorian towns, and submitted to the conditions imposed by the Lacedæmonians. But when Nicomedes should have returned to Sparta, the Athenians, joining the Argives and Thessalians, shut up the passes into Peloponnesus. Nicomedes was much at a loss what to do; but having well considered the matter, he resolved to wait an opportunity, and therefore wintered in Bœotia.

The Athenians and their allies, having expected that the severe season of the year, and the impatience of the troops, would have compelled Nicomedes to attempt the passage of the mountains, resolved in the spring to attack him in the plain. Collecting, therefore, all the auxiliary troops they could, they formed a body of fourteen thousand heavy armed foot. These, with the cavalry, and the attending slaves, would make an army of scarcely less than thirty thousand men, with which they marched in Bœotia. Nicomedes met them at Tanagra, and a severe action ensued, in which neither of the contending parties could claim the victory. The next day it was again renewed, and the Thessalian horse treacherously deserting their allies, the Athenians were compelled to leave the Peloponnesians masters of the field, after a terrible slaughter on both sides. Previous to this battle, Cimon met the troops of Athens before they quitted the Attic border; and, as the law of his exile did not absolutely forbid it, requested to fight as a volunteer amongst them. His request, however, was denied, and he was commanded to leave the army. But before he retired, he addressed himself to Euthippus, and the rest of his friends, who had been considered as accessaries with him in the

B. C.
456.

conspiracy against the state, and desired them to act in such a manner, as to wipe off all aspersion, and convince the Athenians, that they had not amongst them either more brave or more honest men, than Cimon and his friends. They made him no other answer, than by requesting him to leave his armour with them, since their generals would not allow him to fight at their head. Accordingly, when the army was routed, the friends of Cimon continued to combat around his panoply, until they were killed to a man.

Neither the force nor the spirit of Athens, however, were broken by the defeat at Tanagra. Myronides was appointed general of the Athenians. On the sixty-second day after the former unfortunate battle, he met the Thebans and their allies, composing a numerous and well disciplined army. After a long and obstinate engagement with these troops, Myronides prevailed; and obtained a glorious and complete victory. The Athenian general then marched to Tanagra, stormed the town, and, to make even the defeats of his country terrible to its enemies, razed it to the ground. He then plundered all Bœotia; and vanquished an army, which had been drawn together, in order to compel him to retreat. He afterward fell upon the Locrians, entered Thessaly, and having chastised the inhabitants of that country for their treacherous conduct to the Athenians, returned home laden with riches and glory. This campaign of Myronides, though no detail of it existed in the time of Diodorus Siculus, was esteemed equal to, if not surpassing, the most brilliant achievements of the Athenian arms.

About this time also the little barren island of

Ægina surrendered to the Athenians. Cut off from all relief by the powerful armaments which Athens possessed, the Æginetans were obliged. at length to capitulate: their ships of war were given up; their fortifications demolished; and they bound themselves to the payment of an annual tribute. In the same summer, the great work of the long walls, which connected the city with the Piræus, was completed.

B. C. 455. Tolmides, the Athenian admiral, sailing round Peloponnesus with a strong squadron, attacked and burnt Gythium, a naval arsenal of the Lacedæmonians. He then proceeded into the Corinthian gulf, disembarked his forces, and having obtained a victory over the Sicyonians by land, took Chalchis in Ætolia. In the tenth year of the war, the Lacedæmonians were obliged to turn the siege of Ithome into a blockade; and at last to hearken to terms of accommodation; by which it was agreed, that the Helotes should depart from Peloponnesus, never to return. The Athenians collected these fugitives, and settled them at Naupactus, on the northern shore of the Corinthian gulf. Having resumed the name of Messenians, which indeed they had never entirely lost, they became a free republick, under the protection of Athens, and were once more reckoned a Grecian people.

While success attended the Athenian forces in Greece, the troops of the republick, engaged in the distant operations in Egypt, experienced various turns of fortune. Grecian valour and Grecian discipline at first triumphed over all opposition, and the Persian government was driven almost to despair. Megabazus was sent with large sums of money to Lacedæmon, to endeavour by bribes to obtain the alliance of that state, and to procure the invasion of Attica by a Spartan army. An Athenian writer, however, almost contemporary, informs us, that the Lacedæmonians refused to accede to a proposal, to which resentment, ambition, and political intrigue, it might have been supposed, would have contributed so powerfully to incite them.

At length, therefore, the Persians assembled a numerous and powerful army on the confines of Cilicia and Syria; and a fleet was prepared in Phenicia and other maritime provinces. Megabazus led his troops into the field, early in the spring; and the Egyptians, venturing a battle, were defeated. The little army of Greeks, compelled to raise the siege, retired into an island of the Nile, where their fleet joined them. The Persians could not act against them here. Megabazus having formed dikes, and cut water-courses, drained the channel in which lay the Athenian gallies. The fleet being by these means rendered unserviceable, the Grecian army was left open to attack; and after a siege of eighteen months, the island was taken; part of the Grecian troops forcing their way, escaped, but the greater part perished.

B. C. 456.

B. C. 454.

Fifty trireme gallies also, sailing to Egypt, to relieve an equal number there, entered the mouth of the Nile, ignorant of what had happened. The Phenician squadron instantly attacked them, and being assisted by the army on shore, very few were saved.

A reconciliation between the aristocratical and democratical parties in Athens appears to have taken place about this time. Pericles proposed in an assembly of the people to recal Cimon from banishment, after the expiration of only five years of his exile. A cessation of hostilities between the Athenians and the other states of Greece was an immediate consequence of his restoration. Where, however, there were so many jarring interests, a reconciliation could not be easily effected. Before any treaty of peace with the Peloponnesian confederacy could be brought to a conclusion, three years of intermitted war elapsed; and then only a truce for five years was agreed on.

Such was become the constitution of the Athenian commonwealth, and so great the effects which the continuance of war had produced on the minds of the people, that, in order to preserve quiet at home, Cimon saw the necessity of turning the spirit of enterprise towards foreign conquest, and against the common enemy of Greece. He, therefore, determined to make an attack upon Cyprus, that his countrymen might desist from making war upon the Lacedæmonians, or oppressing their allies. Two hundred gallies were equipped, of which he took the command. Sixty of them were detached to Egypt to distract the attention of the Persian government. With his remaining force he attacked Citium and Malum, of which he made himself master. After this success, he defeated the Phenician fleet, obtained a victory over the Persian army encamped in Cilicia, and re-embarking his troops, returned to Cyprus, and laid siege to the principal city. In the camp, however, before that place, Cimon died in the arms of victory. It is not known whether his death was occasioned by sickness, or by a wound he had received. His remains were carried to Athens, and buried there; and a magnificent monument was erected to his memory.

The death of this great man was not less honourable than had been his life. When he found that he was about to expire, he gave suitable directions to the principal commanders; ordered them to conceal his decease, and to embark immediately for Athens. Great as was the military character of Cimon, his wisdom, integrity, moderation, and conciliatory conduct, were virtues for which his loss was most severely felt and deplored. Others might command fleets and armies, and obtain victories; but they could not, or did not, free Greece from civil feuds, and domestick wars.

After the death of Cimon, Pericles became the principal person in the state. But the aristocratical party never ceased to molest and oppose him. Thucydides, the brother-in-law of Cimon, was the chief leader of the party in opposition. He was a man of very respectable character, not without reputation for military talents; but more known as an experienced statesman and able speaker. Pericles, however, obtained the ascendency in directing the affairs of government.

Pericles, conceived an idea of improving the constitution of the Athenian empire, or rather of that of all Greece. For this purpose, he proposed to form of the several little republicks, one great commonwealth, of which Athens should be the head. But the pride of the Peloponnesians, and particularly of the Lacedæmonians, who opposed the measure with all their power, compelled him to abandon the project; and he was reduced to the necessity of adhering to the former policy of the Grecian states.

The Megarians having revolted from the Athenians, and entered into an alliance with the Lacedæmonians, occasioned a war between Athens and Sparta. The Eubæans also having revolted, Pericles marched an army into Euboea, and quickly reduced the whole of that island. The Hestiæans were ejected from their city, and an Athenian colony was settled in it. A negotiation between the Athenians and Lacedæmonians was soon after proposed, and a cessation of hostilities concluded for thirty years.

B. C. 446.

CHAP. VIII.

The Affairs of Greece from the Truce for thirty Years, to the Peace of Nicias.

SCARCELY had six years of the truce expired, when Athens, by the dissentions of the Samians and Milesians was led into another war. The inhabitants of Miletus applied to Athens for redress against the Samians; and the Athenian government, in consequence, required the inhabitants of Samos to appear and answer to the charges of which they were accused. This they refusing to do, the Athenians sent a fleet of forty gallies, which brought them to submission; and their government was changed into a democracy. Pericles, it is reported, engaged the Athenians in this war, in order to gratify his mistress Aspasia, a Milesian, the handsomest woman of her age, who had such an ascendency over him, that for her sake he weakly and wickedly sacrificed his family and his peace. The democratical form of government, however, being soon overturned after the return of Pericles, a second expedition was fitted out; and after besieging Samos for nine months, the place surrendered. Pericles razed the fortifications, bound the inhabitants to the payment of a certain sum for the expenses of the war, and received hostages as pledges of their fidelity to Athens. Flushed with his successes, he returned home, buried the dead with great solemnity, and pronounced their funeral oration with so much eloquence and pathos, that, when he descended the rostrum, the women crowned him with chaplets.

From a spark excited in a remote corner of the country arose that general conflagration in Greece, distinguished by the name of the Peloponnesian war. The island of Corcyra, originally occupied by a colony of Corinthians, had become independent, and a rival and enemy of its parent state, in maritime commerce. The Corcyreans, however, intending to settle some of their people on the Illyrian coast, requested for this purpose a leader from the Corinthians, who was granted them. In process of time, Epidamnus (for this was the name of the colony) grew populous and wealthy, asserted its independence, and maintained the claim. An intestine war breaking out amongst the citizens of Epidamnus, one party requested the assistance of the Illyrians, whilst the other made application to Corcyra. The Corcyreans, however, refusing to intermeddle in the dispute, the Epidamnians sent to desire succours from Corinth, and acknowledged that city as the foundress of their colony. The Corinthians, more actuated by hatred to Corcyra, than good will to Epidamnus, sent a numerous and powerful fleet to the assistance of those that had applied, and reinstated them in possession of the island. As soon as the Corcyreans were made acquainted with the proceedings of Corinth, they equipped a still larger and more powerful fleet, and expelled the party which had sought the aid of the Corinthians.

Corinth not being possessed of so great a naval force as Corcyra, application was made to the republicks her allies. When the Corcyreans received advice of these proceedings they immediately dispatched messengers to Athens, to request the interference of that state, while the Corinthians also did the same. The Athenians entered into a defensive alliance with the Corcyreans, and sent them assistance; but an engagement ensuing, the Corinthians were victorious.

The Corcyrean war was followed by the revolt of Potidæa, a town in Macedonia, founded by the Corinthians, but joined in alliance with Athens. The Athenians had sent orders to the inhabitants of Potidæa, to raze the fortifications, to send back the magistrates they received from Corinth, and to give hostages for their future good conduct and fidelity. The Potidæans, very averse to obey, yet afraid to dispute these commands, attempted to impose upon the Athenians by duplicity. But being detected, a battle followed, in which the Potidæans were discomfited. In this engagement, Alcibiades, who was but a very young man, and Socrates his master, chiefly distinguished themselves. That philosopher was observed to endure the fatigues of war with an ease, that must have been a consequence of the sober and temperate life to which he had inured himself; and he acted with a courage and resolution, that would have done hon-

our to a veteran in arms. Wishing to inspire
his pupil with a love of glory, he obtained the
prize of valour to be adjudged to Alcibiades,
though Socrates himself was much more deserving of that reward. After this victory, the
Athenians besieged Potidæa.

The Corinthians now applied to Sparta, and
accompanied by the deputies of the several republicks who had experienced the arrogance of
Athens, pleaded their cause before the Lacedæmonian assembly. They urged the several
wrongs they had received, and inveighed against
the cruelty and injustice of that state. The
Spartans having heard all the complaints that
the several communities of Greece had to make
against the Athenians, embassadors were dispatched to Athens to demand reparation of injuries; or, in case of refusal, to denounce war
against that republick. The Lacedæmonian embassy required the Athenians to raise the siege
of Potidæa; to repeal a prohibitory decree against
Megara ; to withdraw their garrison from Ægina; and, in fine, to declare the independence of
their colonies.

These demands were heard at Athens with
mingled indignation and terrour. The inconstant
multitude who had hitherto approved and ad-
mired the views and actions of Pericles, now
trembled on the brink of the precipice, to which
he had conducted them. The factions, adverse
to the governing party, embraced the opportunity which these discontented murmurs afforded,
to traduce the character and administration of
that statesman. His most valuable friends were
impeached in the courts of justice ; and the accusation of them was only preparatory to that
of himself. Unshaken and undismayed, how-

ever, amidst the storm, Pericles pleaded the cause of his friends; and vindicated his conduct in a very eloquent and famous, but fatal, discourse, which unalterably decided the war of Peloponnesus.

He informed the Athenians, that whatever the Lacedæmonians might pretend, with respect to the complaints of the allies, the true reason of their resentment was the prosperity of Athens, a state they had always hated, and to destroy which they now sought an opportunity; but as, from reasons accurately and judiciously stated by him, it appeared the Athenians were more able than the Peloponnesians to support an expensive and protracted war, he urged, that it would be scarcely in the power of fortune to rob his countrymen of victory. He, therefore, advised, as the most just and equitable satisfaction which could be given, to answer the Peloponnesians, that the Athenians would not forbid the Megarians their ports and markets, if the Spartans, and other Grecian states abolished their exclusive and inhospitable laws; that they would restore independence to the cities and communities, provided the Lacedæmonians would engage to do the same; that future disputes should be submitted to arbitration; and that, though these condescending overtures should be rejected, they would not commence hostilities, but would repel them with vigour. This reply, moderate as it seemed to the Athenian statesman, was considered by the Spartans and their allies little short of a declaration of war.

Matters being in this situation, the Thebans, who were the most powerful and the most daring of the Spartan allies, undertook a military enterprise against the small but magnanimous republick of Platæa. This state had been always remarkable for its fidelity to Athens, whose toils and triumphs the Platæans had shared in the Persian war. The Thebans conceiving that this republick, would, in the event of the commencement of hostilities, be a troublesome and dangerous neighbour, sent Eurymachus with three hundred men to surprise the place. The town was betrayed to the Thebans by a factious party of the people; but the Platæans, perceiving the small number of the conspirators, attacked them, killed many, and obliged the rest to surrender themselves prisoners at discretion. In the mean time, a considerable body of Thebans advanced to cooperate with their fellow-citizens. The Platæans, foreseeing the injury the Thebans would do to their country, sent a herald to command them to leave their territory; and to denounce, in case of refusal, the cruel death that should be inflicted on their comrades. This stratagem, not less audacious than artful, induced the enemy to repass the Æsopus. The Platæans, however, lost not a moment to assemble within their walls their scattered inhabitants; and braving the Theban resentment, massacred the prisoners to the number of one hundred and eighty. The Athenians, being informed of the attempt of the Thebans, caused all the Bœotians to be arrested. They afterward supplied the Platæans with provision and a considerable reinforcement of troops; transported their wives and children to the island of Athens; and greatly strengthened the works of the place.

The league being now broken on both sides, each party prepared for war. Both the Spartans and the Athenians solicited the assistance of Persia; and both summoned their confederates to arms. Most of the Grecian states were inclined to the Lacedæmonians, because they professed, on this occasion, to be the deliverers of Greece. All the Peloponnesians joined the Spartans, the Argives and part of the Achæans only excepted; and north of the isthmus, the Megarians, Phocians, Locrians, Bœotians, Ambracotes, Leucadians, and Anactorians, declared themselves on the same side. On the other hand, the Athenians numbered among their allies the Chians, Lesbians, Platæans, Messenians, Acarnanians, Corcyrians, Zacynthians, Carians, Dorians, Thracians, most of the islands, and all the Cyclades, excepting Melus and Thera, with Eubœa and Samos. Such was the ardour of preparation, that, only a few weeks after the surprise of Platæa, the Lacedæmonians and their confederates assembled an army of sixty thousand men at the isthmus of Corinth. The several states appointed a leader for their own troops; but the general conduct of the war was intrusted to Archidamus, the Spartan king.

In a council of the chiefs, this prince warmly approved the alacrity and readiness of the troops in taking the field, extolled the greatness and formidable appearance of an army, the most numerous and best provided that had ever followed a Grecian standard. But, however great their exertions and preparations, they were not more than proportionable to the difficult and dangerous enterprise, in which they were about to engage. The people with whom they had to wage war, were powerful, active, and daring. They had discernment to perceive, and ability to improve every opportunity of advantage. Their pride would be wounded, and their resentment inflamed by the approach of hostil-

B. C.
431.

ity and invasion. The Athenians were little
likely to suffer their lands and property to be
wasted and destroyed, without endeavouring to
defend them. It was, therefore, necessary, that
the confederates should be always prepared and
on their guard; and that their discipline should
be strict, regular and uniform, if they hoped to
elude the skill, and oppose the strength and vigour of Athens.

Pericles, in the mean time, having engaged
his countrymen in the war, found it absolutely
requisite to use his utmost exertions against an
enemy far superiour in numbers, and with whom
he feared to contend in the field; he, therefore,
advised, that, leaving their villas and gardens,
and transporting themselves, their cattle, furniture, and valuable effects to Athens, they should
employ themselves in equipping a fleet, and in
fortifying and defending the city. This singular
plan of defence, so ably and boldly traced by
the lofty genius of Pericles, obtained universal
approbation, and was immediately put into execution. The numerous inhabitants of the country
towns and villages, where the more wealthy Athenians were wont to spend their time, flocked to
the capital. Athens, however, though furnished with the means of subsistence, could but illy
afford accomodation for such an influx and increase of families, servants, and slaves. The
publick halls, the groves and temples, with the
walls and battlements, were occupied by many
people of the lower rank of life. The dwellings
of persons of distinction were mean and confined.
Yet such was the resentment against the common enemy, and so great the publick spirit of
the people, that not a single murmur was heard
amongst them.

Archidamus, at the head of his numerous army, marched into Attica; and penetrated within a few miles of Athens. Being still desirous to avoid the war, if possible, he dispatched a messenger to that city; but the Athenians commanded him to return, without hearing his proposals. The enemies of Archidamus insinuating, that, on account of his friendship and respect for the Athenians, he was injuring and betraying the cause of the confederates, the Spartan king immediately ravaged and laid waste the Eleusinian and Thrasian plains. Having desolated these fruitful and valuable districts with fire and sword, the army advanced to Acharnæ. The people in that borough formed no fewer than three thousand heavy armed foot; and as they could not but have great influence in the Athenian assembly, Archidamus thought the impending destruction of their property and estates would make them eager to leave the city, and to give battle to the confederates. His judgment in this respect was accurate and just. No sooner did the Peloponnesian army appear in sight of Athens, and the rich Acharnian plain be known to be the next object of its devastation, than the city was filled with tumult and uproar. Some were vehement for marching out and defending their property. Others warmly contended against a measure, which would endanger the commonwealth. But all condemned Pericles as the author of their misfortunes.

Amidst this popular commotion, the Athenian general and statesman remained firm and immovable, bravely resisting the storm, or eluding its force. Though determined to risk no general engagement with the confederate troops, he omitted no opportunity of beating up their quarters, intercepting their convoys, or surprising their advanced parties. The Athenian and Thessalian cavalry generally formed these detachments. A fleet of one hundred gallies, with a number of land forces on board, ravaged the defenceless coast of Peloponnesus. Another squadron invaded Locris. The inhabitants of Ægina were driven from their possessions, and the island was repeopled from Athens. These several enterprises tended to amuse and divert the publick mind, and to appease faction.

Intelligence of the proceedings of the Athenians in Peloponnesus, but still more a scarcity of provision, that prevailed in the army, induced the confederates to disperse and return to their respective republicks. Having entered Attica on the east, they retired along the western frontier, and spread desolation over the whole Athenian territory. After the Peloponnesian army had retreated, Pericles led out the Athenians, who ravaged and despoiled the neighbouring and hostile province of Megara. The fleet returning from the coast of Peloponnesus, perceived the invading army, and the sailors hastened to share the danger and the plunder of the place. The whole Athenian force amounted now to near twenty thousand men. Thus, in the end of the year, the Athenians repaid the insults and ravages, which, at the commencement of it, the confederates had committed in Attica.

The winter was not distinguished by any important expedition on either side. During the inactivity of this season, the two hostile parties employed themselves in celebrating the memory of the dead, with much funeral pomp, and high encomiums on their valour and martial exploits.

They also distributed prizes and rewards among the survivors, who had distinguished themselves in battle; cemented the alliances and friendships they had formed with other states; and fortified those places in the frontiers of their country, which seemed most defenceless and open to attack.

The spring of the next year was doubly fatal to the Athenians. The Peloponnesian army returned to commit its ravages in the territory about Athens; and a destructive pestilence, imported, as was afterwards supposed, from Egypt, desolated the city. It broke out first in the Piræus, and the inhabitants conjectured, that the enemies had poisoned their wells. It soon spread over the whole adjacent country, and raged with peculiar violence in the populous districts that surrounded the citadel. This disease appeared in various forms, according to the constitution of the person attacked with it, but its specifick symptoms were invariably the same. A burning heat in the head was the sure indication of its approach. The eyes then became red and inflamed; and the tongue and mouth assumed the colour of blood. The pain and inflammation descended to the stomach and lower parts of the body; the skin was covered with ulcers; and the external heat not sensible to the touch, but the internal so violent, that the slightest covering could not be endured.—The patients were attacked with an insatiable thirst, which, when indulged, increased the disorder. Some existed seven or nine days under this distemper, and then expired with apparent remains of strength. Others, whose bowels were attacked, died in debility. Those, who once recovered, were never dangerously ill af-

terward. The disorder, which was always accompanied with an extreme dejection of spirits,
frequently impaired the judgment and the memory. All remedies human and divine were employed to stop the raging malady, but in vain.
The crowds rushed to the temples, and implored the assistance of their gods, but without effect. Near the fountains, whither they had
come to quench their thirst, and around the altars of their divinities, were the dead and the
dying. At length all medical assistance was
despised, and all ceremonies of religion were
neglected. Wherever the doctrine of retribu-
tion in a life to come is believed, a general calamity strongly tends to check the passions, to
inspire serious thoughts, and to direct the attention to a future state of existence; but in Athens,
where the deity was considered as a dispenser
of temporal good and evil only, it was otherwise.
The fear of offending the divine power immediately ceased. For to worship, or not worship
the gods; to obey, or not obey the dictates of
morality; availed nothing. All died alike; and
if there were any difference, the virtuous and
the good, who exposed themselves for the sake
of others, were the first and the surest victims.
A licentiousness of manners succeeded; and the
only pursuit was that of pleasure. To beings,
whose existence was not thought to be protracted beyond the present moment, the dread of
punishment formed no restraint, and the scru-
ples of conscience raised no terrours. The prevailing maxim was, "let us eat, drink, and be
merry, for to-morrow we die." Athens thus exhibited a spectacle the most distressful and
alarming, that can possibly be conceived; for
wretchedness and vice, disease and unbridled

passions, were united. This relaxation, and almost dissolution of morals, was a lasting and lamentable effect of the pestilence at Athens.

While the plague thus raged in the metropolis, the Peloponnesian army was ravaging and desolating the whole Attic territory. The firm mind of Pericles, conscious of its wisdom and rectitude, was scarcely, however, to be depressed by any casualties and calamities that befel either his country or himself. His fortitude was still superiour to the publick and domestick sufferings by which he was surrounded. The dreadful and rapacious pestilence snatched away successively his numerous and flourishing family; and he beheld with a decent and magnanimous composure its baneful and unhappy effects. At the funeral, however, of the last of his sons, the manly mind of Pericles appeared dejected, and when he approached to place a chaplet of flowers on the head of the corpse, he dropped a few reluctant tears of paternal tenderness; but ashamed of his weakness, he immediately bent his whole study to the affairs of his country. He took the command of an armament destined to act against Peloponnesus; and making descents successively upon the Epidaurian and Argian coasts, ravaged all the neighbouring countries.

In the mean time, the Peloponnesians being informed of the force that Pericles had carried against their country, and not unacquainted with the terrible havock which the plague was at that time making in Athens, withdrew their troops from Attica. The Athenian armament, that had returned home, again sailed, to co-operate in the siege of Potidæa with the army of Phormion, which at that time blockaded the place. This measure seemed to be ill-judged, and was certainly unfortunate. The fresh troops, carrying with them the plague from Athens, not only perished themselves in great numbers, but infected the army of Phormion, which had been hitherto healthy.

Accumulated evils, publick and private, irritated beyond sufferance the minds of the Athenian people. Popular discontent always finds some object on which to vent its spleen and resentment, and that object now was Pericles. The bulk of the people desired peace, on whatever terms it could be procured. Embassadors were sent to Sparta, to endeavour to negotiate with that republick; but in proportion as the Athenians were depressed by the circumstances that surrounded them, the Lacedæmonians and their allies became arrogant, and the embassadors were not admitted to an audience. Hereupon a popular ferment was raised in Athens, and the orators clamoured, and traduced Pericles. In his capacity of general of the commonwealth, he had full powers to convene the assembly of the people whenever he deemed it advisable. He, therefore, summoned the people, and, for the last time, mounted the publick tribunal.

But the speech of Pericles, though excellently adapted to the circumstances of the occasion, did not produce the effects, with which he had flattered himself. It prevailed, however, with the people, to determine to offer again no proposals of peace to Sparta. But the irritation excited by the private sufferings of the Athenians could not be so easily appeased. Many of the poor were reduced to almost total want; the rich bore not without extreme uneasiness and dissatisfaction the loss and destruction of their estates; and the popular ferment did not subside, until Pericles had been deposed from his military command, and mulcted in a heavy fine.

The people, however, had no sooner vented their spleen and resentment against Pericles, than they repented of what they had done. There was no other person, whose abilities and integrity were equal to the great and important charge of directing the publick affairs. As soon, therefore, as the anger of the Athenians against Pericles had evaporated and spent its strength, he was reelected general, and invested with the same power which he before possessed. He restored, by his manly and incorrupt conduct, the fainting courage of the republick; but though the Athenians rescued the dignity of Pericles from the popular tumult, they could not preserve his life from the infectious malignity of the pestilence. This disease destroyed him by degrees, and preyed at once on the constitution of his body, and the faculties of his mind. Two years and six months after the commencement of the war, died Pericles. He was inferiour to none in wisdom to ascertain, and abilities to explain and enforce, what was useful and advantageous for the state. He was a sincere and ardent lover of the republick, unbiassed by the dictates of selfishness, unseduced by any partial or sinister views, and superiour to the temptations and allurements of avarice. When the Peloponnesians first invaded Attica, he declared that he would restore his lands to the publick, if on account of the gratitude and kindness of Archidamus, they should be excepted from the general devastation. During his last moments, many of his friends surrounded his death-bed, and supposing him to have lost all knowledge and recollection, dwelt with complacence on the great and illustrious events and exploits of his glorious life. When they recounted the wisdom and incorruption of his administration, and his victories by sea and land, the dying statesman and sage, raising himself on the bed, said to them, "You forget the best and noblest part of my character; no one of my fellow-citizens was ever compelled, on my account, to wear a mourning robe." He expired, teaching an important lesson to the human race, that in the most awful moment, the hour of death, when all other objects fade and disappear, or lose their value, the recollection of those parts of life, which seem to have been most innocent and inoffensive, will be present to the mind. His trophies and victories, his long and prosperous government, the depth of his political wisdom, the perfection of his naval and military knowledge, his unrivalled eloquence, and all the attainments of which he was possessed, could not give or procure to Pericles a consolation, equal to that of the other more valuable, but less dazzling virtues.

By the death of Pericles, the dignity and vigour of the Athenian state seemed for some time also to perish. In the third spring of the war, the Peloponnesians changed their plan of offence. They found, that, by invading and ravaging Attica, though the Athenians were thereby greatly injured and distressed, little advantage had ultimately accrued to themselves. The plunder they acquired was not equivalent to the expenses of the war. The enemy could not be compelled to hazard an engagement. It was therefore deemed expedient, to make an attempt upon some of the continental dependencies of Athens; and as none appeared so open to attack, and so completely excluded from all naval protection, as Platæa, it was resolved to direct their principal efforts against that place.

Accordingly, Archidamus, with the confederate army, entered the Platæan territory, and began to ravage the country. The Platæans sent ministers to deprecate the hostilities and invasion of the Peloponnesians. They urged their exploits and bravery in the defence of Greece against the Persian monarch; and the privileges granted to them, after the famous battle in their territory. Archidamus, therefore, offered them neutrality. The Platæans professed, that they would most willingly have embraced his offer; but that if they offended the Athenians, they could have no assistance against the Thebans, their declared and inveterate enemies, when the Peloponnesian army was departed. To this objection Archidamus replied, " Take an inventory of all your effects, and transport yourselves whither you think proper, during the continuance of the war; and we will engage that your lands shall be cultivated, yourselves subsisted; and, when hostilities shall finally cease, every thing be restored." The Platæans agreed to accept the conditions, provided the consent of the Athenians could be obtained. But when they applied to Athens for leave to accept these offers of the Peloponnesian general, that republick required them to abide by the terms of their confederacy with the Athenians; and promised them every support and assistance. In consequence of this, the Platæans resolved to continue their alliance with the Athenians.

Archidamus, having first invoked the gods, to witness that he did not transgress the articles of the Grecian league, prepared to lay siege to the place. The town itself was small, and the garrison amounted to no more than four hundred Platæans, and eighty Athenians. Beside these, there were one hundred and ten women to prepare provision, and no other person, free or slave. The first operation of the besiegers was to erect palisades; and for this the forest of Cithæron afforded them sufficient materials.—They next broke ground for making approaches. The business was to fill the ditch of the town, and to raise a mound of earth, upon which to mount for making an attack. The extremities of the mound were made firm, with interwoven piles, and the interstices were filled with wood, stones, and earth. For seventy days did the Lacedæmonian army employ itself unremittingly in this work. Reliefs were established, and the Lacedæmonian officers superintended; but the principal reliance of the besiegers was on the great superiority of their numbers.

That the besieged might oppose this mode of attack, they raised, upon that part of the wall opposite to which the mound was forming, a wooden frame, covered in front with leather and hides. Within this they also made a rampart, formed of bricks from the neighbouring houses. The wooden frame bound the whole, and kept it firm to a considerable height. The covering of hides protected both the work and the workmen. But, as the mound still rose, in proportion as the superstructure upon the wall was augmented, and as this superstructure became weaker through increasing height, it was necessary to devise other means of defence. Accordingly, within the wall of their town they built a second wall, in the form of a half moon, connected with the first at the extremities. These extended, on both sides, beyond the mound. If, therefore, the outer wall should be scaled by the besiegers, they would have to renew their work in a less favourable situation.

In the mean time, the besiegers began to batter, from the mound, the superstructure upon the Platæan rampart; but though they shook the wall violently, and alarmed the garrison, no serious effect was produced. The ram, and other machines of the same kind, were also employed against different parts of the wall, but to little purpose. The Platæans, by means of ropes, dragged some out of their directions; others were broken by beams thrown down from the walls. The besiegers, however, put in practice every invention they could devise for effecting their purpose; but after they had consumed great part of the summer in this siege, they found their efforts so completely baffled by the vigilance and activity of the garrison, that they began to despair of success. Before, however, they had recourse to the tedious operations of blockade, they determined to try another expedient. They filled the town ditch, in the parts adjoining to their mound, with faggots, on which were put sulphur and tar, and then set the whole on fire. The conflagration was such, as had never before been prepared by the hands of man. Had the wind favoured, it would have produced the desired effect; but, fortunately for the garrison, a heavy rain, brought on by a thunderstorm, without wind, extinguished the fire, and relieved them from this most formidable attack.

This attempt having failed, the Peloponne-

sians turned the siege into a blockade. A contravallation was added to the palisades already
surrounding the town; and a sufficient number
of troops was appointed to the guard of these
works, of which half were Bœotians, the others
were drafted from the Peloponnesians. The
rest of the confederate forces returned home.
The Platæans, being thus cooped in, began to be
distressed. Their stores were nearly consumed;
relief could not be expected; and their besiegers
would show them no mercy. It was, therefore,
proposed to attempt an escape, by forcing a
passage across the enemy's walls. This proposal was at first joyfully accepted by the whole
garrison; but the enterprise appearing more difficult and hazardous than was expected, many
retracted. Two hundred and twenty, however,
persevered. Ladders were, therefore, prepared,
equal to the height of the wall, which was known
by counting the rows of bricks. The interval
between the circumvallation and contravallation
was sixteen feet, which, being roofed, formed
barracks for the besieging army; and it had
the appearance of one thick wall, with a parapet
and battlements on each side. There were also
occasional towers, in which the guards lodged.

In a dark and stormy night, the adventurers
left the garrison. They were compactly armed,
and had the right foot bare, that they might
tread the more surely. They kept at a distance
from one another, to avoid the clashing of arms.
Their march was directed to the space between
two towers. The ditch being passed, they placed
the ladders, and twelve, light-armed, mounted
the wall. When they had reached the top, they
divided, and six marched towards each tower,
and there waited. Others, in the mean while,

hastened to their assistance; and had their shields borne by those behind, that they might climb the more nimbly. Many of them had already mounted the wall unperceived, for the noise of the storm and the darkness of the night prevented a discovery. A tile, however, which had been accidentally thrown from a battlement, fell with so much noise, that it alarmed the next guard. Immediately there was a call to arms, and the whole of the besieging army was presently in motion. The remaining garrison, according to the plan concerted, sallied from the opposite part of the town, and made a feigned attack upon the circumvallation. The besieging army, distracted and confused amidst the darkness and tempest of the night, knew not whither to move; and a body of three hundred men only went without the trenches, and directed their march according to their opinion and the clamour they heard. Fire signals were made, to give notice to Thebes; but in order to render these ineffectual, the garrison set up signals also in different parts of the town.

In the mean time, the Platæans, who had reached the top of the wall, killed the guards in both towers; and having scaled the wall with their ladders, discharged missile weapons against those that attempted to hinder the passage of their comrades. The parapet between the towers was thrown down to make the passage easier, ladders were placed on the outside, and each, as he passed the outer ditch, formed on the counterscarp, and assisted those upon the towers in protecting the rest. The water in the ditch was frozen, but not so as to bear, and, therefore, the passage over it was tedious and difficult; and the three hundred men who acted as a corps

de reserve, approached the place, before those
upon the towers had descended to cross it. The
torches which they carried in their hands did
them, however, very little service; but they enabled the Platæans to see the number and position of the enemy. They accordingly directed
missile weapons against them with so much effect, that an opportunity was afforded to the
last of their people to get over the ditch. This
was no sooner done, than they hastened off, and
struck directly into the Theban road, as that
which they would be the least suspected to take.
The stratagem was crowned with the completest
success; and they could perceive the Peloponnesians with torches pursuing along the Athenian road. The Platæans having followed the
way to Thebes, for some time, turned to the
right, regained the mountains, and arrived safe
at Athens.

The number of those who engaged in this
perilous, but well planned, and ably executed
enterprise, and profited by its success, amounted
to two hundred and twelve. None were killed.
One only was taken upon the counterscarp; and
six or seven returned without attempting to
scale the wall. These informed the garrison,
that all their comrades who persevered in the
undertaking were cut off to a man. In consequence of this, a herald was sent to demand the
bodies of their companions, in order to have
them buried; but the besiegers candidly unde-
ceived him, and acquainted him with the success
of their enterprise.

The garrison in the town, however, was at
length compelled by famine to think of capitulating. The proposal was first made by the
Lacedæmonian general, who assured them, that

if they would voluntarily submit themselves to the Spartans, and take them for their judges, none should be punished without a trial, and the innocent be set free. The Platæans, utterly incapable of contending for better terms, acceded to these, and the town and the remnant of its inhabitants were accordingly surrendered to the Lacedæmonians. Soon after, commissioners arrived from Sparta, authorized to decide, or rather to pronounce their doom ; for the mode of trial promised nothing equitable. The only question put to them was, whether they had rendered the Peloponnesians any service during the present war ? Startled at such a question, and at a loss what to answer, they urged their confidence in the justice of the Lacedæmonians, and the expectation of a different kind of trial, which had induced them to surrender. They pleaded the acknowledged merit of their commonwealth with Sparta and with all Greece in the Persian wars ; and they made particular mention of their assisting Sparta in the rebellion of the Helotes. They stated, that the refusal of the Lacedæmonians to protect them against the Thebans, had obliged them to seek the friendship and the alliance of Athens ; and they therefore expatiated on the cruelty of punishing them, because they had not deserted a confederacy, to abandon which would have been a mark of the basest ingratitude. They besought the Lacedæmonians not to lay waste those temples, in which thanksgiving had been offered up to the gods for blessing Greece with liberty, and freeing them from the dread of the Persian yoke. And if their commonwealth should be destroyed, the solemn and sacred rites of united Greece, which had been appointed to be performed by the Platæan people, would immediately cease, and be 'abolished. Finally, adjuring the Lacedæmon-ians by every thing human and divine, they deprecated being delivered up to the vengeance of their ancient and inveterate enemies the Thebans, whose treacherous and insidious conduct they had successfully resisted, and justly punished. They requested also, that the possession of the town should rather be given to them, according to the terms of a capitulation ; and they might be at liberty to choose what mode of perishing they thought proper : they would, however, willingly throw themselves on the mercy and justice of the Spartans.

The Thebans, whose hatred of the Platæans could not be effaced by time, replied to what had been urged. They asserted their ancient claim of sovereignty over Platæa ; and affirmed that the connexion with Athens could not excuse the Platæans for their defection from the general confederacy of Greece. "With regard to the attempt to surprise your city," continued the Theban orator, "the most respectable of your citizens invited us, opened your gates to us, and under their authority we acted. Nothing hostile was meditated against you ; our sole aim was, to detach you from a foreign connection, and reunite you to the body of the Bœotian people. Nevertheless our citizens were butchered, contrary to the promise you had given. The fathers of those youths, whom the Platæans murdered after they had submitted to mercy, were the very men that rescued Bœotia from the Attic yoke, and restored it to the Grecian confederacy. Their lamentations and tears demand of you, Lacedæmonians, the punishment of these men, and that justice, to which, by the laws and customs of Greece, the Thebans are entitled."

The Lacedæmonian commissioners, according to the instructions received from Sparta, resolved that the sentence should rest upon the answer, that could be given and supported, to the simple question which was at first proposed. The Platæans were, therefore called on, one by one, to say, Whether, in the present war, they had done any service to the Lacedæmonians, or their allies? All answering in the negative, they were severally led aside, and immediately put to death. The number of the Platæans amounted to two hundred, and that of the Athenians to twenty-five. The women were condemned to slavery; and the town and territory given to the Thebans. A few Platæan refugees however, of the aristocratical party, and some Megarean exiles, were permitted to inhabit the place during one year. After this the lands, being confiscated to the publick use of the Thebans, were leased out for ten years to the citizens of that state; the town was levelled with the ground, but the temples were carefully preserved; and an inn, two hundred feet square, not unlike the modern caravanseras in the east, was built with the materials. Such was the fate of Platæa, in the ninety-third year after its alliance with Athens.

B. C. 427. About this time happened a revolt in the isle of Lesbos, which had been subject to Athens. The Athenians, thereupon, sent a fleet of gallies to reduce the island, which, after some time, was effected. We have already noticed the commotions in Corcyra, which gave rise to the Peloponnesian war. The Corinthians had taken a great number of Corcyrean prisoners, some of whom were sold for slaves; but the rest were well treated, and had their freedom promised them, provided they

Q 2

would endeavour to influence their countrymen to espouse the interest of the Corinthians and their allies, and to prejudice them against Athens and democratical administrations in general.— The Corcyrean nobles readily acceded to the proposal ; and the Corinthians accordingly set them at liberty. Every Corcyrean was examined separately by them, relative to his support in the general assembly, for renouncing the alliance with Athens, and renewing the ancient connexion of Corcyra with Corinth, its metropolis. Success in these overtures was various ; but party soon grew warm, and the whole island was presently in commotion. The aristocratical party, at first, prevailed, and destroyed great numbers of those who inclined to a democracy. The Athenians, however, sending two powerful fleets to the assistance of the distressed faction, the Peloponnesians, who aided the aristocracy, were obliged to leave the island. The democratical party immediately prepared for revenging the injuries received from those that differed from it in opinion. One of the most horrid massacres recorded in history followed. Neither temples, nor altars, afforded protection. The miserable victims were dragged from the most revered and sacred fanes, the walls and pavements of which were, for the first time, stained with human blood. Many withdrew themselves, by a voluntary death, from the fury of their enemies. In every house, and in every family, scenes of bloodshed were exhibited, too numerous and too tragical to be described. Parents, children, brothers, and pretended friends, seized the desired moment to gratify their latent malignity, and to perpetrate crimes without a name. Eurymedon, the Athenian admiral, showed neither ability nor inclination to stop the carnage. For six days did the Athenian fleet remain in the harbour of Corcyra, during which time, the actors in this horrible tragedy hourly aggravated the enormity of their guilt, and improved in the refinement of their cruelty.

A dreadful calm succeeded this violent commotion; and five hundred of the aristocratical faction escaped to Epirus. They procured assistance from Corinth and Lacedæmon, and the Athenian fleet having retired, the party that inclined to democracy was in its turn persecuted by the opposite faction. But another armament arriving from Athens, enabled the former again to obtain the ascendancy. Those of the aristocratical faction being thus obliged to submit to the justice and mercy of their enemies, were confined in a dungeon, whence they were dragged by parties of twenty at a time. They were then compelled to pass, in pairs, with their hands tied behind their backs, between two ranks of their enemies, who tortured them with whips, prongs, and every instrument of licentious and disgraceful torment. As soon as the wretches, that had been left in the prison, understood what ignominious cruelty was inflicted on their companions, and the abominable scenes transacted, they refused to quit their confinement, but invited the Athenians to destroy them where they were. This the Athenians refused to do; and the populace, not daring to force a passage guarded by despair, unroofed the prison, and overwhelmed those below with stones, darts, and arrows. The miserable prisoners attempted, at first, to defend themselves, but finding all their endeavours vain and fruitless, and that the animosity of their enemies did not relax, they de-

termined to finish their existence and their misfortunes at once. During the night, therefore,
they destroyed themselves; and when the morning arose, the Corcyreans found them all dead.
The corpses, piled upon waggons, were carried
out of the city, and no funeral services appointed for them. Eurymedon, after acting a very
conspicuous part in these tragical occurrences,
again set sail, and quitted the Corcyrean harbour.

Thus ended the sedition of Corcyra, but the
consequences it produced were not so soon terminated. Almost all the states of Greece experienced, in their turn, the like commotions. In
every republick, and in almost every city, the
ambitious and the intriguing found means of
procuring the assistance of Sparta, or of Athens,
according as they espoused and favoured the
aristocratical or democratical interest. A virtuous and moderate oligarchy, and a free and
impartial freedom, were the specious pretences
under which they acted. Sheltered by these
names, the prodigal assassin freed himself from
the clamours and the threats of his creditor; the
parent with unnatural cruelty punished the extravagance and dissipation of the son; the son
avenged, by parricide, the severity and inflexibility of the parent. Publick assemblies, that
met to consult the welfare of the state, decided
their debates by the sword. Men thirsted for
blood. And this general disorder overwhelmed
all laws human and divine. Such are the wretched and detestable delusions, by which individuals
ruin the publick and themselves.

The picture of the Peloponnesian war would
be more agreeable, if diversified by scenes of a
milder and more pleasing nature. But, alas!
the occurrences and transactions of this period

present us only with a dark and melancholy prospect; and the episodes commonly reflect the same colour with the principal action. At this B. C. 426. time happened innumerable earthquakes in Greece; and the pestilence returning swept off great numbers of the Athenians. An army, under the command of Demosthenes, an Athenian general, undertook an expedition against Ætolia. But the operations necessary for this purpose were obstructed by the jealousies and dissensions of the confederates; each state, in alliance with Athens, insisting, that the whole force of the war should be directed against its particular enemies. Demosthenes, however, after having been defeated in Ætolia, obtained some very considerable victories over the Ambracians, a brave and warlike people; after which he returned with honour to Athens.

Though the term of the command of Demosthenes had expired, his mind could not brook inactivity, and he requested permission to accompany the armament, as a volunteer, which was about to sail around the coast of Peloponnesus. By a decree, therefore, of the people, Demosthenes was authorized to embark in the fleet, with leave to employ the Messenians as he should think proper. Whilst the fleet coasted along the Peloponnesian shores, Demosthenes advised the Athenian commanders to land, and rebuild Pylus, which, though it enjoyed a convenient haven, and was strongly fortified by nature, the Spartans had abandoned. They, however, answered him, "that there were many barren capes on the coast of Peloponnesus, which those might fortify, who wished to entail a useless expense on their country." He desisted, therefore, from any farther intreaties, till a storm accidentally drove the whole fleet towards the Pylian harbour. This circumstance induced him to renew his request. At length the soldiers and sailors, weary of idleness, began the work, and carried it on with such activity and zeal, that they fortified the place in six days. The fleet then sailed to Corcyra, and Demosthenes remained, with five ships, to guard this new acquisition.

No sooner were the Spartans made sensible of this measure, than they immediately withdrew their army from its annual invasion of Attica, and recalled their fleet from Corcyra. The citizens flew to arms, and marched to Pylus. But the place was so well fortified, that nothing could be done against it, until the whole Spartan army arrived. As soon as all their forces were assembled, Pylus was vigorously assaulted by sea and land. The walls being weakest at the entrance of the harbour, the most furious attack was made there, and the resistance was no less obstinate; for only two ships could sail abreast into the harbour.

Demosthenes encouraged his men by his voice and action. The gallant Brasidas exhorted the Lacedæmonians to save the honour of their country, and commanded the pilots to drive their ships against the beach. In endeavouring, however, to enforce these commands by his own example, he received a wound, and fell into the sea, apparently without life. But some of his attendants recovered him; and when his senses returned, he perceived that his shield was gone. The shield of Brasidas, however, was lost with more glory, than ever shield was defended.

Demosthenes, with few troops, and very unequal strength, resisted the attack of the enemy for three days. At length, however, the fleet, which had been apprised of his danger, returned from Corcyra, and terminated the incredible labours of his small and exhausted garrison. The Athenian and Lacedæmonian armaments immediately engaged, and the Spartans were defeated. An event, however, which principally arose from a want of vigilance and foresight, was calculated to depress the minds of the Spartans, more than the loss of five ships that were destroyed in this battle, the total dispersion of their fleet, and the unexpected relief of the place.

· Before the harbour of Pylus, lies an island, about two miles in circumference, called Sphacteria, which is barren, woody, and uninhabited. In this island the Spartans had imprudently posted a detachment of four hundred and twenty heavy armed men, with a much greater proportion of Helotes. They did not reflect, that as soon as the Athenians obtained the command of the neighbouring sea, these forces must be at their mercy. This consideration did not occur to the Lacedæmonians, till their fleet was defeated. It then produced the most poignant affliction; as the Spartans in the island belonged to the first families of the commonwealth.

Immediate notice of this disaster was dispatched to Sparta. The annual magistrates, with a deputation from the senate, hastened to examine matters on the spot. The misfortune appeared to admit of no remedy; and such was the value of this body of citizens to the community at large, that it was universally resolved to solicit a truce, until embassadors could be sent to Athens, to treat for a general peace. The Athenians accordingly agreed to a suspension of hostilities, provided the Spartans, as a

pledge of the sincerity of their intentions, would
consent to deliver up the whole of their fleet,
amounting to sixty vessels. This mortifying
and humiliating condition was accepted. During
the space of twenty days consumed in this embassy, the Lacedæmonian troops intercepted in
Sphacteria were supplied with a stated proportion of food and wine.

. When the Spartan embassadors were admitted
to an audience, they reminded the Athenians of
the advantages which would result to all Greece,
and in a more particular manner to Athens, if
they embraced the spontaneous friendship—the
proffered treaty and alliance of the Ladedæmon-
ian republick. The proposals of conciliation, if
accepted in the moment of victory, would greatly
redound to the glory of Athens; but if rejected,
would completely ascertain, not only who were
the real aggressors and promoters of the war, but
to whom the calamities that would thence ensue
ought in justice to be imputed.

The meek and submissive spirit of this discourse tended to discover to the Athenians the
full extent of the value of their victory. Cleon,
a clamorous demagogue, therefore, instigated
the people, to demand, as the preliminaries of
peace, that the Spartans in Sphacteria, should be
sent to Athens, and that many fortified and important places belonging to the Lacedæmonians
should be surrendered. These lofty pretensions
did not appear to the Spartan negotiators justified by the military events which had taken
place; and they returned with disgust. The
Athenians, on various and groundless pretences,
refused to restore the fleet, which had been surrendered as a pledge of the treaty; and both
parties prepared to recommence hostilities. The

Athenians, that they might vindicate the arrogance of their pretensions; and the Spartans, that they might avenge it.

It was determined, to attempt the reduction of the soldiers in Sphacteria, by famine, rather than by the sword. The Athenian fleet, therefore, guarded the island night and day. But, notwithstanding its vigilance, supplies were often thrown into the place, during storms and darkness. The blockade was fruitlessly protracted for several weeks; and the besiegers began to suffer equally with the besieged. In the mean time, many clamours were raised in Athens against Demosthenes, who blockaded Sphacteria, and Cleon, who prevented an advantageous peace. Cleon, in order to elude what was directed against him, asserted, that if he were appointed general, he would sail to the island with a small force, and take it at the first onset.

This proposal was no sooner made, than instantly agreed to; and the chief command was ceded to him. Cleon, more clamorous than courageous, and little expecting that the Athenians would have accepted his offer, was at a loss what measure to pursue. Not forsaken, however, by his impudence, he advanced to the middle of the assembly, and declared, that he was not afraid of the Lacedæmonians; and engaged, in twenty days, to bring the Spartans prisoners to Athens, or die in the attempt. This declaration excited the ridicule of the multitude; while the discerning rejoiced, that they should either be freed from the clamours of a turbulent demagogue, or that the Spartans in Sphacteria would be subdued.

Some of the Lacedæmonian soldiers in the island, in dressing their victuals, happened to

VOL. III.   R

set the wood on fire, and a brisk gale springing up, a most violent conflagration ensued, and the whole place was threatened with destruction.—— This unforeseen disaster disclosed to the enemy the strength and situation of the Spartans; and Demosthenes was actually preparing to embrace the favourable moment, and to attack them, when Cleon, with his troops, arrived in the camp. During the night, the island was invaded; and in the morning the Athenians made a descent from seventy ships. The Lacedæmonians, involved in the ashes of the burnt wood, which, mounting high into the air, intercepted the sight on all sides, endeavoured to make good their retreat to a strong post opposite to Pylus, but were greatly harassed in their march by showers of arrows, stones, and darts. Being closely embodied, however, and presenting a dreadful and threatening front to the enemy, they retreated, in good order, and with comparatively little loss. Having gained possession of the post, they repelled with vigour and bravery the enemy, wherever they approached; for the nature of the ground was such, that they could not easily be surrounded. During the whole day, the contending parties fought with the greatest obstinacy, under the painful pressures of thirst and a scorching sun. At length the Messenians discovered an unknown path, that led to the enemy's rear, and immediately climbed the eminence. The Spartans, thus encompassed on all sides, and reduced to a similar situation with their brave countrymen at Thermopylæ, were attacked by the Athenians in front, and the Messenians behind.

Nor did this devoted band disgrace the country of Leonidas. Many of the commanders were slain; and those who were wounded exhorted their soldiers to persevere in the battle. Demosthenes and Cleon, perceiving that the Spartans were resolved to fight till every man was slain, and being desirous of carrying them prisoners to Athens, checked the Athenian troops. A herald was therefore sent to offer them quarter, provided they would surrender themselves to the mercy of the Athenian people, and lay down their arms. It was doubted, however, whether the Lacedæmonians would submit to such a proposal; but the greater part dropped their shields, and waved their hands, in token of compliance. Styphon, on whom the command of the Spartans had devolved, requested leave to dispatch a herald to the Lacedæmonian army on the continent, that he might know how to act. This was refused, but a conference followed, and the Athenian generals sent for a herald from the Lacedæmonian army.—Several messages having passed between them, a final answer was received by the garrison in the island, to this effect: "The Lacedæmonians permit you to consult your own safety, provided you submit to nothing disgraceful." As soon as the Spartans in Sphacteria received this message, they surrendered their arms and themselves.

B. C. 425.

On the next day, the dead were given up to be buried, and the Athenians erected their trophy. The Spartans, who had been made prisoners, were carried to Athens; and, by a decree of the people, it was resolved that they should be kept in chains, until peace between the two states should be established. But, if the Peloponnesians invaded Attica in the mean time, the decree declared, in order to intimidate the Lacedæmonian publick, they should be immediately put to death. The Athenian commanders left a strong garrison in Pylus, which was soon reinforced by an enterprising body of Messenians, from Naupactus. The Messenians, though possessed of only a barren cape on their native and once happy coast, infested the neighbouring country with continual incursions; and the Helotes, attracted by their affection for their ancient kinsmen, and animated by every principle of resentment against their tyrannical masters, revolted to them in great numbers. Pylus was now so fortified, that while supplies could be received by sea, no impression could be made upon it by land. In this situation of things, the Lacedæmonian government, anxiously desirous of peace, expected that the Athenians would only insult them, if they made any publick proposals for an accommodation between the two states. They, therefore, secretly offered terms, and requested a peace might be negotiated. But the victories and successes of the Athenians served only to inflame their ambition ; and, while the wiser and more moderate among the people, would gladly have profited of the present happy posture of their affairs, to make an advantageous agreement, the populace, instigated by the boisterous eloquence of Cleon, dismissed the Spartans with greater insolence than ever.

Indeed the war had now become popular at Athens, on account of the success which had lately attended it. The Lacedæmonians, depressed by misfortunes, remained inactive ; but B. C. 424. the spring no sooner approached, than the Athenians made all the preparations possible for a vigorous campaign. The first operations of the Athenians were directed against Cythera, a very important appendage of the Lacedæmonian dominion. This fertile and populous island, which was governed by a Spartan administration, and possessed a Spartan garrison, was taken by Nicias; and no other capitulation was made by the inhabitants, except for their lives.

Soon after this important conquest, the Athenians, under the command of Demosthenes and Hippocrates, reduced the town of Nicæa, a seaport belonging to the Megareans, and the fleet ravaged all the eastern coasts of Peloponnesus. Their attack was next directed against Thyrea, a city that had been granted to the miserable natives of Ægina, where the cruelty of the Athenians still continued to pursue them. The city was taken, the houses were burned, and the inhabitants, without distinction, put to the sword.

Hitherto the Athenians had been every where successful, but they now suffered a defeat in Bœotia. Demosthenes and Hippocrates had, for some time, been tampering with the political factions of that country; and the insurgents had promised to take up arms in their behalf. The Athenian commanders, therefore, sailed to the eastern parts of that province, with a great number of gallies and men. As the insurgents had agreed to deliver up the western coast of Bœotia, it was expected, that, before the Thebans should be in readiness to take the field, the invaders and their abettors, advancing from opposite extremities of the country, would unite in the centre, and proceed to attack Thebes, of which they might probably make themselves masters.

The whole contrivance, however, was betrayed to the Spartans by a Phocian; and the Lacedæmonians communicated it to the inhabitants of Bœotia. The cities that meditated a revolt were therefore timely secured. Hippocrates, having quitted Attica, entered the eastern frontier of Bœotia, and attacked and took Delium, a place sacred to Apollo. The principal design of the enterprise having failed, he fortified and garrisoned this post, and prepared to return home. The Thebans, however, with a force of eighteen thousand men, under the command of Pagondas, a brave and skilful leader, marched with great rapidity from Tanagra, in order to intercept their retreat; an engagement ensued, in which the Athenians were routed, and left in the field of battle one thousand pikemen, with their general Hippocrates. The Thebans, after this victory, laid siege to Delium, and took it; and the Athenian garrison, reduced by death or desertion, to two hundred men, surrendered themselves prisoners of war.

The Athenians had scarcely time to lament over these calamities, when they were informed of others still greater, and more to be deplored. The citizens of Olynthus, and other places of the Chalcidice, had embraced the earliest opportunity of revolting from Athens. When, therefore, the victories of Demosthénes and Nicias, in the eighth year of the war, were made known to them, they feared the vengeance of the Athenians, and craved assistance from their Peloponnesian allies. At the same time, Perdiccas, king of Macedonia, by whom the Athenians were regarded as his ancient and natural enemies, and the rapacious invaders of his coast, sent to hire soldiers in Greece, whom he intended to employ in resisting the attempts of that ambitious people, and in subduing the several barbarous tribes, that had not yet submitted to the Macedonian tyranny.

Brasidas was therefore appointed by the Spartans to undertake this expedition; who having joined forces with Perdiccas, the army marched against Arribæus, the king of the Lyncestians. This prince, however, having offered to submit the differences between Perdiccas and himself, to Brasidas, and to abide by his determination, the Spartan general listened to a proposal, which seemed so highly reasonable. Accordingly a negotiation was opened; but Perdiccas, having more ambitious prospects, refused to accept as a judge, the man whom he had hired to be an auxiliary. Brasidas, on the other hand, avowed that he could not think of waging war with those who implored his justice and protection; and, therefore, a treaty was soon after concluded, and Arribæus was numbered among the allies of Sparta. Perdiccas, unable to prevent this measure, was nevertheless, highly incensed; and the generals parted in mutual disgust.

Brasidas having joined the Chalcidians, offensive operations were commenced against those states in alliance with Athens. Acanthus, in which some of the principal persons were known to incline to the Lacedæmonian interest, was intended to be attacked first. This place being summoned, after some deliberations among the people, the Spartan commander was permitted to enter the town, and allowed to declare his proposals before the general assembly. Brasidas having made a very eloquent and judicious speech, in which he inveighed bitterly against the ambition and tyranny of Athens, and boasted of the great superiority of the Lacedæmonians, with respect to their military force, engaged the

Acanthians to accept the friendship and alliance of Sparta. Stagirus, another city on the Strymonic gulph, readily followed the example, and became a member of the Lacedæmonian confederacy. During the winter season, the Spartan commander signalized himself with equal ability and enterprise. His operations against the inland towns facilitated in a very considerable degree the reduction of such places, as by their maritime, or insular situation, were most exposed to the vengeance of Athens, and, therefore, most averse to recede from the alliance of that state. At length, however, by the success of his arms, the moderate use he made of victory, and his behaviour to the vanquished, all of which contributed to render him uniformly prosperous, Brasidas became master of most places in the peninsulas of Acta, Sithonia, and Pallene.

The loss of Amphipolis was what the Athenian people most severely felt, and for which they were most afflicted. The government of Thasos had been committed to Thucydides, the celebrated Greek historian ; and he had also the direction of the gold and silver mines, on the opposite coast. As soon as this distinguished character received information, that the Amphipolitan territory was invaded by a Spartan army, he hastened to relieve the town, but arrived too late to be of any signal service. When the success of the expedition of Brasidas was known at Athens, the popular tumult was extremely great. A truce for one year, however, was agreed on soon after, between the two contending republicks. This transaction was wholly unexpected by Brasidas, who received the submission of two considerable places in the peninsula of Pallene, after hostilities had been suspended.

This action of the Spartan general, and the worthlessness of Cleon, promoted the renewal of the war. The Athenian demagogue was continually extolling the greatness and power of Athens. He was always instigating his countrymen to punish the insolence and perfidy of Sparta, in abetting the revolt of those places in Macedonia, after the truce had been agreed on. They were at length influenced by the advice of this turbulent declaimer, and he was sent with a fleet of thirty gallies, twelve hundred citizens heavy armed, a squadron of three hundred horse, and a powerful body of light-armed auxiliaries. Cleon, thus vested with a very important command, after having taken one or two places, proceeded against Amphipolis. He applied to Perdiccas, king of Macedonia, for succours, which, according to treaty, he was to furnish. But Brasidas, aware of the inferiority of his troops in arms and discipline, and more confident of the resources of his own genius, as he knew the inability of the general he had to oppose, wished to join battle before the expected assistance should arrive. Accordingly the Spartan general, perceiving that Cleon advanced towards the city in a negligent and disorderly manner, gave orders to attack the Athenians by surprise, and in different parts of the army. This was instantly done; and the enemy, confounded with the rapidity and complicated charge, fled amain, while Cleon, though foremost, was killed in the pursuit. Brasidas, being also wounded, died soon after.

Scarcely any Spartan recorded in history, and few, indeed, of any nation, have been endowed with such talents to command armies, to persuade citizens, to make and to maintain con-

quests, as Brasidas.   The estimation, in which
the different states and communities held this
great and extraordinary man may be collected
from the sorrow which they expressed at his
death, and the honours paid to his memory.
His funeral was performed with the utmost solemnity, amidst the tears of those who considered his virtues and abilities as the surest pledges
of their own happiness and security.   The citizens of Amphipolis erected a monument to per-
petuate his memory ; and by way of distinction,
every other testimony of their former leaders
and patriots was carefully destroyed. Annual
games, with sacrifices, were appointed to be celebrated at his tomb; and worship was decreed to
him, as the hero and founder of their community.   It is related, that his mother, hearing
Brasidas praised by some Thracians, who asserted that no person alive was equal to him, replied, " You are mistaken ; my son was a man
of great merit, but there are many superiour to
him in Sparta."

By the death of Cleon and Brasidas, the principal obstacles to peace were removed.   The
Athenians, dejected by defeat, wanted the im-
posing eloquence of Cleon to disguise their weakness, and varnish their misfortunes.   Their armament was greatly enfeebled, and there appeared no prospect of regaining their possessions
in Macedonia.   The greatest part, therefore, of
those who returned home, seemed sufficiently
desirous of forwarding an accommodation with
the enemy.   Nicias, who had succeeded to the
influence of Cleon, was inclined to pacific measures ; and happily for the sufferings of mankind, the same moderation was observable in
Pleistoanax, king of Sparta.   Several confer-

ences were held during winter; the negotiation, however, did not appear likely to be soon successful, and, therefore, towards spring the Lacedæmonians circulated a report, that they would fortify Attica; but immediately after, preliminaries of peace were agreed on. In B. C. 421. consequence of this negotiation, all places and prisoners taken in the course of the war were to be mutually restored. The several states of Greece were supposed to be included in this treaty; but each of the other communities refused to make any restitution. The peace was to continue for fifty years; and as Nicias was the great promoter of it, people universally called it the peace of Nicias. The disposition of this man was exactly the reverse of that of Cleon. The latter was violent and turbulent, and a vehement enemy of the Lacedæmonians: Nicias was gentle in his manners, a friend to the Spartans, and advised his countrymen to pursue moderate and peaceful measures. He was a man of a virtuous, but timid disposition, endowed with much prudence, and little enterprise; possessed of moderate abilities, but immensely rich.

CHAP. IX.

From the Peace of Nicias to the total overthrow of the Expedition against Sicily.

THE treaty of peace thus concluded, after a war of ten years, was at last ill calculated to give general satisfaction, and to fix and establish permanent and universal quiet. The

Lacedæmonians had stipulated for themselves, that all places and possessions, of which they had been deprived during the war, should be restored. But their allies, and especially the Corinthians and Megareans, were left to suffer very considerably; and the Eleians considered themselves treated with the greatest injustice and oppression. With all this, however, the Lacedæmonians could not carry into effect some of the most important articles of the treaty.— Amphipolis, and the other towns in that neighbourhood, refused to enter again into an alliance with the Athenians. They were also equally unsuccessful in endeavouring to accommodate matters with the Argives; and a war with that state, in which the greatest part of the Peloponnesians would probably be against them, seemed inevitable. Alarmed by these considerations, the Spartans sent proposals to Athens, relative to a defensive alliance between the two states, which was immediately concluded.

The Corinthians, irritated now against the Lacedæmonians, and equally indignant with Athens, dispatched deputies to Argos, as soon as the convention of the confederacy was dismissed. These having roused the ambition of the Argives, conjured them to vindicate the honour of Peloponnesus, which had been shamefully abandoned by the pusillanimity, or betrayed by the selfishness, of the Spartans. The Argives were well disposed to listen to what was recommended. Having observed a prudent neutrality, during the events of the Peloponnesian war, Argos was grown wealthy and strong. The protection of this state was courted by most of the other smaller communities of Greece, which, before the conclusion of peace, had been the friends and the allies of Sparta. To this association of popular governments, an accession still more important was soon acquired; and Athens was received into the confederacy. The means, by which this was effected, it is proper to explain.

Amidst the factious turbulence of senates and assemblies, whatever was proposed and adopted by one party was certain to meet with opposition from another, however prudent and necessary the measure proposed might be.—Those who opposed the peace of Nicias were many; but among the Athenians, one person eclipsed the rest, who, on this occasion, first displayed those singular, but unhappy talents, which proved fatal to himself and to his country. By the constitutions of Solon, every Athenian ought to be thirty years of age before he was permitted to speak in publick; but Alcibiades had not yet reached this period. Every circumstance, however, which could plead an exception to that law, united in this youth. His birth and fortune, his natural and acquired abilities, the accomplishments of his mind and body, all conspired to render him the favourite of the people. Amidst the crowd of rhetoricians and sophists, at that time inhabiting Athens, Alcibiades distinguished the superiour merit of Socrates, who, rejecting all fictitious and abstruse studies, confined himself to matters of real importance and utility. He was, however, more charmed with the eloquence, than with the innocence and integrity of Socrates; and the youthful levity of Alcibiades was chiefly delighted with the splendour of particular actions. But the invincible and astonishing intrepidity of Socrates, when quitting the shade of speculation and the groves of Academus, and grasping his spear, he justified, by his martial exploits, the useful lessons of his philosophy, could not but attract the esteem and reverence of his young disciple.

And if Alcibiades were fascinated by the abilities and superiority of Socrates, that philosopher entertained no less respect and affection for his pupil. Alcibiades was beautiful....his beauty however depended, not on that transient flower of youth, and the seductive elegance of effeminate graces, but on the ineffable harmony of a form, which seemed to recal to mind and realise the fabulous divinities of Homer, and the productions of Phidias. The affection of Socrates, though pure as his principles, resembled rather the ardour of love, than the moderation of friendship. The company of the sage was courted by his other disciples, but he himself scrupled not to seek the friendship and conversation of Alcibiades: and when the ungrateful youth sometimes escaped to his licentious companions, the philosopher pursued to reclaim him, with the eagerness and anxiety of a father or a master, desirous of recovering a fugitive son or slave. At the fatal battle at Delium, it is said, that Alcibiades repaid the kindness and favour Socrates displayed at the battle of Potidæa, by saving the precious life of the sage. This interchange of noble and important offices would doubtless cement the bands of mutual friendship, during which the powers of reason and fancy were directed, with unremitting attention, to improve the understanding of Alcibiades, and excite in him the love and practice of virtue.

But this favourite youth laboured under a lamentable defect, which neither his birth and for-tone, nor his great mental and bodily accomplishments, nor even the friendship of Socrates, could compensate. He wanted a sincere and honest heart. The talents of Socrates had led him to admire, and attach himself to that philosopher; and the hopes of becoming by his instructions, not a wise and good, but a great and able man, induced him to continue the appearance of amity. Some inclination to virtue he might in such company feel, or rather feign; for he was capable of adopting at pleasure, the most opposite manners; and, while he surpassed, at times, the splendid magnificence of Athens, he could conform himself, at others, to a more rigid frugality, than even Sparta required. He could assume the soft and effeminate manners of an eastern potentate, or rival the vices of the Thracians.

It was generally reckoned important for those, who sought eminence in the state, to extend and strengthen their political connexions with other Grecian communities. The family of Alcibiades had been long united, in friendly and hospitable intercourse, with the Spartan republick, and he had been assiduous in kind attention to the Lacedæmonian prisoners, taken at Sphacteria. The Spartan government, however, little partial to youth in political eminence, and not less averse to the wild and luxurious extravagance of Alcibiades, disregarded his advances, and paid him no respect. Whenever the Lacedæmonians had any business to transact with the republick of Athens, they generally made their suit to Nicias, for whom they testified the highest regard.

This line of conduct pursued by the Spartan government, induced Alcibiades, in order to gratify at once his resentment, his ambition, and his jealousy, to renew the war, and to oppose the Spartans and Nicias. We have before noticed the obstacles, with which the Spartans had to contend, in carrying the treaty of peace into effect. It belonged to the Lacedæmonians, to cede first the places and possessions to the Athenians; the latter, though the prisoners taken at Sphacteria had been set at liberty, refused to surrender Pylus, until the conditions stipulated in return, had been performed. Mutual reluctance, or, what perhaps is more likely, inability, to comply with the articles of peace, produced animosity and disagreement between the two states. In their eagerness to recover Pylus, without which, they were sensible, it would be impossible to contend with any advantage against Athens, the Spartans renewed their alliance with the Thebans, from whom they received Panactum. In this transaction, however, they forgot an important clause in the treaty with Athens, " that neither state should, without mutual consent, conclude any new confederacy."

That they might excuse what they termed an apparent infringement of the treaty, they sent embassadors to Athens to plead their defence, and to request that state to accept Panactum, which they had carefully dismantled, in exchange for Pylus. And as these men declared in the senate, that they were invested with full powers for embracing and cementing a present and permanent friendship between the two communities, their proposal was heard without emotion or surprise. After this audience, Alcibiades, having invited the Lacedæmonian embassadors to an entertainment, pretended to be a great admirer and friend of the Spartan state, and professed his readiness to coöperate with them, in obtaining the object of their mission. But there was one circumstance, he observed, that occurred in the speech they had made, that gave him much concern, and which, it would have been their advantage, entirely to have suppressed. This was their mentioning the full powers, with which they were invested. They must beware of repeating that errour in the popular assembly, for the rapacity of the populace was such, that if they should be apprised of this circumstance, their demands would be so great, that the honour and the safety of Sparta could not possibly allow them to be complied with. If they concealed the extent of their commission, to declare which would only indicate timidity, and provoke insolence, he pledged himself to support their cause, and to procure for them the full gratification of their wishes.

. The Spartans, ignorant of the character of the man, who had been formerly irritated with the neglect and ingratitude of their country, confided in Alcibiades, as the friend of Lacedæmon. When, therefore, they appeared before the people, the artful Athenian interrogated them, with a loud voice, as to the object and extent of their commission. They replied, that they had no full powers granted to them. Alcibiades, affecting a transport of indignation, arraigned the baseness and audacity of a people, by whom his own unsuspecting credulity had been abused. "It is but yesterday," cried he, "they declared in the senate the full powers with which they were invested; and to-day they deny what they so lately asserted. It is thus, that they have infringed the articles of the treaty. Amphipolis is not restored. An alliance is entered into with the Theban state; and they offer the Athenians Panactum, after they have demolished its walls and fortifications. Can you tamely submit, men of Athens! to such indignities? Will you not expel such traitors from your presence, and from your city?" This extraordinary and unexpected harangue, wholly disconcerted the Spartans, and they retired abruptly from the assembly. Nicias and others, who were known to favour the Lacedæmonian republick, shared their disgrace; and Alcibiades endeavoured to persuade the people to embrace the Argive alliance. But, before this was effected, Nicias proposed, that he might be sent as embassador to Lacedæmon. To this proposal, the assembly immediately consented. The instructions, however, given to Nicias, by the Athenian people, were such, that, upon his arrival at Lacedæmon, his demands were ill received, and he returned to Athens, without obtaining for the commonwealth, or for himself, any one object of his mission. A league, offensive and defensive, between the Argives and the Athenians, was instantly concluded, for one hundred years; in which the several independent allies of each contracting power were included; and, by this transaction, Athens, not Lacedæmon, became the head of the Dorian states, and of the principal confederacy in Peloponnesus.

This alliance, though it did not cancel that subsisting between Sparta and Athens, was, nevertheless, wholly inimical to the former state. Though the friends of Alcibiades could not commend the method, by which he had attained his purpose, yet they considered it as a masterpiece in politicks, to divide and shake all Peloponnesus. By these means, the war would

be removed to a great distance from Athens;
and if the Spartans should be conquerors, success would avail them little ; but if they suffered
a defeat, Lacedæmon itself would be in danger.

It might be expected, that the weight of such
a powerful confederacy should have speedily
crushed the weakness of Sparta, already enfeebled and exhausted by the former war. But the
military operations of Greece depended not so
much on the relative strength of the contending
powers, as on the alternate preponderance of
faction. The Spartans, fearing the confederacy,
which was united against them, resolved to endeavour to crush the evil at once, and thereby
intimidate other cities from revolting. A numerous and formidable army was therefore collected, and as Pleistoanax had been a promoter
of the peace of Nicias, the command was given
to Agis, his more warlike colleague. The Spartan allies showed unusual ardour in the cause,
and mustered all their troops to join the Lacedæmonian army.

The Argives observed the approaching storm,
and prepared to resist its force. The Eleans
and Mantineans joined their troops to the Argives,
who, without waiting for the Athenian auxiliaries, boldly took the field to oppose the invaders.
The skilful manœuvres of Agis completely cut
off their return to Argos ; and a battle seemed
inevitable. But whether the Argive commanders were disconcerted by the judicious position
of the enemy, and saw the danger of their situation; whether they were touched with com-
punction, on viewing such numerous bodies of
men, principally natives of the same country, of
the same extraction, and speaking the same
language, about to embrue their parricidal

hands in kindred blood, is unknown. Certain, however, it is, that they went privately to Agis, and pledging themselves to endeavour to procure a reconciliation and alliance between Argos and Lacedæmon, upon satisfactory terms to the latter state, prevailed with him to grant, by his sole authority, a truce for four months. The Lacedæmonian army, therefore, to the astonishment of every one present, was immediately ordered to retreat.

B. C. 417. This measure occasioned universal discontent, which was followed by loud and licentious clamours. The Spartans and their allies complained, " That, after having assembled such a body of forces as had scarcely ever been seen in Peloponnesus, whose attachment to their cause was ardent, and whose numbers and courage were invincible ; and, after surrounding their enemies on every side, and depriving them of every resource ; the glorious hope, or rather certainty of the most complete and important victory, was snatched from their grasp, by the treachery, the cowardice, or the caprice of their general." On the other hand, the Argives lamented, that their numerous enemies, inadvertently enclosed between the allied army and the garrison of Argos, who might easily have been subdued and cut to pieces, should have been allowed to escape, by a hasty and imprudent composition ; nor was their resentment confined to vain and fruitless complaints. The publick indignation, apparently stimulated by the democratical leaders, rose so high, that the houses of Thrasyllus and Alciphron were attacked by the most daring and seditious of the populace. Thrasyllus and his colleague, however, saved their lives by fleeing to the protection of an altar; but a decree of the people declared all their effects confiscated.

Soon after the retreat of the Lacedæmonians, the Athenian auxiliaries arrived at Argos. Alcibiades was invested with the character of embassador to that state. His activity would not fail to promote the popular tumult, in which his own and the Athenian interests were concerned. His eloquence prevailed over the few, who seemed desirous of pursuing moderate and pacific measures. He reproached the Argives with their breach of faith towards Athens; represented the irresistible and matchless strength of the confederacy; showed them how peculiarly favourable the circumstances were for continuing the war; and concluded by suggesting, that they might now make an important attempt, with a certain prospect of success. To this proposal they summarily acceded: and thus encouraged by the Athenian embassador, the Argives and their allies were persuaded to break the truce with Sparta. The army marched to Orchomenus, an ancient and wealthy town of Arcadia. The fortifications of the place were weak; and the people, alarmed by the greatness of the force prepared to attack them, and apprehensive of being overpowered before succours could arrive, agreed to a capitulation.

The Eleans were now urgent, that the combined army should endeavour to recover Lepreum, a district upon their own borders; but the allies paid no regard to their solicitations. The Mantineans proposed the much more important acquisition of Tegea; and giving assurance, that they carried on a correspondence with a faction in the town, the Argives and Athenians concurred with them. The Eleans were so.

much dissatisfied with this preference of the great concerns of the confederacy to their own particular interests, that they returned home, and the army proceeded to lay siege to Tegea.

It was not without indignation, that the Lacedæmonians heard of the submission of Orchomenus, the siege of Tegea, and the open and daring infraction of the treaty. They had been displeased with the truce granted by their general, but whilst peace was the apparent consequence of the measure, they had confined their resentment merely to expressions of disapprobation. No sooner, however, did they feel the ruinous and disgraceful effects of his misconduct, than their indignation became outrageous. He was called to an account with a degree of hostile warmth not usual with the Lacedæmonians. They had determined to destroy his house, and to condemn him in a fine of several thousand pounds. But considering his former diligence and service, and the general deportment of his conduct, he was again received into favour. His known talents for war recommended him to the command of the army, and he promised his countrymen, that his future services should speedily wipe off the late aspersion from his character. The Spartans, however, appointed ten counsellors, without whose concurrence he could not lead the forces beyond the Lacedæmonian territory.

The whole force of Laconia, with that of the allied states, was assembled with great celerity; and as the Spartans were desirous of withdrawing the Argives from the siege of Tegea, the army immediately marched to Mantinea. By these means the enemy were compelled to defend that place, or permit it to fall into the hands of the Lacedæmonians. The Argives withdrew their troops from before Tegea, and approached the Mantinean frontier. Both armies, whose ambition or resentment had been so lately disappointed of an opportunity to display their force, eagerly prepared for an engagement.

The ancient custom, previous to the commencement of a battle, was for the leaders of the respective nations to harangue their soldiers in a moving and appropriate speech. The Mantineans were exhorted, valiantly to contend for the defence of their city, and the safety of their wives and children. The event of this battle, they were told, would determine the very important alternative of dominion or servitude; a dominion which they had lately assumed over several cities of Arcadia, or a servitude which they had already suffered under the galling yoke of Sparta. The Argives were reminded of that preeminence they had formerly held in Peloponnesus, and which they had lately recovered. They were put in mind of the long and bloody wars carried on for the defence of their liberty and property, and to repel the usurpations of a powerful and ambitious neighbour. This was the same enemy they were now about to attack, who had provoked their arms, and whose crimes and injustice, exercised for several centuries, they were about to revenge. The Athenians heard, and repeated, that it was glorious to march at the head of warlike and faithful allies, and to prove they were worthy of the ancient renown of Athens. They were inferiour to no nation, in point of bravery and courage. Their power was unrivalled, and, when they had conquered the Lacedæmonians in Peloponnesus, their dominion would not only be more extensive, but more secure.

The Spartans, sensible that discipline, long and carefully exercised, will give more confidence to troops, than the most eloquent and appropriate harangue, briefly exhorted their followers to exert that innate ardour and valour, which could receive no additional assistance from the laborious display of useless words.— Thus saying, they marched in silent and in perfect order, and moved to the sound of numerous flutes, with their front compact and even, to meet the impetuous onset of the Argives and Athenians. Never in Peloponnesus had two such numerous and powerful armies been seen before. Above a thousand Argives, chosen from amongst their noblest youths, had been for a long time employed in the constant exercise of arms, that they might maintain the honourable pretensions of their country. These behaved in the bravest manner, while the Athenians proved that they were not inferiour in courage, and that the fame their country had obtained for martial exploits was justly founded. The Mantineans strenuously defended every thing dear and valuable to them. The Eleans, however, having seceded from the confederacy, the allied army was greatly weakened; and the martial enthusiasm of king Agis, aided by the valour of the Spartans, decided the fate of the battle. The allies were repulsed, thrown into confusion, and completely defeated. Agis, true to the institutions of Lycurgus, observed the ancient maxim, which enjoined the Spartans to make a bridge for a fleeing enemy; and therefore pursued the foes no farther, than to make the victory sure. In consequence of this, the killed were not numerous in proportion to the numbers engaged, and the completeness of the success. The Spartans lost three, and the allies eleven, hundred men. The events of this battle restored the lustre of the Lacedæmonian character; and the misfortunes, the misconduct, and the apparent slackness of the Spartans, in the course of the war with Athens, were no longer attributed to any degeneracy of the people, but to the mismanagement of the leaders, and the chance of war.

The unfortunate battle of Mantinea strengthened the oligarchical interest in Argos. The dread of such another event, and of the consequences that generally followed the termination of an unsuccessful war in Greece, induced the Argives to think of an accommodation with Lacedæmon. Accordingly, the popular form of government was abolished, the partisans of Athens were destroyed, the league with that state was abjured, and an alliance offensive and defensive entered into with Sparta. During the two following years, however, Argos paid dearly for a moment of transient splendour.— This state underwent three bloody revolutions, in which the atrocities committed in the Corcyrean sedition seemed to be renewed. The contest ended, as in Corcyra, in favour of Athens and democracy.

The island of Melos, the largest of the Cyclades, and which lies directly opposite to the cape of Malea, the southern promontory of Laconia, was next attacked by the Athenian arms. This beautiful island, of an agreeable temperature, and affording the usual productions of a fine climate, had early invited the Spartans to send a colony thither, which had enjoyed political independence for seven hundred years. Before, however, they commenced hostilities, embassadors were sent, to persuade the Melians to surrender, without incurring the punishment

VOL. III.   T

which would necessarily follow a vain and fruitless resistance. The Melians would not consent to join the Athenian alliance, and declared
their resolution not to betray, in an unguarded
moment, the liberty they had so long maintained.
But they entreated the Athenians to accept their
offers of neutrality, and to abstain from an un-
provoked violence. The embassadors only replied by a sarcastick threat, that the Melians, of
all men, considered the future more certain than
the past, and that they would grievously lament
their folly and presumption, in hoping to avert
and resist the just vengeance of their republick.
The Athenians, irritated by opposition, invested
the capital of Melos, and blocked it up by sea
and land. The besieged, having suffered greatly
by famine, made several desperate sallies upon
the besiegers, seized the Athenian magazines,
and destroyed the works they had raised. They
were, however, partly by domestick faction, but
chiefly by the vigorous efforts of the enemy,
compelled soon after to surrender. The citizens of Melos became the victims of a revenge
equally cruel and impolitick. All the males
above the age of puberty were put to the sword;
the women and children were dragged into servitude; and an Athenian colony replaced the
unfortunate Melians!

Plutarch, an instructive, but often an inaccur-
ate, biographer, has ascribed the inhuman massacre of the inhabitants of Melos to the pride
and ambition of Alcibiades. But more ancient
and authentick writers, whose silence on this
part of the subject seems to exculpate the son
of Clinias from this atrocious deed, uniformly
represent him as the promoter of the expedition
against Sicily; an expedition unjust in its principles, and unfortunate in its consequences.

Before, however, we commence the narration of those important events, which were the result of this expedition, it will be proper to take a brief review of the Grecian colony settled in

B. C. 1084.
Sicily. Corinth had early acquired considerable reputation and power as a maritime state; and it is universally seen, that the improvement of navigation tends to discovery, to commerce, and to colonization. It produced all these effects upon the Corinthians. The coast of Sicily had not been long known to them, when they projected a scheme to settle a colony of Peloponnesians in that country. Archias, therefore, one of the Heraclidæ, or descendants of Hercules, was sent with a fleet, and had every thing provided for accomplishing the enterprise. He built and peopled Syracuse, the metropolis of Sicily, and, according to Cicero, the greatest and most wealthy of all the cities possessed by the Greeks. Thucydides, indeed, equals it to Athens, when at the summit of its glory; and Strabo says, that for its advantageous situation, the stateliness of its buildings, and the immense wealth of the inhabitants, it was one of the most famous cities of the world. It consisted of three principal divisions; the island, which lay on the south side, and communicated with the main land by a bridge; Achradina, which stretched along the sea-coast, and was the strongest and most beautiful part of the city; and Tyche, which stood between Achradina and the hill Epipole. It was long subject to the Corinthians; but does not appear to have exercised, for any great length of time after its foundation, a democratical form of government. As it increased in power, it became proud and insolent, and, by degrees, renounced its depend-

ence on Corinth. To its emancipation are owing the occurrences, which we have to relate.

As the names of Sicily and Cyrenaica will seldom occur in the subsequent parts of this history, it may be necessary and proper to notice, in a brief manner, the causes that withdrew from the sphere of Grecian politicks a fruitful and extensive coast, and an island equally fruitful and extensive, and much more populous and powerful. The Greeks found it very inconvenient to interfere in the affairs of these remote provinces, on account of their insulated situation. And the colonies, being far removed from any assistance or protection, that could be afforded them from their parent country, were frequently obliged to submit to the oppression of domestick tyranny, and to the ravages of foreign barbarians.

The Cyrenaicans waged alternate war with the Lybians and Carthaginians. The tyrant Ariston oppressed them. Soon after, however, they recovered their civil liberty, but were frequently compelled to contend for the independence of their state. Though often attacked by the barbarians, they never submitted to their oppression ; and it was not until after the time of Alexander, that they were deprived of their liberties. The person that first subjected them to his dominion was the fortunate general, who, in the division of Alexander's conquests, succeeded his master in the government of Egypt.

The revolutions that happened in the affairs of Sicily are much better known. The Syracusans had been induced, by the assistance granted them by the Lacedæmonians for the defence of their country, to engage in the Peloponnesian war. But the Carthaginians having made some formidable descents on Sicily, by which the safety of the island and of the capital was endangered, the Syracusans were under the necessity of recalling their armament from the assistance of the Peloponnesians, in order to repel the invaders of their country. The Carthaginians had entered into this war for the purpose of acquiring at once those valuable commodities, the annual purchase of which had drained Africa of such immense treasures, and also to support the pretensions of Segesta and other inferiour cities, at variance with Syracuse.

Hannibal, the grandson of Hamilcar, was appointed general of the Carthaginians. He commenced operations in the four hundred and tenth, which continued, without intermission, until the four hundred and fourth, year before the christian æra. Considerable levies were made from the native Italians and Spaniards, who naturally envied the splendour and dreaded the power of the Greeks, to whose conquests and colonies they saw no bounds. The whole army, therefore, of Hannibal amounted in the spring to three hundred thousand men, who were transported into Sicily in a proportionable number of ships.

It would seem, that the designs of Hannibal were, to possess himself of the inferiour and more defenceless cities, before he attempted the reduction of Syracuse, which, being naturally strong, had been lately fortified by art, and could not be taken otherwise than by a blockade. In B. C. 409. the first campaign, the Carthaginian general made himself master of Selinus and Himera, and most of the inhabitants of these places were cruelly put to death by the victors. Every one they met, without regard

T 2

to sex or age, was inhumanly killed; and the slaughter was so terrible in the streets of Himera, that the channels flowed with blood. After plundering the temples and houses, and levelling the city with the ground, Hannibal caused three thousand of the captives to be carried to the place where his grandfather had been defeated and killed by the cavalry of Gelon, in the first Carthaginian invasion. These miserable wretches were then exposed to the insults of the barbarians, and sacrificed, by the cruelty of Hannibal to the manes of Hamilcar.

This success emboldened the Carthaginians, and revived the design they had always entertained of subduing the whole island of Sicily. They therefore began to make new preparations, and committed the whole management of the war to the same general; but he, pleading his advanced age, as an excuse for not taking upon him the sole command, they joined in commission with him Hamilcar, the son of Hanno, and a person of the same family. Every thing being ready, the numerous and formidable armament sailed for Sicily, landed on the coast of Agrigentum, and immediately marched to that city.

The Syracusans and their confederates had sent embassadors to Carthage, to make complaints of the late hostilities committed against them by Hannibal, and to persuade the senate to forbear sending any more troops into Sicily. The Carthaginians, however, having returned a doubtful answer to this embassy, the Syracusans had made preparations for a defence, and were ready to receive the enemy. The Agrigentines also, expecting that the attack would first be made on their city, had carefully provided every thing necessary for sustaining a siege, and had followed the directions of Dexippus, a Lacedæmonian, and an officer of great bravery and experience.

Hannibal sent embassadors to the Agrigentines, with a proposal either to join his standard, or to remain neuter; and declared that he would be satisfied with their conduct, and forbear all hostilities, provided they would agree to a treaty of friendship. This offer being rejected, the two generals began to lay siege to the place. But a plague broke out in the Carthaginian army, which carried off a great number of the soldiers and their general Hannibal. This was declared, by the soothsayers, a punishment for the injuries and indignities inflicted on the dead; whereupon sacrifices were appointed for appeasing the gods. The Agrigentines expected an army of Syracusans to march to their relief, under the command of Daphneus. Hamilcar, having received intelligence of their approach, detached all the Iberians and Campanians in his army, together with forty thousand Carthaginians, and commanded them to engage the enemy in the plains of the river Himera. Accordingly the Syracusans were attacked soon after they had crossed the river, and as they advanced in good order, through the plains, towards Agrigentum. The contest was fierce and bloody, and the victory for some time doubtful. At length, however, the Syracusans, being greatly superiour in point of numbers, routed the Carthaginians, and pursued them, with great slaughter, to the walls of Agrigentum. On their approach to that city, the besiegers fled with precipitation to the camp of Hamiclar, pitched upon the neighbouring hills. Daphneus followed, with an intention of forcing the camp; but finding it

strongly fortified, he thought it more advisable
to guard the avenues leading to it with his cavalry, and thereby starve the enemy, or compel
them to venture an engagement.

Whilst the numerous army of Carthaginians
was thus blockaded, and greatly straitened for
provision, a Syracusan fleet of sixty transports,
laden with corn, and all kinds of necessaries, was
intercepted by the gallies belonging to Hamilcar. Agrigentum, being thus deprived of the
provision sent for its relief, the mercenary soldiers in the city passed over to the enemy ; and
the inhabitants desponding for want of necessaries, an assembly was convened, and it was
resolved, that they should abandon the town,
and transport themselves to some place of safety.
Accordingly, the greater part of the inhabitants
left the city the next night, and, under the escort
of the Syracusan army, arrived safe at Gela,
where they were received with kindness and
humanity, and plentifully supplied with necessaries. They had the city of Leontini and its
fertile territory afterward granted to them.

When the Syracusan army was departed,
Hamilcar marched out of the trenches, and entered the city, but not without betraying
some fear and suspicion. Those who
were found in Agrigentum were massacred, without regarding sex, age, or condition.
Gellias, a humane and hospitable man, and the
richest citizen in Agrigentum, whose opulence
enabled him to lodge and entertain five hundred
guests, and to supply them with coats and
cloaks out of his wardrobe ; and whose cellars,
consisting of three hundred spacious reservoirs,
invited all to be his guests, betook himself for
protection to the temple of Minerva. But when

B. C.
406.

he understood the universal desolation of his country, and that the temples were profaned and plundered, and those murdered who had sought refuge in them, he set fire to the sacred edifice, and chose to perish by the flames, rather than fall into the hands of the cruel and merciless foe.

Near fourscore years before the demolition of Agrigentum, Sicily acquired great renown, by resisting more numerous invaders. But the efforts of the whole island were then directed against the common enemy. Whereas, now, amidst the universal danger and consternation of the Carthaginian war, the Sicilians were distracted with domestic factions. Hermocrates, whose prudence, valour, and integrity, were well known, was the only man able to direct the helm in the present tempestuous juncture, and he had been banished his country. In the interval, however, between the taking of Himera and Agrigentum, he made a forcible attempt, at the head of his numerous adherents, to gain admission into Syracuse. But the attempt proved fatal to himself; and, in its consequences, destroyed the freedom of his country. Though his partisans were discomfited and banished, they soon found a leader qualified to avenge their cause, and to punish the ingratitude of the Syracusans.

Dionysius, a native of Syracuse, of mean extraction, but unbounded ambition, contrived to usurp the sovereignty of his country. He is said to have been a man destitute of almost every virtue, and possessed of almost every talent; and it was his fortune to live amidst those perturbed circumstances of foreign and intestine war, which call great and superiour abilities into action, and favour their elevation. Though he was caressed by Hermocrates, more capable of appreciating his abilities, than of discovering his dangerous ambition, Dionysius had obtained friends in the opposite faction, whose influence procured his recal. He distinguished himself in a very particular manner, at the battle near Agrigentum. He was possessed of great bravery. His eloquence was unrivalled. In the object of his pursuit he persevered with inflexibility; but the means of obtaining his purpose were various, and suited to the exigency of his affairs. Professing himself a patriot and a lover of his country, he acquired the esteem and affection of the people, and employed the authority he had over them, to restore his banished friends. Many perceived the object he had in view, but durst not oppose his proceedings, because he had now gained so much popularity, that all resistance would prove not only ineffectual, but involve them in certain destruction.

Soon after this, he had the address to procure himself to be elected commander in chief of the army, with absolute and unbounded authority. In order to secure himself against the change of disposition, which he saw many of the Syracusans manifest, when they reflected on what they had done, he pretended to be afraid of assassination, during his abode at the castle of Leontini, whither he had purposely repaired, and therefore desired that a guard of soldiers might be granted him. He requested no more than six hundred, but chose a thousand men, whom he caused to be completely armed, and flattered them with great promises. The mercenary soldiers also were attached to him. With this train **B. C. 404.** he entered Syracuse, the citizens of which were greatly alarmed at his approach. They were, however, no longer able to oppose his designs, or dispute his authority.

Thus did Dionysius, by his crafty and daring ambition, raise himself to the sovereignty of the greatest and most opulent city of Sicily.

In the mean time, the Carthaginians under the command of Hamilcar, having razed the city of Agrigentum, marched with all their forces against Gela. This city, though indifferently fortified, resisted for a long time an army of three thousand men, without receiving assistance from any of its allies. At length, however, Dionysius marched an army of fifty thousand foot, and a thousand horse to its relief; but not caring to risk a general engagement, he persuaded the inhabitants to abandon their country, as the only means of saving their lives. As soon as they departed, the Carthaginians entered the city, and put to death, or crucified, all they found in it. Camarina shared the same fate as Gela. The affecting sight of the aged and infirm, who were obliged, however unable, to hasten from two several cities, in one and the same country, and all the citizens deprived of their wealth and possessions, raised compassion in the hearts of the soldiers, and incensed them against Dionysius. They considered him as acting in concert with the Carthaginians; and, therefore, the Italians, in a body, left his camp and returned home; while the Syracusan cavalry, having attempted his death on the march, rode with all speed to their city, blocked up the gates, forced the tyrant's palace, and ransacked and plundered all his treasures. Dionysius, suspecting their designs, followed them with all expedition, and having made himself master of the city, scoured the streets with his cavalry, and put to the sword all that came in his way. He even entered the houses of those whom he suspected to be hostile to his tyranny; and destroyed whole families together.

In the mean time a plague broke out in the Carthaginian camp, and Hamilcar, finding himself unable to continue the war, sent a herald to Dionysius to offer terms of peace. These unexpected overtures were very acceptable to the tyrant. And a peace being concluded between the two contending parties, the Carthaginian commander, having lost more than half of his men by the plague, which afterward made dreadful havock in Africa, embarked the remains of his troops, and sailed for Carthage.

During the long and active reign of Dionysius, he was generally engaged in war; sometimes with the Carthaginians, and at other times with his disaffected and seditious subjects : but he was uniformly victorious. The Carthaginian power in Sicily he greatly diminished, and appeased or intimidated domestick faction. His present condition, however, he only considered as a preparation for still higher grandeur. Being under no apprehensions of the Carthaginians, he turned all his thoughts to the reduction of Rhegium, the key of Italy. His design in this was, to reduce under his dominion the Grecian cities in that country. Having, therefore, laid siege to the city, the inhabitants held out for eleven months, against the whole force of Dionysius; but for want of provision, were at length reduced to the utmost extremity; till, overcome by famine, they were compelled to surrender at discretion. When Dionysius entered the city, he was astonished and terrified at the meagre appearance of the survivors, and the number of the dead. He collected, however, about six thousand prisoners, whom he sent to Syracuse, where such as were unable to redeem themselves were sold for slaves. But the cruelty of the tyrant did not end here. He resolved to take revenge on Phyto, the chief magistrate of the place, by whose bravery and counsel Rhegium had resisted his efforts for so long a time. He caused his son to be thrown headlong into the sea. The next day Phyto was scourged through the city, underwent innumerable other cruelties, and was also thrown into the sea.

It is probable, that the feeble confederacy of the Italian Greeks could not have prevented the conquest of that country by the arms of Dionysius, had not the renewed hostilities of the Carthaginians, and domestick faction, hindered the execution of his designs. This growing storm he resisted as successfully as before, and transmitted to his son the peaceful inheritance of the greatest part of Sicily. The fortifications of the capital, Dionysius strengthened with wonderful art. He enlarged and improved the form of the Syracusan gallies. He invented the military catapults*, an engine of war, which he employed very advantageously in reducing the towns of Motya and Rhegium. And he not only defended his native island against all foreign invasion, but rendered its power formidable to the neighbouring countries.

In the intervals of leisure, Dionysius unbent his mind with the study of the liberal arts and sciences, and especially poetry, and valued himself highly for the extent of his genius, and the

* The catapults here mentioned were engines, from which vollies of arrows and stones were discharged against the besieged. But this word is sometimes used simply for arrows. *See Potter's Gree. Ant.*

eloquence of his performances. Philoxenus was the only person about his court, that attempted to undeceive him, and was, therefore, ordered to be carried to the quarries, or common prison. Being released, however, the next day, Philoxenus was again desired to give his opinion of some verses, that Dionysius had composed. Upon which, Philoxenus immediately cried out, " carry me back to the quarries." This pleasantry Dionysius took in good part, and told Philoxenus, that his wit atoned for his freedom.

Notwithstanding the endeavours of Philoxenus to undeceive him, Dionysius still considered himself as one of the greatest of poets, and therefore sent his brother, Thearides, to the Olympic games, to dispute in his name the prizes adjudged to the muses, and to the chariot-races. The most skilful rhapsodists of the age were chosen for reciting his verses. The audience was, at first, charmed with the poems of Dionysius. But when they considered, not the manner of delivery, but the sense and composition, the rhapsodist was immediately hissed off the stage ; and the embassador of the tyrant insulted with the most humiliating indignities. Lysias, the celebrated orator, who was then at Olympia, pronounced a discourse, in which he maintained, that it was inconsistent with the honour of Greece, and therefore improper, to admit the representative of an impious tyrant, to assist at a solemnity consecrated to religion, virtue, and liberty.

The oration of Lysias gives ground to suspect, that the plenitude of Dionysius's power, rather than the defect of his poetry, exposed him to the censure and derision of the Olympic audience. Certain it is, that having caused a tragedy, which he had written, to be acted at Athens, in the last year of his reign, he obtained a poetic crown from the Athenian assembly ; which was always considered as impartial in its literary decisions.

It is remarkable, that, with a mind active, vigorous, and comprehensive ; with a variety of talents, and an accumulation of glory, Dionysius should be universally held out and branded, as the most odious and miserable tyrant that ever existed ; the object of terrour in his own, and of hatred in after ages. But though he was vicious and cruel in some respects, history will bear sufficient testimony, that his character was not decisively flagitious. It is probable, that his situation rendered it artificial ; and he is acknowledged to have assumed the appearance of virtue. He was always crafty and cautious. Sometimes, and when it suited his purpose, he was mild, affable, and condescending. At other times, he was the cruel, arrogant, and imperious tyrant. It was not until the Syracusans had provoked his indignation, by insulting and maltreating his wife and children during an insurrection, that they felt the rigour and cruelty of Dionysius. There are two circumstances observable in the character of Dionysius, which in all probability have excited the indignation of the Greek and Roman moralists, and occasioned them to consider him more tyrannical and oppressive than he really was. These are, the usurpation of the government of a free republick, and the profession of contempt for the religion of his country. The bare suspicion of the latter crime had brought to death, as we have seen, the most amiable, most innocent, and most respected of men. But the impiety, which

Dionysius professed, was nothing more than the child of his interest, and sometimes the parent of his wit.

A celebrated statue of Jupiter he stripped of a robe of gold, and observed, that it was too heavy in summer, and too cold in winter. For a reason not less ingenious, he ordered a statue of Æsculapius to be deprived of its golden beard, and asserted, that such a venerable ornament ill became the son of the beardless Apollo. If, however, he deprived the statues and temples of what belonged to them, it is certain that he augmented the fleets and armies of Syracuse, which were successfully employed against the common enemy. Against the general current of satire and invective, with which the character of this extraordinary man is treated, it is necessary only to mention, that the opinion of Polybius and Scipio Africanus was, that no man ever concerted his schemes with greater prudence, and no man ever executed them with greater promptitude and boldness, than Dionysius the elder.

His son, Dionysius the younger, succeeded, on the demise of his father, to the government of Syracuse. He is said to have exceeded his father's vices, without possessing his abilities. The reign of this latter tyrant was distracted and inglorious. His disposition was mild and temperate, but this proceeded more from indolence, than a wise and judicious understanding. Dion, who was well acquainted with him, and knew that he was naturally inclined to virtue, had a taste for arts and sciences, and was a lover of learning and learned men, proposed to correct the mean and imperfect education he had received under his father. The young prince, by the advice of Dion, invited

B. C.
366.

Plato to his court. But to correct the vices of Dionysius was a task too hard for both Plato and Dion. The latter, unable to restrain the excesses of Dionysius, became advocate for the people. The former was driven back into Greece, by the tyrannical conduct of the prince. But the patriotism of Dion, though it served to interrupt, did not finally destroy, the tyranny of Dionysius. The magnanimity of Timoleon, however, abolished the government of the tyrant in Syracuse; and Dionysius, who was once king of one of the most wealthy states then known, became a private person, and lived during the rest of his life an exile at Corinth. Timoleon no sooner perceived himself master of Syracuse, than he invited the citizens to demolish the castles and citadel, which he considered as places fit only for the refuge and protection of tyrants. Timoleon having demolished the forts and palaces, and destroyed every vestige of tyranny, enacted many wise and salutary laws, and settled the city in peace and tranquillity. He then prepared to carry his arms against the Carthaginians, and gained a very considerable and important victory over that people, in which thirteen thousand were slain, and fourteen thousand of the enemy made prisoners. All the baggage and provision, with a thousand coats of mail, and ten thousand shields, fell into the hands of the conquerors. Timoleon, however, divided amongst the soldiers all the gold and silver plate, and other things of value, and reserved nothing for himself beside the glory of the victory. He concluded a peace with the Carthaginians, in which it was stipulated, that all the Greek cities in Sicily should be set free.

B. C.
348.

The Syracusans enjoyed for the space of twenty years the fruits of Timoleon's victories. But after the death of that general, new tyrants started up in that, and almost every city of Sicily, and held a precarious sway under the alternate protection of the Carthaginians and Romans. The Syracusans, not forgetful of their ancient fame, dethroned their usurpers, and enjoyed considerable intervals of liberty. At

B. C. 200. length, however, the Romans gained possession of the city. They had besieged Syracuse for three years. Nor would the perseverance of Marcellus have prevailed over the bold efforts of mechanical power, directed by the inventive mind of Archimedes, had not the garrison been corrupted by the gold of the Roman general, which treacherously delivered up the city to the enemy. During the sacking of Acradina, Archimedes was shut up in his closet, and so intent on the demonstration of a geometrical problem, that neither the tumult and noise of the soldiers, nor the cries and lamentations of the people, could divert his attention. He was very deliberately drawing his lines and figures, when a soldier entered his apartment, and clapped a sword to his throat. "Hold, friend," said Archimedes, "for one moment, and my demonstration will be finished." The soldier, astonished at the unconcern and intrepidity of the philosopher in such imminent danger, resolved to carry him to the proconsul. But Archimedes unfortunately taking with him a small box of mathematical and astronomical instruments, the soldier supposing it contained silver and gold, and not being able to resist the force of temptation, killed him on the spot. His death was much lamented by Marcellus, who caused his funeral to be performed with the greatest pomp and solemnity, and ordered a monument to be erected to his memory, among those illustrious men, who had distinguished themselves in Syracuse.

The passion of this philosopher for mathematical knowledge was so strong, that he devoted himself entirely to the pleasures of study. This gave occasion to the report, that he was so charmed with the soothing songs of a domestick tyrant, that he neglected the common concerns and occupations of life. Every other object he despised; and that he might not interrupt his pursuits, he frequently denied himself the necessaries of life. Hiero, king of Syracuse, prevailed by intreaties on the speculative geometrician, to descend to mechanicks; and Archimedes constructed those wonderful machines for the defence of cities, the effects of which retarded, and might, perhaps, have completely impeded, the taking of Syracuse.* He is also said to have been the inventor of a sphere of glass, on which the periodical and synodical motions of the stars and planets were represented.

After the reduction of Syracuse, most of the cities of Sicily voluntarily submitted to the power of Marcellus; and the whole island became in a little time a Roman province, and was the first conquest that republick made out of Italy. B. C. 198. Sicily was obliged to the payment of a certain tribute to Rome; but was suffered to enjoy its ancient privileges, and to retain all its former rights.

During the time of the invasion of Greece, by the forces of Xerxes, the Greek settlements

* It is not known how those machines were constructed, or in what manner they were employed.

in this island bravely defended their liberty, and asserted their independence ; and the salutary union of the princes of Syracuse and Agrigentum triumphed over the ambition and the resources of Carthage. Sicily flourished under the virtuous administration of Gelon and Theron ; but the tranquillity of the island was disturbed by the dissensions that afterward arose between their successors. Hiero, king of Syracuse, proved victorious in a long and bloody war, during which the incapacity and misfortunes of the prince of Agrigentum emboldened the resentment of his subjects, which his injustice and cruelty had already provoked; and, expelling him from his kingdom, they instituted a republican form of policy.

This Hiero was, in the latter part of his life, a model of wisdom and virtue ; and adorned the history of Sicily and the age in which he lived. The poets Simonides, Æschylus, and Bacchilides, frequented his court, and paid their homage to the greatness of his mind rather than of his fortune. Pindar has celebrated the magnificent generosity of his patron ; and Xenophon, who had nothing to hope or fear from the ashes of a king of Sicily, has represented Hiero as a prince of the most consummate virtue and prudence. His successor, however, was a wretch, that disgraced both the throne and human nature; and was expelled from Sicily by the just indignation of his subjects, who, forgetting the fame of Gelon, and the merit of Hiero, exchanged the odious power of kings for a furious democracy.

Distracted by internal discord, and harassed by external hostilities, the Greek settlements could not attend to the politicks of Greece; and

Syracuse, imitating the ambition of Athens, had obliged most of the Dorian states to become confederates, or rather tributaries. Not satisfied, however, with having reduced these communities to dependence, they exerted their valour against the Ionic settlements of Leontium, Catana, and Naxos. In the sixth year of the Peloponnesian war, the Leontines sent to Athens, to solicit the assistance of that republick against the injustice and usurpations of Syracuse. The Athenians immediately complied with their request, and twenty ships of war were sent to the aid of their Ionic brethren. Two years afterward, the Leontines again importuned the assistance of Athens; and that republick was about to engage in the war with vigour, when the Syracusans, alarmed at the intrusion of these ambitious strangers, promoted a general congress of the states of Sicily. In this convention, the general interest of the island was regarded, and all parties were engaged to terminate their domestick contests lest the power of Athens should subvert and destroy their independence.

This plan of union, so seasonable and salutary, was not, however, of long duration. Leontium was soon after taken and destroyed, its inhabitants were driven into banishment, and the Egesteans, their confederates, closely besieged by the arms of Selinus and Syracuse. The unfortunate communities again sent to implore the aid of Athens. They pleaded the rights of consanguinity, and addressed not only the passions, but the interest of the Athenians. They insisted, that their allies were bound to assist them by every principle of sound policy. They further urged, that the growing greatness of Syracuse, if not repressed, would become a form-

B.C. 416.

idable accession to the Peloponnesian league; and that, while their Ionian kinsmen were capable of acting with vigour against the Syracusans, it was the proper time for undertaking the enterprise. That they might add weight to these arguments, the embassadors of Egesta, gave an ostentatious and a very false description of the wealth of their state, which, they assured the Athenians, was capable of furnishing the whole expenses of the war. The Athenians, however, deemed it advisable to send deputies to Sicily, who might inquire into the state of the island, and particularly into that of the Egesteans.

Upon the arrival of the embassadors at Egesta, that state borrowed the riches of their neighbours; which they displayed to the Athenians; and in the spring following, the commissioners returned with new ministers from Egesta, who brought with them about sixty talents of silver, as a month's pay in advance for sixty triremes. With this money in their hands, which they asserted their state would monthly repeat, they were introduced into the assembly of the Athenians. Allured by the extravagant but flattering prospects of grandeur, the people of Athens held two successive assemblies, in which the reasons for and against the Sicilian expedition were considered. In the latter the Athenians came to a resolution, to raise such a naval and military force, that the war might be prosecuted with vigour and success.

While, however, they deliberated on the means for carrying this resolve into execution, Nicias, who had been appointed with Alcibiades and Lamachus to the command of the armament, omitted nothing which prudence could suggest;

or patriotism enforce, to deter his countrymen
from this dangerous and fatal design. He urged
the impossibility of contending with the Spartans,
and of sending, at the same time, so great a body
of forces in Sicily. He expatiated on the mad-
ness and folly of attempting to subdue so populous and powerful an island, when they had not
been able to reduce Greece. The assembly,
he said, ought not to be moved by the arguments
and entreaties of which the Egesteans had made
use, heightened as they were by resentment and
misery. In short, the question, he asserted,
ought to be again debated ; the decree that had
passed, be rescinded ; and the cause of the
Egestians be forever abandoned by the Athenians.

This discourse called up Alcibiades, who held
an opinion diametrically opposite to what Nicias
had proposed. The undertaking which he advised, he said, was founded in justice and prudence, and no reasonable objection could be
made against it : The Egesteans and other confederates would furnish the expenses of the war ;
and the danger could not be great, because Sicily, however extensive, populous, and powerful,
was inhabited by different nations, who had
never been exercised in the discipline requisite
for obtaining victory, and were without arms,
devoid of patriotism, and incapable of union.

The assembly murmured their applause of
the sentiments of Alcibiades, ratified the decree
they had already passed, and testified greater
alacrity for the war than before. Nicias perceived the violence of the popular current ; but
he determined to make one last, though ineffectual effort, to resist the torrent of publick opinion, and to bring the Athenians to a due sense

of the danger and difficulty of the enterprise. The success of an invader, he observed, generally depended on the force and rapidity with which his first impressions were made. By these means, the confidence of friends was confirmed, and the terrour and dismay of enemies were excited. If the Athenians were determined to invade Sicily, in spite of the dangers and difficulties that would attend the undertaking, they ought to remember, that the utmost vigour would be requisite for carrying their designs into execution. They would have to contend with seven large and powerful cities, against which no naval armament would be sufficient. Great numbers of pikemen, with a proportional number of archers and cavalry, could not render the invasion successful. The towns in Sicily must be stormed or besieged; workmen, with all kinds of implements necessary for this kind of warfare, must be collected, and transported to an island, from which, for four months in the year, even a messenger could not be sent to Athens.* To collect and transport such an immense mass of war, required great ardour and perseverance; but, if the Athenians did not pursue the most vigorous and decisive measures, for rendering the invasion of Sicily prosperous and successful, or should they presume to make the attempt with a less force than he had supposed adequate to the purpose, he would decline the command, and they must elect another general in his room.

This last attempt of Nicias to deter his countrymen from their mad design, by magnifying the dangers and difficulties to which the enter-

* This proves the miserable state of navigation at that period.

prise was liable, produced a quite different effect from what he proposed to himself. The obstacles, which he affirmed it would be difficult or impossible for Athens to surmount, only served to animate the courage of the assembly. The generals were directed by a decree of the people, to raise such sums of money, and levy such a body of forces, as they might suppose sufficient for ensuring success. The domestick strength of Athens, however, was not equal to the undertaking. They sent, therefore, to demand the assistance and supplies of their several dependent states, and to summon the reluctant aid of their more warlike allies. Corcyra was appointed to be the general rendezvous of the Grecian fleet. The levies were carried on at Athens, and in the confederate cities, with so much success and expedition, that in a few days the proposed number of troops was completed, and the gallies manned and fitted for sea.

Such were the general expectations on raising this great and powerful armament, that the hopes and ardour of all ranks can scarcely be conceived. The aged supposed, that nothing could withstand or resist such a numerous and well equipped force. The young eagerly seized the opportunity of gratifying their curiosity and love of knowledge, in a distant navigation, and of sharing the honours and dangers of so glorious an enterprise. The rich embraced the means of displaying their magnificence and liberality; and the poor rejoiced, that the success of this expedition would procure for them the materials of future ease and happiness. In completing the levies, the greatest difficulty appeared in deciding amongst those that solicited to serve, to whom the preference of valour and merit belonged; and the whole compliment of forces, intended to be employed by sea and land, was composed of men chosen for the purpose.

Socrates was the only person, who dared openly and boldly to deliver his opinion, to condemn the expedition, and to predict the future misfortunes and disgraces, that would attend it. The authority and sentiments of the sage philosopher, however, could not damp that universal ardour and enthusiasm, that had seized all ranks and degrees of persons; and which not even the anniversary festival of Adonis, a sacred and melancholy rite, had been permitted to check or interrupt. This solemnity inauspiciously happened a few days preceding the embarcation. The dreary ceremony was performed through the streets of Athens; spectres appeared in funeral robes; the domes and temples resounded with loud and lamenting vociferations; and the Grecian matrons, tearing their dishevelled hair, and beating their naked bosoms, bewailed in mournful strains the untimely death of Adonis, the lover and the favourite of Venus.

B. C. 415. All the citizens enrolled for the expedition appeared early on the morning of the day appointed for the embarcation. The whole city accompanied them to Piræus. The Athenians were divided between hope and fear, when they reflected on so great a proportion of the strength of Athens, in which every one had a friend or relation, committed to the uncertainty of the elements, and the chance of war. But no sooner were the men put on board, and the fleet prepared to get under way, than the trumpets sounded, as a signal of silence. Immediately prayers were offered up to the gods with great solemnity; and the numerous spectators upon the shore answered with corresponding vows. Libations were then poured out, in goblets of silver and gold. This ceremony being performed, triumphant pæans were sung in full chorus; and the whole fleet moved to Ægina, thence to take its departure for Corcyra.

When the whole armament of the Athenians and their allies had arrived at Corcyra, it consisted of one hundred and thirty-four ships of war, with a proportionable number of transports and tenders. The heavy armed troops amounted to five thousand, to which were added a sufficient body of slingers and archers. The whole military and naval strength of this expedition may be computed at twenty thousand men.

With this powerful host, had the Athenians attacked the Syracusans in their present security, and ignorance of the armament coming against them, there would have been a greater probability, that the enterprise, adventurous and imprudent as it certainly was, might have been successful. But the Grecian mariners, unaccustomed to make long voyages, would not have been prevailed on to trust so great an armament on the wide expanse of the Ionian sea. They, therefore, determined to coast along the eastern shores of Italy until they reached Messina, and then to cross the strait for Sicily. That they might execute this design with the greater safety, three ships were dispatched to the Italian and Sicilian shores, to inquire which of the cities would give them a reception, and afterward to rejoin the fleet as soon as possible, and acquaint the commanders with the information they had been able to collect.

After crossing the gulf, and making the Japygian promontory without any disaster, they dispersed to seek supplies around the bay of Tarentum ; but not a single town would admit them within its walls, or even furnish them, for money, with the necessaries of life. The towns of Tarentum and Locris would not grant them the use of their harbours, and refused even to supply them with water. At length, the whole fleet reassembled at the port of Rhegium, without accident. The magistrates of Rhegium allowed them to purchase the commodities, of which they were in immediate need ; but cautiously denied them admittance within their walls. Alcibiades, however, strongly remonstrated against this conduct, and exhorted them, as a colony of Eubœa, to assist their brethren of Leontium, to aid and defend whom the Athenians had fitted out this expedition ; but his remonstrances were vain and ineffectual.

In the mean time, the three Athenian ships had sailed as far as the Egestean territory, and rejoined the fleet in the harbour of Rhegium. They brought information, that the inhabitants of Egestia, notwithstanding the boasted accounts of their riches, were poor, and had grossly deceived the commissioners, sent by the Athenian government to inquire into the real state of their treasury. This disagreeable intelligence, and the unexpected reception they had met with from the cities on the Italian coast, induced the commanders to call a council of war, to consider how they should act in this matter. The opinion of Nicias was, that the Egesteans ought to be supplied with such a number of ships only, the charges of which their treasury was able to defray ; and that the Athenian fleet, after having settled, by arms or persuasion, the quarrels among them, and exhibited to the Sicilians their ability and readiness to aid and protect their allies, should return to Athens.

Alcibiades, who had formed his plan of procedure, and whom a slight disappointment could not deject, declared, that it would be disgraceful to the Athenian republick, to dissolve so great an armament, without having performed some exploits worthy of the vast preparations; that they should solicit the cities of Sicily to a confederacy against Syracuse and Selinus; and attack the former if it refused to restore the Leontines; and the latter, if it did not conclude a peace with the Egesteans. Lamachus, much of a soldier, and little of a politician, differed from both his colleagues. He said, that what appeared to him the most prudent and likely measure to be pursued was, to sail directly for Syracuse, and lay siege to the city, while yet in a state of impromptitude and surprise, and before the inhabitants had time to prepare for their defence. And, if they immediately attacked Syracuse, it would not only be the first, but the last city, which they would have occasion to besiege in Sicily.

This advice, which does honour to the abilities of Lamachus, was rejected by both the other commanders; and the opinion of Alcibiades prevailed. The fleet now sailed from Rhegium, to execute the plan which had been formed, and to promote, if possible, a confederacy of the Sicilian cities against Syracuse. A considerable detachment was sent to examine the fortifications and strength of that city, and to proclaim liberty, and offer protection, to all the captives within its walls.

Naxos was persuaded to accept the alliance of Athens. Thence Alcibiades proceeded to

x 2

Catana; but the prevalence of the Syracusan party in that place procured, at first, a refusal even to treat with the Athenians. The Cataneans, apprehensive, however, of the Athenian armament, or of a faction among themselves, consented, at length, to admit Alcibiades to a declaration of his proposals in the general assembly. The forces were therefore disembarked, and ordered to remain without the gate of the city. The artful Athenian transported the people of Catana with his eloquence. While he was speaking, the citizens flocked from every quarter, to hear a discourse purposely protracted. Some of the Athenian soldiers, observing a gateway unguarded, burst into the town, and became masters of the city. The sight of these men, in the place where the assembly was held, made the Cataneans believe, that the town was betrayed by the party in opposition to Syracuse. Some, therefore, of those who favoured the Syracusans, hastily, but silently, withdrew. The rest, fearing the dreadful consequences and calamities, that generally attended the weaker party of those who promoted factions in Grecian cities, concurred in a decree, which was speedily proposed, that the Cataneans should conclude an offensive and defensive alliance with Athens. It was soon apparent, that the scheme of Alcibiades, to strengthen the Athenian interest by negotiation, was justly and extensively founded. A faction in Camarina, encouraged by what had happened in Naxos and Catana, and awed by the strength of the Athenian armament, sent to request assistance for attempting a revolution. The fleet accordingly sailed to that place; but it was found, that the innovators had been too hasty in their measures, and that the project was not sufficiently ripe for execution; an Athenian party, however, still remained in Camarina.

The fleet, proceeding to Catana, discovered there the Salaminian galley, appropriated to purposes of sacred and solemn office. By this ship Alcibiades was informed, that the Athenian people had ordered his immediate return to Athens, in order to stand trial for his life.

The cause of this we find in the subsequent incident. The night preceding the sailing of the armament for Sicily, the numerous statues of Mercury, erected in the streets of Athens, as boundaries of different edifices and tenements, where thrown down, broken, and defaced. Only one large and beautiful image of the god, which was called Andocides, because it stood before the house of the orator of that name, had been saved from the general wreck. This insult, this act of impiety, was at first ascribed to the wicked and sacrilegious contrivances of the Corinthians, that they might deter the armament from sailing to the relief of Egesta. The enemies of Alcibiades, however, succeeded in making the people believe, that he had been guilty of this atrocious deed; for, on the evidence of slaves, he was accused of having treated with rude familiarity other adored images of the gods, and was therefore most likely to be guilty of this sacrilege.

During the terrour which these accusations produced in the minds of the Athenians, it happened that some movements in Bœotia occasioned a small body of Peloponnesians, to march toward the isthmus of Corinth. This circumstance seemed to justify suspicion, and redoubled fear. Androcles, and other artful demagogues, persuaded the Athenians, that the profanation of the mysteries, the defacing of the statues, and the movements of the Lacedæmonian army, all tended to indicate a conspiracy to demolish the present form of government, the preservation of which, ever since the expulsion of the Pisistradids, had been an object of universal and anxious regard.

The eloquence and address of Alcibiades were boldly and instantly employed in defending himself against the malignity of his enemies, and these charges of impiety and treachery; while the soldiers and sailors, who were eager for the expedition against Sicily, interceded for him; and the Argives and Mantineans refused to leave the Athenian coast, unless Alcibiades was permitted to accompany them. These combinations in his favour disappointed the present hopes, but did not disconcert the future project, of his enemies. They perceived, that were he brought to a trial at this time the populace would set him at liberty. They therefore urged, that Alcibiades might be permitted to sail for Sicily, where his presence would be so much wanted; and that, after his return home, he should either vindicate his innocence, or suffer the punishment of guilt. Alcibiades perceived the drift of his enemies in acting in this manner, and testified his reluctance to leave behind him such materials for malice; but was obliged to comply with the publick wish.

No sooner, however, was Alcibiades removed from Athens, than the people were continually convened, to consider of, and inquire into, the violation of the statues. Every one was desirous that his personal enemies should be found traitors and criminals against the state. Resentment was invited to accuse them falsely. A decree of the assembly was passed, by which rewards were offered to those who should discover the guilty, and even to the guilty themselves, that would give up their accomplices. Among the persons on whom suspicion fell, and who had been seized and put in prison, was Andocides, a profligate and impious person, before whose house the statue of Mercury had escaped the general destruction. Andocides, in order to avoid the punishment for which his character had marked him out, like a true villain, turned informer; and denounced many persons as guilty of the mutilation of the statues. The persons whom he named were either banished or put to death. The absent, among whom was Alcibiades, were recalled, in order to stand their trial. They did not obey, however, the commands which had been transmitted by the Salaminian galley. Alcibiades, to escape the fury of the storm, first fled to Argos; but being informed that the Athenians had promised a reward to any one who should apprehend him, he finally took refuge in Sparta. It was here that his active and enterprising genius seized the opportunity to advise and to promote measures, which, while they gratified his private resentment, occasioned the ruin and subversion of his country.

It was soon apparent, that the removal of Alcibiades occasioned a languor and delay in the operations of the expedition against Sicily. Lamachus, whose character was warlike and daring, was compelled, on account of his poverty, to be subject to the wealth, eloquence, and authority of the timid and cautious Nicias. Instead of attempting any thing against Selinus or Syracuse, the possession of the colony of Hyccara, a small and inconsiderable town of the Sicanians, fully contented him. He ravaged, or laid under contribution, some places of less note; and obtained thirty thousand pounds sterling from the Egesteans towards defraying the expenses of the war. This sum, with the booty collected from the cities in Sicily, might, indeed, be of some service, but could not compensate for the unsuccessful attempts against Hybla and Himera, and the inactivity and delay at Naxos and Catana.

The Athenian troops murmured at these dilatory and ignoble proceedings. Nicias, therefore, contrary to the timid caution of his disposition, was obliged to comply with the demands of the Athenians, and to make greater and more vigorous exertions. Syracuse was now intended as the object of his attack; and, as this city formed the main obstacle to their ambition, and the reduction would seem to decide the fate not only of Sicily, but of the Italian and African coasts, this attempt might well stimulate emulation and provoke energy.

When the Syracusans were first informed of the powerful armament fitted out against them, they despised, or pretended to despise, the rumour, and considered it as an idle tale, invented to amuse and deceive the people. But when the fleet arrived at Rhegium, their scepticism was at an end. Hermocrates, one of the principal persons in the place, now persuaded the people to provide against a danger, which their presumption and folly had hitherto represented as imaginary and chimerical. When they received intelligence, that the Athenian armament had reached the Italian coast, and they beheld this numerous and powerful fleet stretching along the shores of Sicily, and ready to make a descent on the defenceless island, they were struck with consternation and dismay. From the height of presumption and security, they plunged into the most abject fear and dejection; while Hermocrates, who was not less prudent in prosperity than intrepid in danger, could scarcely animate the minds of his countrymen, and inspire the requisite resolution to attempt a resistance.

They were, however, at length prevailed on to prepare their arms, equip their fleet, garrison their towns, and summon their allies to assist them. These necessary preliminaries were at length carried on with ardour and persevering activity; while the tardy operations of the enemy not only served to remove the fear and dejection, which had at first overwhelmed the minds of the Syracusans, but to restore them to their long lost vigour and intrepidity. They appointed fifteen generals, whom they desired to lead them instantly against the Athenians at Catana. The chiefs, however, did not think it prudent and safe to comply with the request of the troops; but parties of horse were sent out, to beat up the quarters of the enemy, to intercept their convoys, and repel their advanced posts. In these incursions, the Syracusans would frequently approach the main body of the Athenians, and, insulting them with taunting and sarcastick language, ask, Whether the boasted lords of Greece had left their native country, that they might settle at Catana.

Though provoked at these indignities, and excited by the resentment and resolution of his troops, Nicias would neither hazard an engagement in the plain, nor march against Syracuse. He therefore formed a stratagem, which he hoped would in some measure divide the difficulties and dangers of the enterprise. A Catanean undertook to go over to the enemy as a deserter from his native city. This man pretended to the Syracusans, that a numerous and powerful body of the inhabitants of Catana, weary with the disgraceful yoke of the Athenians, longed to take up arms, and to repel the invaders of their country. He observed, that if the Syracusans would join and assist this body of Cataneans, the design could scarcely fail of success; for the Athenians were extremely remiss in their military duties; their posts were forsaken, and their fleet was left unguarded. The people of Syracuse, therefore, were persuaded to appoint a day on which they would attack the city; and the artful Catanean returned home, to revive the hopes, and confirm the resolution, of his pretended associates.

On the day appointed by the inhabitants of Syracuse for assaulting the Athenians in Catana, Nicias sailed with his whole armament. They had marched already with this view to the plain of Leontium, when the fleet of Athens arrived in the great harbour, the troops were disembarked, and a camp was formed without the western wall of the city of Syracuse. In the mean time the cavalry of the Syracusans, having proceeded to the walls of Catana, discovered that the Athenians had departed. Their infantry, being informed of this, marched back with all expedition, to protect the city of Syracuse. The warlike youths having thus returned, and being joined by the forces of Gela, Selinus, and Camarina, it was determined, without loss of time, to attack the hostile encampment.

Only a few days had elapsed before the Athenians and Syracusans prepared to engage. The former relied on their superiour discipline and habitual victory; the latter, on their courage and numbers. The Syracusans formed their troops sixteen, and the Athenians eight, deep. The latter, however, kept a body of reserve in the camp, which was ready to engage on the first signal. Nicias, having harangued his troops, led them towards the enemy; the priests brought forth the accustomed sacrifices; and the trumpets sounded to engage.

Dreadful and furious was the attack, which continued with perseverance for several hours. Every thing that could animate and impel to great and vigorous exertions, inspired the minds of the combatants. The Syracusans fought in defence of their country, their liberty, and independence; and the Athenians were no less strongly impelled by resentment and ambitious prospects. The battle, however, was still doubtful, when a tempest suddenly arose, accompanied with tremendous peals of thunder. The Athenians were unconcerned at the event; but the Syracusans, struck with consternation and dismay, were broken and put to the rout. Nicias restrained the troops from the pursuit, lest a body of cavalry belonging to the enemy should assault them when in disorder. The Syracusans lost two hundred and sixty men, and the Athenians only fifty. The former took refuge in the city; and the latter returned to their camps.

The voyage, the encampment, and the battle, employed the dangerous activity, and gratified the impetuous ardour of the Athenian troops, but did not in any essential degree contribute to facilitate the conquest of Syracuse; and, without more powerful assistance, Nicias began to despair of being able to storm the place, or to take it by siege. Soon after this successful onset, the Athenian fleet returned to Naxos and Catana to winter there; and Nicias expected that the inferiour states of Sicily would now more readily submit, or render assistance. Emissaries were sent to Tuscany, in which some Grecian colonies had been founded; embassadors were likewise dispatched to Carthage, the enemy and the rival of Syracuse. The messengers sent to Athens returned with three hundred talents, and several troops of cavalry; and the Egesteans provided them also with a reinforcement of horse and all kinds of provision.

While the Athenians were thus preparing for the attack of Syracuse, the citizens of that place exerted equal vigour in providing for their defence. Instead of fifteen, they appointed three generals, Hermocrates, Heraclides, and Sicanus. These commanders were invested with unlimited power, according to the exigency of affairs.— They dispatched embassadors to Corinth, and also to Lacedæmon, to implore their assistance against an enemy that aimed at no less than the sovereignty of all Greece. The Syracusans received a very favourable reception at both places, and especially at Sparta, where Alcibiades enforced their request with all his credit and eloquence. At his persuasion, Gylippus, an able and experienced officer, was appointed to command the reinforcement destined for Sicily; and troops were raised with a design to invade the Attic territory, and thereby make a powerful diversion in that part, in favour of the Syracusans.

The importance of Camerina, on the southern coast of Sicily, engaged, in the mean time, the attention of Nicias and of Hermocrates. The Camerineans had given a very feeble and reluctant assistance to their allies of Syracuse; and both parties were desirous of attaching them to their interest. They dreaded, however, the distant ambition of Athens, and the neighbouring hostility of Syracuse; and requested that they might be allowed to preserve a strict and impartial neutrality between the contending parties. By these means they hoped to avoid the resentment of either of the two, and, nevertheless, defeat the intentions of both.

Before any supplies from Greece could reach B. C. 414. Syracuse, Nicias, leaving his winter quarters, set sail for that place, and arriving there in the night, before the inhabitants of the city were aware of his departure from Catana, possessed himself of the important post of Epipole. The Syracusans, being quickly informed that the Athenians had surprised that place, immediately attempted to dislodge them. A fierce conflict ensued : tumultuous valour, however, could not overcome steady discipline. The Syracusans were compelled to retreat with the loss of three hundred men; and the near refuge of their walls prevented a still greater slaughter. Encouraged by this success, Nicias began to execute the plan he had formed for conquering the city. It was intended to surround the besieged place by a wall from Epipole to the sea, on each side; to the Trogilian port on the north, and to the great port on the south. When these circumvallations should be completed, Nicias expected that his numerous fleet would be able to block up the harbour. As the necessary materials had been provided during the winter, the work rose with such rapidity, that the Syracusans were not less astonished than terrified. Their former, as well as their recent defeat, deterred them from again risking a general engagement; but, by the advice of Hermocrates, they raised walls, which traversed and interrupted those of the Athenians. The workmen, urged by imminent danger, forwarded the work with great activity; the hostile bulwarks approached each other; frequent skirmishes happened, in one of which the brave and enterprising Lamachus lost his life; but the Athenian troops were again victorious.

The circumvallation was at length completed, and the town blocked up on all sides. The canals that conveyed water into the city were interrupted, and by these means Syracuse was greatly distressed. The inhabitants, seeing themselves on the brink of ruin, and no hopes of relief, began to think of a capitulation. Accordingly an assembly was convened to propose and settle the articles, which circumstances seemed to require should be sent to Nicias. While, however, they deliberated on the execution of this measure, a Corinthian galley, commanded by Gongylus, entered the harbour. All the citizens crowded around the Corinthian, that they might learn the design of his voyage, and the intentions of their Peloponnesian allies. Gongylus acquainted them, that they might soon expect a speedy and effectual relief to their besieged city. He informed the Syracusans, that the Corinthians had warmly espoused the cause of their kinsmen, and most respectable colony; and had fitted out a very considerable armament, which might be looked for every hour. The Spartans, also, had joined a small squadron to the ships from Corinth, and the whole armament was conducted by Gylippus, a Lacedæmonian, and an officer of great abilities and experience.

The joy which this unexpected intelligence diffused in the city, is incredible. The Syracusans proceeded from one extremity to another. Instead of capitulating, they prepared to make sallies upon the enemy, that Gylippus might have a better opportunity for entering the city. Soon after, a messenger arrived from the Spartan commander himself. He had landed his troops on the western coast of Sicily, that the Athenians might not intercept his passage; and approached Syracuse on the side of Epipole, where the line of contravallation was yet unfinished, with several thousand men.

The transverse wall was extended with the greatest diligence; and Nicias having fortified himself in the castle of Labdalus, Gylippus drew up his army under the walls, and sent a herald to inform the Athenian general, that he would only allow him five days to embark his troops, and to leave Sicily. To this message Nicias did not condescend to return an answer. Gylippus, therefore, attacking the fort, stormed it, and put all the Athenians found therein to the sword. Nicias, perceiving the necessity of bringing the war to a speedy and decisive conclusion, offered battle to the Spartan and Syracusan army. Gylippus did not decline the engagement. In the first action, the Athenians were victorious. This was principally occasioned by the unfavourable situation of the Syracusan forces, who had been imprudently posted in the narrow defiles between the two walls, which rendered their cavalry and archers unserviceable. The magnanimity of Gylippus led him to acknowledge this errour, and declare, that he, and not the troops, had been the cause of this defeat. The next day he drew up his forces in a more advantageous posture.

The Athenians were now repulsed, thrown into confusion, and pursued to their camp; and Gylippus obtained a very considerable victory.

This success of the Spartan general produced the most important consequences. The Syracusans extended their works beoynd the circumvallation, insomuch that, unless the Athenians forced the ramparts, they could not hope to block up their city. While the besiegers maintained the superiority of arms over their enemies, the neighbouring territory had abundantly supplied them with every necessary; but no sooner was their defeat known, than every place was alike hostile, and provision could not be procured without the greatest difficulty. The soldiers that went out in quest of wood and water were unexpectedly attacked by the enemy's cavalry, or by the reinforcements which daily arrived from every quarter, to the assistance of Syracuse; and the army was soon obliged to depend for every necessary supply on the uncertain bounty of the Italian coast.

Nicias, finding his troops dwindling away in proportion as those of the enemy increased, became greatly disheartened, and dispatched a very desponding letter to the Athenians. He, honestly, and without disguise, described and lamented the misfortunes and miseries of the army. Great numbers of the slaves deserted t the mercenary troops, that fought only for pay and subsistence, saw the reasonableness of preferring the more secure and lucrative service of the Syracusans. The Athenian citizens, tired of the war, and of the hardships to which it subjected them, left the care of the gallies to unexperienced persons. Nicias frankly confessed his inability to check these disorders; and observed, that the Athenians to whom he wrote, were equally competent to judge how difficult it was to govern the licentious disposition of domestick troops. Finally, he exhorted the assembly to recal the forces immediately, or, otherwise, to send, without delay, a second armament, not less powerful than the first.

This letter made a great impression on the minds of the Athenians. They chose Demosthenes and Eurymedon to succeed Alcibiades and Lamachus in the command. The latter sailed immediately with ten gallies, and a considerable sum of money, to assure Nicias, that speedy and powerful supplies should be sent him, while the former was employed in raising troops, and equipping ships, in order that a numerous armament might sail the spring following.

In the mean time, the Lacedæmonian and Syracusan generals were acquainted with the actual distress of the Athenian army, and with the future hopes which they entertained, in consequence of the letter of Nicias. It was possible that more supplies might be received from Attica, than the besieged could expect from Peloponnesus. Prompted, therefore, by interest and inclination, they resolved to press the Athenians on all sides, by sea and land. Beside the weak condition of the fleet of Athens, several of their gallies were detached to conduct the convoys of provision. The Corinthian fleet, long and anxiously expected, at length arrived; and consisted of twelve sail. The whole naval strength of Sicily, in the ensuing spring, filled the harbours of Syracuse. Hermocrates persuaded his countrymen that the advantages of skill and experience, which he candidly acknowledged the Athenians possessed, could not compensate their tenrour and confusion at being suddenly attacked by a superiour force.

The principal squadrons of Syracuse lay in the harbour of Ortygia, which was separated from the station of the Athenian fleet by an island of the same name. Hermocrates sailed out with a fleet of eighty gallies, to venture a naval engage-, ment; and being met by the Athenians, a severe action ensued. While great numbers of the soldiers had withdrawn themselves from their fortifications at Plemmyrum, that they might be spectators of the fight, Gylippus unexpectedly attacked the forts. He made himself master of them without experiencing much opposition, and slew all those who hastened from the shore to assist their companions. Upon this, a noise and tumult arising in the camp, the Athenians at sea, were struck with consternation and dismay; they endeavoured to gain the shore, that they might defend the forts and repel the enemy; but perceiving the fortifications already in the possession of Gylippus, with their whole fleet in line of battle, they attacked the ships of the enemy, which were pursuing them in disorder, Eleven vessels of the Syracusans were sunk, great numbers of their forces were killed, and a complete victory at sea, made the Athenians ample amends for the defeat they had experienced by land. The Athenians lost, in the forts that were taken, a large quantity of military and naval stores, and a considerable sum of money. Both parties, however, erected trophies: the Athenians for their victory at sea, and the Syracusans for their success on shore.

The Syracusans, notwithstanding the defeat they had suffered, determined to hazard a second naval engagement, before Demosthenes should arrive with the supplies from Athens. In order, therefore, that they might provoke the Athenians to an attack, they drew up their fleet daily before the great harbour, in line of battle. But Nicias was averse to venture a second engagement. He expected, he said, a fresh fleet every moment, with a strong reinforcement of troops. If he, therefore, hazarded a battle, unless compelled to it, when his forces were inferiour in number to those of the enemy, and already fatigued, he should justly be censured for imprudence and temerity. On the other hand, Menander and Euthydemus, who had been appointed to take part in the command until the arrival of Demosthenes, eager to perform some exploit before they resigned their commission, represented to Nicias, that, should they decline a battle, the Athenians would lose their reputation, and be forsaken by all their allies in Sicily. They pressed him so much, that, at length, he was obliged to comply. Accordingly, the fleet, consisting of twenty-five gallies, sailed out of the harbour. The first day, the two hostile armaments continued in sight of each other, without engaging. On the second day, a few vessels only attacked each other; and neither side gained any considerable advantage. On the third day, the Syracusans formed their ships in order of battle earlier than usual; and having continued in this manner until the evening, withdrew as before. The Athenians, supposing that they would not return that day, retired in disorder. But the enemies fleet sailing out of the little harbour, attacked the Athenians before they had time to draw up in order of battle. Victory did not continue long in suspense. Seven Athenian ships were sunk, and many more were disabled. Nicias saved the remains of his shattered and disgraced fleet, by retiring behind a line of merchantmen and transports. From the masts of these vessels were suspended huge masses of lead, which, on account of their form, were named dolphins. These were sufficient to crush, by their falling weight, the stoutest gallies of antiquity. This unexpected obstacle arrested the progress of the conquerors; but the advantages already obtained, raised their hopes to the highest pitch, and sunk the minds of the Athenians into the greatest dejection and despondency.

Great as were the misfortunes that befel the Athenians in Sicily, the calamities of the republick at home were still more alarming and more dreadful. Alcibiades first acquired the esteem and confidence of the Spartans, by condemning, in the strongest manner, the ambition and injustice of the Athenians, in their hostility with Lacedæmon, and cruelty towards himself. He, moreover, informed the Spartans, in what manner they might disarm and disappoint the Athenian republick. The town of Decelia was situated between Thebes and Athens, about fifteen miles from each, and belonged to the Attic territory. He, therefore, advised, that the Spartans should surprise and fortify this place, which commanded an extensive and fertile plain; and from it they might infest the Athenians by a continual war, instead of an annual incursion.

Alcibiades often proposed and urged this measure; and, at length, Agis led a powerful army into the Attic territory. The defenceless inhabitants fled before him; but, instead of pursuing them as before, he stopped at Decelia. The necessary materials having been provided, previous to the marching of the army, the town was speedily fortified, and the walls bade defiance to those of Athens. The watchful garrison continually alarmed the Athenian republick. The Athenians could neither plough nor sow; or, if they did, the Spartans deprived them of the fruit of their labour. The valuable island of Eubœa, too, from which, in seasons of scarcity, or during the ravages of war, they had been accustomed to derive the necessary supplies of corn, wine, and oil, was cut off from any communication with them. Harassed by unremitting service, and in want of bread, the slaves murmured, complained, and in great numbers revolted to the enemy. By their defection, Athens was deprived of twenty thousand useful artisans. Since the latter part of the administration of Pericles, the Athenians had never suffered such misery and distress; while the inextinguishable hatred of a cruel and unrelenting enemy still persecuted them.

These signal calamities at Athens, did not, however, prevent the most vigorous exertions abroad. The Syracusans had scarcely time to rejoice at their victory, or Nicias to bewail his misfortunes, when a numerous and powerful armament was descried on the coast of Sicily. All the vessels were richly trimmed, and had their prows adorned with gaudy streamers. This fleet, consisting of seventy-three Athenian gallies, beside innumerable foreign vessels and transports, commanded by experienced officers, and furnished, at a vast expense, with all kinds of warlike machines then used in maritime engagements, pursued a secure course towards the harbours of Syracuse. The emulation of the rowers, and the splendour of the scene, exhibited a pompous spectacle of naval triumph. As they approached the shore, the sound of the trumpets and clarions, mingled with repeated shouts and loud acclamations from the fleet and the camp, reechoed through the town. This air of pomp and triumph Demosthenes purposely affected, that he might strike the enemy with terrour.— The number of pikemen on board the fleet exceeded five thousand; the light-armed troops were nearly as numerous; and the whole armament was equal to that sent with Nicias, which amounted to more than twenty thousand men.

B. C. 413. The besieged, notwithstanding their late success, considering the power and vigour of the enemy with whom they had to contend, became dispirited, and acknowledged, that Athens was the only city in the world that could furnish such a formidable and magnificent contribution. The Syracusans now conceived the design of capitulating, before the city was reduced to extremities, and whilst they could hope to obtain reasonable and tolerable terms. But Demosthenes did not give them time for putting their scheme into execution. Thinking it most advisable to take advantage of the consternation and dismay, which his arrival had occasioned, he prepared for an immediate attack of the city.

Nicias, alarmed at this bold and hasty resolution, conjured him not to be too precipitate, but to consider matters maturely before he proceeded to make an attempt against Syracuse. He observed to him, that delays would ruin the enemy; that they were in great want of money and provision; that their allies were now ready to abandon them; and that, in a little time, they would be obliged to surrender. All this Nicias said, not from any conjectures of his own, but from the information and advice he had received of what was transacting in the city. Demosthenes replied, that his intentions were, speedily to decide the fate of the war, or raise the siege, and return to the relief of Athens, which was at that time blockaded by the Lacedæmonians. The known cautious and dilatory disposition of Nicias induced Eurymedon to approve of the opinion of Demosthenes; and Nicias himself was also obliged finally to acquiesce.

After ravaging the banks of the Anapus, and making some fruitless attempts against the fortifications on that side, that the attention of the enemy might be diverted, Demosthenes marched, in the middle of the night, to attack the important post of Epipole. The attempt was at first successful: the outposts were surprised; the guards put to death; and the three separate encampments of the Syracusans, Sicilians, and Peloponnesians, formed a weak and feeble opposition to the ardour and resolution of the Athenian troops.

In the mean time, Gylippus had assembled the whole force of Syracuse, and hastened to the relief of the place; but his troops being seized with a panick, which was increased by the darkness of the night, were easily repulsed, and put to flight. The Athenians pursuing them in disorder, that they might prevent them from rallying, met a body of Bœotians, under the command of Hermocrates, whose resistance checked the fury of the assailants. The sudden and unexpected firmness of the Thebans might alone have decided the fate of the enterprise; but the Athenians were ignorant of the ground; and the glare of the moon shining in the front of the enemy, illumined the splendour of their arms, and mul-

tiplied their numbers. The foremost ranks of
their pursuers were repelled; and as the Athenians retreated to their main body, they met the
Argives and Corcyreans advancing, who, singing
the pœan in their Dorick dialect and accent, were
unfortunately mistaken for enemies. Fear, and
then rage, siezed the Athenians. Thinking themselves surrounded, they determined to force a
passage, and slew many of their allies before the
mistake was discovered. To prevent the repetition of this dreadful errour, they were obliged
to demand the watch-word every moment. In
consequence of this, their enemies became also
acquainted with it. The consequence of this
was doubly fatal. The silent Athenians, at every
rencounter, were slaughtered: the enemies, on
the other hand, knowing their watch-word, declined or joined the battle, according to their
weakness or strength. The terrour and confusion of the Athenians increased; the rout became general; and Gylippus, with his victorious
troops, pursued in good order. The vanquished,
ignorant of the passages through which they had
mounted, lost great numbers who fell from the
rocks, and were dashed in pieces. Others ex-
plored the unknown paths of Epipole. Several
thousands were left dead, or wounded, on the
scene of action; and the Syracusan cavalry, the
next morning, intercepted and cut off all the
stragglers.

By this dreadful and unexpected disaster, the
operations of the siege were suspended. After
this overthrow, Demosthenes was decidedly of
opinion, that they should return immediately to
Athens. The season of the year would yet, he
said, permit their crossing the Ionian sea; and
it would be much more advantageous to compel

the Lacedæmonians to raise the blockade of Athens than to continue the siege of Syracuse; and waste their strength in vain and fruitless foreign attempts. But Nicias dissuaded the design of leaving Sicily, until the republick should recal them by positive authority, and they should be warranted to proceed in this important measure. Those, he said, who were now so earnest for an ignominious flight, and exclaimed so bitterly against the calamities under which they laboured, would, after their return, be the foremost to accuse the weakness or the treachery of their commanders. For his part, he would rather choose to die gloriously by the band of the enemy, than perish by the unjust suffrages of the people.

This reasoning could not, however, convince Demosthenes, who was sensible, that the only means, by which they could hope to save the remains of their distressed forces, was to leave Sicily immediately, and return to Athens. But Nicias, knowing by the secret correspondence maintained in Syracuse, that the treasury was exhausted by the enormous expenses of the war, and that the magistrates had used their utmost to borrow from their allies, hoped that the vigour of their resistance would abate with the decay of their faculties; and that the city would submit in a little time. Demosthenes, therefore, as his former advice had been attended with such ill success, yielded in this instance to the opinion of Nicias.

In the mean time, the Syracusans were reinforced by powerful supplies from the different nations in Sicily; and the transports so long expected from Peloponnesus arrived in the harbour of Ortygia. The Peloponnesian forces had staid for some time on the coast of Cyrenaica; and their fleet was augmented with a few Cyrenian gallies. This armament reached Syracuse in safety, the place of its destination. Neither of the contending parties received, after this, any farther accessions of strength. Nothing was wanting to complete the actors in this dreadful scene : Syracuse was now attacked, or defended, by all the various divisions of the Grecian name; and these formed, in that age, the most civilized portion of the inhabitants of Asia, Africa, and Europe.

These powerful auxiliaries having arrived at Syracuse, and a plague, originating from the effluvia of the fens and marshes, near which the Athenians were encamped, breaking out among the soldiers, Nicias was induced to change his opinion. Accordingly, orders were issued privately, enjoining the officers of the fleet to sail at a minute's warning; and the troops were commanded to be ready to go on board upon a signal that should be given. But the night appointed for their departure was inauspiciously distinguished by an eclipse of the moon. This the superstitious Nicias, and his diviners, considered as an omen of evil tendency. The voyage, therefore, was ordered to be deferred, until thrice nine days were accomplished.

. But before the expiration of that period, which superstition had fixed, it was no longer practicable to depart. The Syracusans, having received notice that the Athenians intended to leave Sicily, resolved to attack them by sea and land.— They attempted to destroy the Athenian fleet by fire-ships; but this enterprise was unsuccessful. After this, they employed superiour numbers, to divide and weaken the strength and resistance of an enfeebled and dejected foe. A perpetual succession of military and naval exploits continued for three days. On the first day the battle was doubtful, and fortune hung in suspense; on the second, the Athenian fleet, commanded by Eurymedon, was deprived of a considerable squadron; and on the third, the Athenians lost eighteen ships, and two thousand men in the number of whom was their admiral.

The Syracusans celebrated their victory with triumphant enthusiasm. They did not consider themselves at this period as an oppressed and unhappy people, struggling in the almost hopeless defence of every thing dear to them; but they now looked forward for that success, which should entitle them the vanquishers of Athens, and vindicators of the liberties of Greece. Accordingly, they applied themselves immediately to block up the port. They were now desirous to prevent the departure of that force, from which they had formerly expected the worst evils of subjugation; and they proposed to themselves no less than to destroy, or reduce to the dreadful condition of prisoners at discretion, the whole of that formidable fleet and navy.

In the mean time, dejection, not only from the sense of disgrace and fear of the resentment of their enemies, but also from the most urgent wants, assailed the Athenians. In consequence of the resolution to raise the siege, they had forbidden further supplies from Catana. Naval superiority being lost, they had now no means of intercourse with Catana; and, therefore, their departure was enforced. A council of war being summoned, it was generally resolved to withdraw the whole armament by sea.

After repeated defeats, and though he was grievously tormented with a nephritic complaint, which had frequently obliged him to solicit his recal, Nicias, whose courage seemed to rise according as evil pressed and dangers threatened, used his utmost diligence to retrieve the affairs of his country. The shattered gallies were speedily refitted, and prepared to the number of one hundred and ten, to risk the event of another battle. And as they had suffered greatly from the hardness and firmness of the enemy's prows, Nicias provided them · with grappling irons, whereby they would be able to prevent the recoil of their opponents, and the repetition of the hostile stroke. Armed men were crowded upon the deck ; a mode of fighting taught them by the Syracusans, who had too successfully used it against them.

No sooner was the fleet ready for sea, than Nicias recalled the troops from the posts and fortresses still occupied, and formed them into one camp on the shore. The behaviour of that commander on this trying occasion was truly great. He was little ambitious, and when fortune was favourable, rather deficient in exertion, and sometimes even culpably remiss in his command ; but at this juncture, none was so warm in exhortations, which might serve to revive the hopes, and restore the drooping courage of the troops. The state of his health would not permit him to take the command of the fleet; but he was sedulous in attending the necessary preparations, and in directing every arrangement. When all was ready for the projected attempt, thinking that he had not yet said sufficient to stimulate the minds of the officers and soldiers, as the importance of the occasion seemed to demand, he went round the whole armament: he exhorted them with a cheerful and magnanimous firmness, to remember the vicissitudes of war and the instability of fortune. Though hitherto unsuccessful, the vastness of the preparations should induce them to hope that victory would again be theirs. Men, who had undergone and surmounted so many and great dangers, should not in the trying and decisive moment darken future success by the remembrance and the regret of past defeat. It was yet in their power to defend their lives, their liberty, their friends, and, what ought to be dearer to them than every thing besides, their country, and the mighty name of Athens. But should this opportunity be neglected or improperly used, the destruction of every thing near and dear to them must follow, and the glory of their nation be no more!

In the mean time, the bustle of preparation in the naval camp of the Athenians had been observed by the Syracusans, who were informed of the grappling irons with which the Athenian prows were armed. They, therefore, prepared to counteract the new mode of action proposed by the Athenians: the forecastles of their gallies they covered with bull-hides, on which the grappling irons would have no effect.

Nicias having led the troops to the shore, committed the last hope of the republick to the active valour of Demosthenes, Meander, and Euthydemus; and returned to the camp, with a feeble and emaciated body, and an anxious mind. The first shock of the Athenians was irresistible, and they made themselves masters of the vessels that opposed their passage, and burst through the bar. As the entrance widened, the Syracusans rushed into the harbour. Thither also the Athen-

ian gallies followed, either repelled by the enemy, or that they might assist their comrades. In
the mouth of the harbour the engagement became general; and in this narrow space, two
hundred gallies fought with an obstinate and
persevering valour during the greatest part of
the day. The battle was not long confined to the
shocks of adverse prows, and to the distant hos-
tilty of darts and arrows. The vessels grap-
pled with each other; and their decks soon flowed with blood. The heavy-armed troops board-
ed the galley with which they contended; and
by that means left their own ships exposed to the
same misfortune. The fleets became massive
clusters of adhering gallies. The Athenians, sensible of the importance of the action, exhorted
one another not to abandon an element on which
their republick had ever acquired victory and
glory, for the dangerous refuge of a hostile
shore; while the Syracusans encouraged each
other not to flee from enemies, whose weakness
or cowardice had caused them for a long time
to meditate retreat. The lamentations of the
wounded, and of those who were perishing in
the water, the noise of the oars, and the acclamations from the ramparts and the shore, prevented any orders from being either heard or
obeyed.

The spectacle of a battle, more fierce and obstinate than had ever before been seen in the
Grecian seas, restrained the activity and wholly
suspended the powers of the numerous and adverse battalions, that lined the coast of the surrounding shore. The spectators and the actors
were alike interested in the result of this singular and tremendous engagement. But the former, who had nothing besides to engage their

attention, felt more deeply, and expressed more forcibly, the various emotions by which they were actuated. The fight was long and dreadful, and the slaughter on both sides incredibly great. But at length, with various fortune at times in various parts, the advantage of the Syracusans became decisive, and the whole Athenian fleet was pursued by the enemy to the shore. Then grief, indignation and dismay, in the highest pitch that can possibly be imagined, seized the Athenian army on land. Their circumstances now were desperate, and they became hopeless. Some of the vanquished escaped to the camp; others fled, not knowing whither to direct their steps. Nicias, however, with a small but fearless troop, remained on the shore, to assist and protect their unfortunate companions. In this well fought battle, the victors lost forty, and the vanquished fifty gallies.

Cicero has justly and elegantly observed, that not only the navy of Athens, but the glory and empire of the republick, perished in the harbour of Syracuse. The dejection of the Athenians, on this disastrous occasion, was so great, and the impending danger so urgent, that they neglected a duty always before observed, and which had formed a very respectable part of their national character. No herald was sent to demand the restoration of the dead; and they abandoned to indignities and insults the bodies of the slain. Amid the general despair, however, Demosthenes did not lose his usual energy and presence of mind. He proposed that, as the Athenians had still sixty, and the enemy only fifty gallies, they should again attempt to force a passage; and he considered the measure as very practicable, if, embarking that night, they made the effort the next morning. Nicias approved of the proposal, but the forces absolutely refused. They would go any where by land, they said, and fight their way, if necessary, but, by sea, the experience of the past sufficiently proved that they could expect nothing but destruction. Thus was the execution of this salutary measure prevented by excess of despondency, arising from the contemplation of previous disasters.

The general opinion among the Syracusans was, that the Athenians would not attempt to escape again by sea, and they supposed, that they would decamp the same night. This justified the proposal of Demosthenes, and testified his prudence and foresight. But the Syracusans, wearied with the labour of the day, and exhilarated with its success, were more eager to enjoy the leisure they had so well earned, than solicitous about any future events. It happened, too, that the following morning was the festival of Hercules. Among such an assemblage of people of Dorian race, and especially in such circumstances as the present, the celebration of the day became an object of great regard, and they refused to quit the religious revel for a nocturnal military enterprise. Hermocrates, therefore, sent some persons upon horseback in the evening to the Athenian camp; these approaching near enough to be heard, though they could not be distinctly seen, pretended they belonged to the same party which had been accustomed to communicate with Nicias. Finding that the Athenians believed what they said, they informed them, that the Syracusans had already occupied all the passes, and that they had better not move that night. The horsemen then desired those to whom this conversation had been addressed, to acquaint the general with this information, that he might wait and concert his measures accordingly. Nicias credited the report, and the next day was spent by the Athenians in various preparations for their march.

But Gylippus and Hermocrates, having yielded for the moment to the pleasure of their people, found means before the morrow ended, to engage them in their own views. Their victorious fleet, sailing to the Athenian station, and meeting with no opposition, burnt or carried off every vessel. The army, at the same time, marched out under the command of the Spartan general, and occupied all the principal passes in that line of country, which it was probable the Athenians would attempt to traverse. The avenues, also, leading to the fordable parts of the rivers, were guarded, the bridges broken down, and detachments of horse placed on the plains, insomuch that whithersoever the Athenians should direct their march, they would be obliged to fight their way.

However, as they could no longer subsist in their present situation, and every thing being prepared as far as circumstances would permit, orders were issued by the Athenian generals, on the third day after the battle, that they should decamp. Forty thousand men, of whom many were afflicted with wounds and diseases, and all exhausted with labour and fatigue, exhibited not even the appearance of a fleeing army ; they rather resembled a large and populous community, driven from their ancient possessions by the cruelty and vengeance of a conqueror. From the lofty expectations with which they first set sail from Piræus to the coast of Sicily, they were now miserably fallen. Deep was the distress which arose from the reflections, that the whole of their fleet had been destroyed; that through their failure, destruction threatened Athens; and that, instead of returning the triumphant conquerors of Sicily, they were obliged to attempt an ignominious flight, as the only hopes they had left of avoiding slavery or death. Their collective sufferings were thus enhanced and exasperated by a thousand dreadful considerations, and the painful sights that obtruded themselves to the view of every individual. The mangled bodies of their relations and friends, deprived of the sacred rites of sepulture, affected them not only with grief but with horrour. No sooner did they remove their eyes from this dreadful spectacle, than a sight still more melancholy and terrifying presented itself. The numerous crowds of sick and wounded, unable to proceed with their companions. intreated, in the accent and language of unutterable anguish, to be delivered from the horrours of famine, or the rage of a cruel and implacable foe. Such affecting scenes as these would have pierced the heart of a stranger, and he could not but have felt sympathetick tenderness and compassion. How much more then must it have afflicted the Athenians, to see their parents, brothers, children, and friends, involved in unexampled misery! to hear them utter their piteous heart-rending complaints; and obliged to throw the clinging victims from their wearied necks and arms! Mutual and self-reproach, for that share they had taken in forwarding the enterprise, or obstructing the retreat, aggravated the bitterness of woe. Such, in short, was the accumulated weight of misery, that the whole multitude were thrown into tears; and their present affecting situation not only absorbed any future apprehensions, but took away the power and even the desire to move.

At length the march was begun. Amid the extreme dejection and anguish which pervaded the troops, Nicias, by his character and sufferings, but still more by the melancholy firmness of his conduct, deserves the regard and esteem of mankind. As an individual, he appeared not to be affected with the distress of the existing circumstances. His whole anxiety was directed to relieve and alleviate the calamities of others. Carried with a quick and rapid pace around every part of the army, the ardour of his mind reanimating his weak and emaciated frame, he exclaimed with a loud and distinct voice,—— " Athenians and allies, there is still room for hope. Many have escaped from greater evils than we suffer, nor ought you rashly to accuse the gods or yourselves. As for me, who am far from being the strongest among you (and you see to what a miserable condition my disorder has reduced me), and who in the blessings of fortune was inferiour to none, I suffer every present calamity equally with the lowest and most abject. Yet I am unconscious of deserving this reverse of prosperity. I have been regular and zealous in my duty towards the gods; and my actions with men have been scrupulously just. I have, therefore, hope and confidence; and the calamities which guilt has not merited, cannot terrify me. If our enterprise has drawn upon us the indignation and vengeance of the gods, we surely suffer more than our iniquities deserve. Other nations have invaded their neighbours with less provocation, and nevertheless have escaped with gentler punishment; nor can

I believe, that for the frailties and errours of passion, Providence will impose penalties too grievous to be borne.

"Confiding thus far in the divine mercy, we ought not to despond, especially when we consider the means which Providence has still left us for our defence. Our numbers, our resolution, and still more our misfortunes, render us objects of terrour and dismay. Our enemies possess not an army able to intercept our course, and therefore much less to expel us from the first friendly territory that shall afford us a reception. If, therefore, we can secure our safety by a speedy, prudent, and courageous retreat, we may still retrieve our lost honour, and restore the fallen glory of Athens. For the strength and support of a state consist not in empty ships, and undefended walls, but in brave and virtuous citizens."

Nicias, having thus spoken, led the march. The army was disposed in two divisions, with the baggage between them. Demosthenes commanded the rear, and Nicias the van. They did not chuse the road to their friends at Naxos and Catana, but that which led to the Sicel country, where they might more readily find food and safety, and have leisure to concert proper measures for their future operation. They forced their passage over the river Anapus, which was vigourously defended by the enemy. But the Syracusan horse and archers, harassing them in the rear, gave them such continued annoyance, that, after marching only five miles, they encamped on a rising ground for the night. The next day they made still less progress. Having marched only two miles and a half, they reached a spacious plain, where they were induced to halt; especially, as they were in need of a supply of water and provision, which might be easily obtained from the surrounding country. But on the third day, when they attempted to proceed, the Syracusan horse and light-armed troops, in larger force than before, annoyed them so much, that, after many hours wasted in fruitless attempts to repulse them, the distressed Athenians were compelled to return to the camp they had occupied: and, on account of the superiority of the enemy's cavalry, they could not even procure supplies as they had done the day before.

On the next morning they moved earlier than usual, and pressed their march to gain the mountain Acræum. But the enemy, who were apprised of their intended course, had sent a detachment to interrupt them, and to fortify the mountain. A small degree of art was capable of rendering this place impregnable, since it was of a steep and rapid ascent, and encompassed on all sides by the rocky channel of a loud and foaming torrent. When, therefore, they arrived at the mountain, they found an armed force ready to oppose them, and the difficulties of the ascent increased by a fortification. An assault was immediately attempted, which was not in the moment successful. A storm coming on was construed by the Athenians, in their present dejected and desponding state, as an ill omen; nor could the generals persuade their troops to renew the attack. For three successive days did the Athenians in vain attempt to force their passage; they were repelled with loss in every fresh assault, which became more feeble than the preceding.

The condition of the Athenians was now become deplorable to the last degree. The numbers of the wounded had been increased, by their late unsuccessful attempts to pass the mountain; and they could no longer procure provision and necessaries in the adjacent country. The generals, therefore, came to a resolution to break up their camp, and pursue a different and more circuitous route, which led through a level and open territory. Accordingly fires being lighted in every part of the camp, to deceive the enemy, the Athenian troops decamped under cover of the night, and marched in the same order which they had hitherto observed; but they had not proceeded far in this nocturnal expedition, when by some unknown fatality, alarm and tumult arose in the division commanded by Demosthenes. Order was after some time restored; but the division unhappily mistook the road, and quitted, never more to rejoin, the rest of the army.

The Syracusans perceiving at the break of day, that the Athenians had deserted their camp, pursued the road which the miserable and unfortunate fugitives had taken. The scouts of Gylippus soon brought intelligence, that the divisions of the enemy had separated. The superiour knowledge of the country, which the Spartan general possessed, enabled him, by the celerity of his motions, to intercept and surround that part of the army under the command of Demosthenes. This took place in the difficult and intricate defiles that led to the ford of the river Erinios. The Athenians were assaulted during the whole of the day, with darts, arrows, and javelins. In the evening, when many were thus wounded, and all worn out with fatigue, hunger, and thirst, Gylippus sent a herald to proclaim liberty to any of the islanders, who would come

to the Syracusan camp, and surrender their
arms; but not many, even in their forlorn situation, and when all the evils which the ancient
warfare of barbarians could inflict were impending, would desert their general and confederates.
At length, he entered into treaty with Demosthenes, who surrendered himself and all his
troops prisoners of war. No other stipulations
were made, than that they should neither suffer
death, imprisonment, nor famine. With their
arms, they gave up all their money, which they
threw into the hollow of their shields, and filled
four broad bucklers. The prisoners, about six
thousand, were sent to Syracuse.

Nicias arrived the same evening at the river
Erinios. Gylippus pursued and overtook him
near the banks of Asinarius. He immediately
sent a herald to acquaint him with the capitulation of Demosthenes, and to exhort him to
imitate the example of his colleague, and to
surrender to his virtuous and irresistible pursuers without further bloodshed. Nicias disbe-
lieved, or affected to disbelieve, the report. He
was therefore allowed to send a confidential person to make the necessary inquiry. When the
messenger returned, and assured him of the fact,
he sent to propose, in the name of the Athenian republick, to reimburse Syracuse for the expenses of the war, and offered to leave a citizen
as a hostage for every talent, that should thus
become due, provided hostilities might immediately cease, and his army be allowed to depart
without molestation.

The proposal was rejected with disdain; and
the Syracusans surrounded the Athenian army.
The former, however, would neither make nor
sustain any regular attack; but they continued

until the evening to annoy the Athenians unceasingly with missile weapons. About midnight, Nicias called to arms as silently as possible, and hoped that the troops might escape under cover of the night; but the watchful enemy perceived his motions, and immediately began to sing the pæan. Upon this the troops returned to their former station, and laid down their arms in despair. A body of about three hundred men, however, of determined courage, without any orders from the general, gallantly broke through the guards, and effected their escape. The return of the morning no sooner appeared, than Nicias pursued his march. The river was still the object they desired to reach; but in their way thither, they were miserably galled with missile weapons, and desultory charges of cavalry. Their distress was most lamentable and incurable; but they nevertheless hoped, that could they reach the opposite bank of the river, they should obtain some respite from the heavy-armed soldiers and the horse of the enemy.

Urged, therefore, also with the desire of assuaging their thirst, they strained every nerve to reach the river; but, notwithstanding every exertion to which such powerful motives impelled, when they reached the fatal banks of Asinarius, the heavy-armed forces of the enemy were close up with them. Discipline then yielded to the pressure of necessity. They hurried down the steep in confusion, and without order; and trod one another to death in the stream. Their first object was to assuage intolerable thirst; and to the gratification of this appetite, even personal safety was sacrificed. In the mean time, the enemy's light-armed troops occupied the opposite banks: and the whole Athenian army, enclosed in the river, was exposed, without the power of resistance, to missile weapons on both sides. The Peloponnesians at length led the way for the Syracusans down to the river, that they might complete the slaughter. The Athenians resisted the foe to the utmost; but here another kind of danger and of horrour presented itself to the eyes of Nicias. In the midst of the action, his soldiers turned their fury against each other, and disputed with the point of the sword the unwholesome draughts of the turbid and bloody stream. At the sight of this, the manly soul of Nicias melted within him: he felt that all was lost.

Already the Athenians were lying dead in heaps in the river, when Nicias found an opportunity to submit to Gylippus. He asked merely for quarter for the miserable remains of his troops, who had not perished in the Asinarius, or upon its banks. According to the barbarous practice of the age, many of the Syracusan soldiers had seized their prisoners as slaves, before the orders of the Lacedæmonian general to give quarter could be known. These Athenian captives were afterward distributed among the communities of Sicily, which had sent assistance to Syracuse. The publick prisoners, with the spoil that could be collected, were carried in triumph to the city.

It would have been a singular and glorious trophy of victory, to have exhibited in Sparta the two Athenian generals, who were the most illustrious men of their time ; and though Nicias had little to expect from the *humanity* of a proud and victorious Spartan, Demosthenes certainly had reason to flatter himself with the hope of *justice.* Both the generals, however, were condemned to death. Demosthenes urged, but urged in vain, the observance of the capitulation, which had been ratified in due form, and according to which he surrendered himself and all his troops prisoners of war. But the fears of those, who had carried on a treasonable correspondence with Nicias, induced them, if not to promote, at least to concur in the decree against the two commanders. The Corinthians also are said to have harboured particular enmity towards Nicias; and for some unknown cause to have been apprehensive, that the restoration of this great but unfortunate man to Athens, would eventually be detrimental to the interest and prosperity of their state.

Hermocrates, the Syracusan general, who is said to have been famous for his probity and justice, attempted to remonstrate against the cruel and tyrannical decree of putting the Athenian commanders to death; but the shouts which echoed from all parts interrupted him; and so much were the multitude incensed against the Athenians for invading their country, that they would not suffer him to continue his speech. At that instant appeared an old man, venerable for his years and gravity, who had lost two sons in the war, the only heirs to his name and estate. He was supported by two of his servants; and the people no sooner saw him, than a profound silence was observed, as no one doubted but he would pronounce a bitter invective against the prisoners.

" You see before you," said the old man, " an " unfortunate father, who has more severely felt " the fatal effects of this war than any other Sy- " racusan. My two sons, who were the hope and " support of my old age, and the only consola-

" tion and comfort of my declining years, have
" both been slain in battle. I cannot but admire
" and commend their courage and patriotism, in
" sacrificing a life, for the defence and welfare
" of their country, of which they must one day
" have been deprived by the common law of
" nature. But, at the same time, I feel myself
" strongly affected with the loss which I have
" suffered; nor can I forbear to detest the Athen-
" ians, as the authors of this unjust war, and
" the destroyers of my children. I cannot, how-
" ever, conceal one circumstance, which is, that
" I am more jealous of the honour of my coun-
" try, than sensible of my private affliction. The
" Athenians, assuredly merit every punishment
" that can be inflicted on them. But have not
" the gods, who are the proper avengers of every
" thing criminal and unjust, sufficiently revenged
" our cause, and retaliated upon them the inju-
" ries they have done us? When the Athenian
" commander surrendered himself and his troops
" prisoners, was it not stipulated, that none of
" them should suffer death, imprisonment, or
" famine? If, therefore, you condemn them to
" die, will you not thereby violate the sanctity
" of your promise and the law of nations, and
" commit an action the most perfidious and in-
" human? Will you suffer the glory you have
" acquired by the war to be thus tarnished; and
" have it said, that a nation which had dedicated
" a temple to clemency in your city, had expe-
" rienced no mercy and pity from you?

" You, doubtless, have not forgotten that Ni-
" cias, whose fate you are about to pronounce,
" was the man who pleaded your cause in the
" Athenian assembly, and used all his credit, in-
" fluence, and eloquence, to dissuade his coun-

" try from embarking in the war. Where then
" would be the justice, or the interest, of pro-
" nouncing sentence of death upon this good
" and worthy man? As for myself, O Syracu-
" sans! I would rather suffer death, than behold
" you guilty of an act fraught with so much
" injustice, tyranny, and dishonour."

Notwithstanding the visible effect which this
magnanimous speech had upon the multitude,
the Athenian generals were consigned to the
executioner, by a solemn decree of the Syracusan people. In the mean time, the miserable
remnant of their once flourishing army, the
greatest ever sent by any one Grecian state, was
doomed to a still severer lot. The prisoners,
who exceeded seven thousand men, were condemned to labour in the mines and quarries of
Sicily. The food that was given them was
scarcely sufficient to support life. But the cruelty of the Syracusans was still more exhibited
in their scanty allowance of water. They had
no shelter to screen them from the inclemency
of the sky; and while they suffered the reflected
heat of the scorching sun, the chill damps of
the autumnal nights were injurious to their
health. No care was taken of those who sick-
ened; and when any died, as many did, the
bodies remained to putrify among their living
companions. After a confinement for about seventy days, an eternal separation was made
between those who should enjoy the happier lot
of being sold for slaves into distant lands, and
those that should be forever confined to their
terrible dungeons. The Athenians, with such
Sicilians and Italians as had unnaturally embraced their cause, were reserved for the latter
doom. The people of Athens of those times

justly regretted the loss of Demosthenes, a gal-
lant and enterprising commander; but all posterity will lament and mourn the fate of Nicias, the most pious, the most virtuous, and the most unfortunate man of his age.

B.C. 413.

Amidst these dreadful and melancholy scenes, which have just passed under review, it would be unjust to omit the mention of a singular act of humanity. The Syracusans, who could punish their helpless captives with such unrelenting severity, had been often affected with the tender and plaintive strains of Euripides, an Athenian poet. Euripides had learned in the school of Socrates, to adorn the lessons of philosophy with the charms of fancy, and was considered by his cotemporaries as the most pathetick, the most philosophical and instructive, of all the tragick writers. The pleasure, which the Syracusans received from his inimitable poetry, induced them to wish that it might be rehearsed by the flexible voices and harmonious pronunciation of the Athenians, which were so unlike, and so superiour to the rudeness and asperity of their own Doric dialect. Their captives were requested to repeat the plaintive and affecting passages of their favourite bard. They obeyed, and in representing the woes of ancient kings and heroes, too faithfully delineated their own. The Syracusans, on account of their taste and sensibility, afterward treated them with great kindness, loosed their bonds, and restored them to their longing and afflicted country. When the captives returned to Athens, they walked in solemn procession to the house of Euripides, and hailed him as their deliverer from slavery. This was an acknowledgment infinitely preferable to all the crowns and splendour that ever surrounded the person of a poet, and even than all the temples and altars that ever immortalized the memory of genius. We attend the career of a hero, like the progress of a comet, with terrour and dismay, but repose with a fond delight on the contemplation of talents, cultivating the arts of peace, and softening the ferocity of martial minds.

CHAP. X.

The Affairs of Greece, from the Defeat of the Expedition against Sicily, to the Conclusion of the Peloponnesian War.

THE news of the total destruction of the most powerful armament, that ever sailed from a Grecian harbour, did not immediately find credit at Athens. So far from supposing that such a dreadful catastrophe could ever happen to it, this fleet was considered as capable of accomplishing almost any conquest. Multiplied concurring testimonies, however, removed, at length, every doubt of the magnitude of the calamity ; and the publick anguish became extreme. In one rash enterprise the Athenians lost their army, their fleet, their best and most exeperienced generals, and the flourishing vigour of their manly youth : in fine, all their proudest hopes perished forever in the harbour of Syracuse. These irreparable disasters disabled them from resisting the confederacy of Peloponnesus, reinforced as it now was by the accession of a resentful and elated enemy. A Syracusan fleet would probably assault

Piræus, while a Lacedæmonian army invested their city; and to these combined attacks the citizens had reason to fear that Athens must finally yield.

It was no wonder, therefore, that the minds of the Athenians should have been seized with consternation and despair, when they were aware of the extent of their losses. The venerable members of the Areopagus expressed their grief in the solemn majesty of silent sorrow; but the piercing cry of woe was heard for several miles along the walls that joined Piræus to the city; and popular rage vented itself against the diviners and orators, whose blind predictions and ambitious language had promoted an expedition eternally fatal to their country.

The distress of the Athenians indeed was too great to admit of any consolation, because it was felt to be deserved; but had they been capable of receiving comfort, there were none who would pity their sorrows, and compassionate their sufferings. What was afflicting to them, gave unspeakable joy to their neighbours. Many feared, most hated, and all envied a people that had long usurped the sovereignty of Greece. Their allies, scattered over so many islands and coasts, prepared to assert their independence. The confederates of Sparta, among whom the Syracusans might justly be considered as holding the first rank, were unsatisfied with victory, and longed for revenge. The republicks, which had hitherto declined the danger and uncertainty of a doubtful contest, considered the present moment proper for deciding to what party they belonged. and meanly solicited to be engaged in the war, that they might assist in the destruction of Athens.

In the mean time, the Lacedæmonians, with the characteristical rancorous coolness of their government, enjoyed with unspeakable satisfaction the view of this various ferment, and prepared to exert themselves, and profit by the misfortunes of their neighbour. They now considered the establishment of their own permanent superiority over all Greece as an acquisition completely within their power. But, should all the efforts of such a powerful confederacy be unable to accomplish the ruin of Athens, there was still another enemy behind, from whose strength and animosity the Athenians had every thing to fear. Darius Nothus, who had now succeeded to the government of the Persian empire, had employed his arms in extending his dominion toward the shores of the Ægean, and of the Hellespont and Propontis. The recent misfortunes of the Athenian people flattered the Persian commanders, who governed in Asia minor, with the hope of restoring the whole of that coast to the authority of the great king. They considered it also as now practicable, to execute exemplary punishment on the proud city, which had resisted the strength, dismembered the empire, and tarnished the glory of Persia.

The terrour of such a powerful combination might well have reduced the Athenians to a state of despair. They afford the only example of a people, who by the virtues and qualities of the mind alone acquired an extensive dominion over men, that were equally skilful with themselves in the arts of war and government. The nations around them considered the Athenians as superiour in courage and capacity to every other people; and by the force of this opinion they were enabled to maintain, with very feeble garrisons, an absolute authority over the islands of the Ægean sea, and the cities of the Asiatic coast. The disasters and disgrace of the expedition against Sicily destroyed, however, at once, every real and ideal support of their power. They thereby lost one-third of their citizens; and they could not supply their garrisons in foreign parts without fresh recruits. The dread of their arms was no more; and their multiplied defeats before the walls, and in the harbour of Syracuse, had converted into contempt that admiration, in which Athens had been long held both by Greeks and barbarians.

But in free governments there are many latent resources, which publick calamities alone can reveal. Adversity also furnishes in the enthusiasm of popular assemblies the greatest opportunity to men of strong and vigorous intellects of displaying national honour and magnanimity. The first spark of generous ardour, excited by the love of virtue, of glory, and of their republick, was diffused and cherished by the natural contagion of sympathy. The whole surrounding multitude caught the patriotick flame; and its social and invigorating warmth was reflected from such a variety of objects, that its intenseness could not be resisted even by the chills and damps of despair. The Athenians resolved with one mind, and one resolution, to brave the severity of fortune, and to withstand every assault of their collective foes.

Nor did this resolution evaporate in useless speculation. The wisest measures, and the most vigorous that circumstances would admit, were immediately put into execution. They began to restore the navy, to collect stores, to raise money, to save and use it, according as the exigency of affairs seemed to demand. They abridged not only private, but publick luxury, which was become immoderate, and therefore pernicious, in the Athenian state. They endeavoured to obviate the defection of the allied and subject states, and particularly of Eubœa, the most valuable dependency of the commonwealth, and without which the city of Athens could not easily subsist. Never were the Athenian people so disposed to listen to, and obey, wise and proper advice. " It was so resolved," says Thucydides, " and it was done; and the summer ended."

The year following the defeat of the expedition against Sicily, the Peloponnesians equipped a fleet of one hundred sail, of which the Spartans furnished twenty-five gallies, the Thebans twenty-five, the Corinthians fifteen, and the Locrians, Phocians, Megareans, with the other inhabitants of the maritime cities in Peloponnesus, the rest. By the defeat in Sicily, it was generally supposed that the command of the sea was completely lost to Athens; and immediately the Greek Asiatic cities began to think of revolting. The Lesbians had commenced the example, and the Chians and Erythræans followed. Diffident, however, of their own strength, their first measure was to communicate with Tissaphernes, one of the Persian governours in Asia-minor; but the satrap did not think himself able, with his own forces, to give them protection. He, therefore, gladly united his interest with theirs, and conjointly they sent ministers to Lacedæmon. The fleet, which the Peloponnesians had prepared, was destined to encourage and support the revolt of the Asiatic subjects of the Athenians.

B. C. 412.

Tissaphernes, on his part, promised, if they would send a part of this armament to the assistance of the Chians, Lesbians, and Erythræans, that he would pay the soldiers, and victual the ships.

At the same time, embassadors arrived from Cyzicus, a populous and opulent city, situated on an island of the Propontis. They requested the Lacedæmonians to send their armament to the safe and capacious harbours, which had long formed the wealth and the ornament of that city, and to expel the Athenian garrisons from their island. Pharnabazus, the Persian governor of the northern district of Asia minor, seconded their proposal, and offered the same terms as Tissaphernes. These satraps, however, were so disunited, that each urged his particular request with a total unconcern about the important interests of their common master. The Lacedæmonians and their allies, unable to come to any resolution, for a great length of time held many consultations. They hesitated, deliberated, resolved, and then changed their determination; but, at length, Alcibiades prevailed upon them to accept the overtures of Tissaphernes and the Ionians, and to abandon, at present, the cause of Pharnabazus and the Hellespontines.

This deliberation was not the only occasion of delay. A variety of private considerations diverted the Peloponnesians from the general aim of the confederacy; and the season was far advanced before the Corinthians, who had distinguished themselves in antipathy and hatred to Athens, were ready to sail. It happened also, that the time for performing the Isthmian games was at hand; and such was the inviolable sanctity of the armistice on that occasion, that the Athenians might come to Corinth, and remain there in safety and security. The preparations, therefore, could not long remain a secret; and even the negotiations would probably also transpire. The movements of the fleet, in the mean time, excited the suspicion of Athens; and the persons coming and going directed the suspicion to its object. Aristocrates, therefore, one of the generals of Athens, was sent to Chios with instructions to inform himself of the present state of things in that island; and, as a precaution for the future conduct of the Chians, to demand the ships, which, according to the terms of the confederacy, they were bound to furnish for the Athenian fleet. The leaders of the revolt, therefore, thus taken unprepared, denied any intention of breaking their ancient connexion with the Athenian republick, and, in conformity to the requisition, sent seven ships to Piræus.

The Athenians who attended at the Isthmian games neglected not the commission, with which their country had entrusted them. The preparations were seen, and the purpose was suspected; and they secretly learned the plan and particular circumstances of the revolt, and the precise time fixed for the departure of the Corinthian fleet. The Athenians took their measures accordingly; intercepted the Corinthians as they sailed through the Saronic gulph; and having attacked and defeated them, pursued and blocked them up in their harbours.

Meanwhile the Spartans and their allies sent squadrons successively to the Ionian coast, under the command of Alcibiades, Chalcideus, and Astyochus. The fleet under Alcibiades sailed to Chios, and on its arrival excited universal astonishment and alarm among the inhabitants, excepting those of the aristocratical party. The council, according to previous concert, was now sitting. Alcibiades boldly asserted, that a large fleet was on its way from Peloponnesus. They had not heard any thing of the defeat on the Corinthian coast. A decree was proposed for renouncing the confederacy with Athens, and entering into an alliance with the Peloponnesians; which, without being materially opposed by the democratical party, was immediately carried. The Erythræans followed their example; and three ships only being sent against Clazomene, that city also surrendered. Alcibiades had an old and hereditary interest at Miletus, and he proposed next to engage the richest and most important of the Asiatic Grecian cities in revolt against his native state. Miletus soon after surrendered. Thus, with the trifling force of a few triremes, did Alcibiades strike a greater blow against his country, than the Lacedæmonians and their confederates, after the signal advantages obtained in Sicily, had almost dared to meditate.

The affairs of Athens were now in so critical a situation, that they voted an expenditure of a thousand talents, which, in the more prosperous times of the commonwealth, had been deposited in the citadel, to be employed in the moment of extreme necessity. By this seasonable supply, the Athenians were enabled to send a fleet, under the command of Phrynichus and other leaders, to the isle of Lesbos. Having secured the fidelity of the Lesbians, they endeavoured to gain possession of Miletus. The Athenians and their allies consisted of two thousand five hundred men. Eight hundred heavy-armed

Milesians under the command of Alcibiades, with the Peloponnesians that had been commanded by Chalcideus, and a force of Asiatic infantry and cavalry, led by the satrap Tissaphernes in person, opposed them; and a bloody battle was fought under the walls of Miletus. The Argians in the Athenian army, thinking that the Ionians would avoid them at the first onset, advanced without order; but the Milesians presently routed them, and killed near three hundred men. In the mean time, the Athenians, who were opposed to the Peloponnesians and Asiatics, fought with great courage and bravery, and having attacked and defeated the former, the latter immediately fled. In both parts of the engagement, therefore, the Ionic race, commonly reckoned by the Greeks the less warlike, prevailed over their Dorian rivals and enemies. The Athenians having erected their trophy, prepared to make an assault upon Miletus. Late, however, in the evening of the same day on which the battle was fought, they received intelligence that a fleet of fifty-five triremes had arrived from Peloponnesus. But the exertions of the Peloponnesians alone had not sent out this powerful armament. Hermocrates had prevailed upon the Syracusans to equip a squadron of twenty triremes; which, being joined by the Peloponnesian gallies, had proceeded to the relief of Miletus. Theramenes, the Spartan, was commander in chief.

Phrynichus, the Athenian commander, considering, that to perform what appeared most conducive to the welfare and interest of his country was in reality most honourable, prudently declined to engage the hostile fleet; and his firmness despised the clamours of the Athenian soldiers, who insulted, under the name of cowardice, his retreat. He calmly retired to Samos, with forty-eight gallies, and refused to commit the last hope of the republick to the danger of an unequal combat.

The superiority which the Peloponnesians now possessed over the fleet of Athens was fully testified, in obliging the armament of that republick to quit the harbours and the coast of Miletus, and was of itself sufficient to acquire or maintain the submission of the neighbouring cities and islands. In other respects also the Peloponnesians had many advantages over their unfortunate rivals. Tissaphernes victualed their ships, and paid their soldiers, and had procured the allies a reinforcement of one hundred and fifty Phœnician gallies, which had already reached Aspendus, a seaport of Pamphilia. In this dangerous and dreadful crisis, Alcibiades, who had so long been the misfortune and courage of Athens, was destined, by a train of singular and almost incredible accidents, to become the defence and saviour of his country; and fortune seemed once more to respect and favour the declining age of the Athenian republick.

During the time of his residence in Sparta, Alcibiades assumed the gravity and the austerity of the Lacedæmonian manners, and used himself to the spare diet, and laborious exercises, which prevailed in that republick. His real character and principles were, however, still the same. His intrigue with Timæa, the wife of Agis, king of Sparta, was discovered by an excess of female vanity: she frequently told her maids, that her son's name ought to be Alcibiades instead of Leotychides; and that the father of her child was the greatest and handsomest

man of his age. This report, which was for a
while confined to the privacy of her female companions, soon spread abroad in the world. Alcibiades, to punish her folly, boasted that he had
been induced to pay attention to the queen, not
from any inclination for her person, but merely
from the vanity of giving a king to Sparta, and
an heir to the race of Hercules. The injured
husband felt the keenest resentment for the dishonour done to his bed; and still more for the
open and shameless avowal of that dishonour.
The magistrates and generals of Sparta, jealous
of the fame, and envious of the merit of a stranger, readily sympathised with the misfortune,
and promoted the revenge of Agis. They re-
sorted to a disgraceful and nefarious expedient,
for obviating the mischief. Private instructions
were sent to Astyochus, to procure the assassination of Alcibiades; but the crafty and active
Athenian had secured too faithful domestick intelligence in the several families of Sparta, to
remain long ignorant of what was transacting,
and to become the victim of their resentment.
With his usual address, he eluded all the attempts of Astyochus, and betook himself to
Tissaphernes.

Alcibiades was not unprepared for the change,
which his new situation induced. Notwithstanding the favour which he had found at Sparta,
and the attention that was daily paid to him, in
the character of a stranger and a fugitive, he
was secretly uneasy; and his sole object was to
restore himself to his country, before that country was reduced so much, as to be unworthy of
receiving him. With this view, therefore, he had
assiduously and successfully courted Tissaphernes. In the selfish breast of the satrap, neither

the advantage of the Persian empire, nor that of the Peloponnesian confederacy, was regarded by him, but as it promoted his own private interest and opulence. An opportunity, therefore, was not wanting for insinuations and advice, that might occasion a difference between Tissaphernes and the Peloponnesians, and render Alcibiades not only agreeable, but useful to the Persian. Tissaphernes, pressed for money by his court and the exigency of his own government, listened with great attention to any suggestions, by which he could hope to spare his treasury, and to amass wealth for himself. Alcibiades told him that the pay to the Peloponnesians was extravagant. The Athenians, he said, allowed their seamen only half a dráchma per day; not from any motives of economy, or inability to afford more; but because they esteemed a larger pay disadvantageous to the service. Should discontent arise among the sailors on account of the reduction of their wages, a sum of money judiciously distributed among the commanders, would prove an easy expedient for silencing the licentious clamours of the seamen.

Tissaphernes heard the proposal, with the attention natural to an avaricious man desirous of saving his money; and the event proved how true a judgment Alcibiades had formed of the Grecian character, when it was found that Hermocrates the Syracusan was the only person, who disdained meanly and perfidiously to betray the interest of the men under his command. Tissaphernes, however, afterward declared, that Hermocrates, though more coy, was not less corruptible; and that the only reason why he undertook the patronage of the sailors was, to obtain for himself a more exorbitant sum. How

far this assertion was true, is uncertain, but it
strongly corresponds with the opinion, that other
nations have formed of the Grecian character.
. Alcibiades now saw the crisis approaching,
that might enable him, not only to return to his
country, but to acquire the glory of restoring
Athens to its former splendour and reputation.
The Athenians in their distress, had made wonderful exertions and bravely contended against
their adversaries; but it was evident that these
exertions had almost exhausted them; and the
more intelligent among the people were sensible that they could not long resist the Peloponnesian confederacy, aided as it then was by the
wealth and power of Persia. At this juncture,
Alcibiades applied secretly to Pisander, and other
persons in the Athenian camp. He gave them
assurance, that he would engage Tissaphernes
in their interest, and, through him, lead the
Persian monarch himself to an alliance with
Athens, provided they would consent to demolish the turbulent democracy, which was odious to Darius.

His overtures excited attention, and a great
majority of the people approved the proposal.
Phrynichus, however, the commander in chief,
firm in the interest of democracy, was not, at
first, made acquainted with the innovation that
menaced the state. But no sooner was he aware
of what was transacting, and perceived how deaf
his colleagues were to every objection against
recalling the friend of Tissaphernes, than he informed Astyochus, the Spartan admiral, of the
divisions of the armament under his command.
Astyochus was become the pensioner and crea-
ture of the satrap, and communicated both to
him and Alcibiades the intelligence he had re-

ceived. Alcibiades immediately informed the Athenians in Samos of the treachery of their general. Phrynichus alarmed, and in great peril, wrote again to Antyochus, complaining that due secrecy had not been observed, and acquainting him with the means of surprising the Athenian fleet at Samos. Phrynichus understanding that the Spartan admiral had communicated this also to Alcibiades, extricated himself with singular boldness and dexterity. The consideration that Samos was unfortified, and that the fleet was stationed without the port, had, he said, induced the enemy to make an attack, of which he had been made acquainted by private intelligence. He, therefore, issued immediate orders to fortify the city. In the mean time Alcibiades sent notice to the people, that the armament was betrayed by its general, and that the enemy were preparing to attack it. This intelligence only served to confirm that which had been communicated by Phrynichus, and to justify his measures.

In the mean time Pisander and his colleagues were endeavouring, at Athens, to overturn the democratical form of government. The compact body of conspirators warmly approved the proposal; but many and loud murmurs of discontent were heard from different quarters of the theatre of Bacchus, where the people had been convened. Pisander asked the reason of this disappointment. " Have you," said he, " any thing better to propose? If you have, come forward, and explain the grounds of your dissent. But, above all, explain how you can save your country, your families, and yourselves, except you comply with the demand of Tissaphernes. The imperious voice of necessity is superiour to every thing besides; and when the danger has subsided, you can reestablish that form of government which you most approve."

A decree was immediately passed by the assembly, investing ten persons with full power to treat with the Persian satrap.

· The embassadors proceeded to Magnesia, where Tissaphernes usually resided, and were admitted to a conference, in which Alcibiades acted for the satrap. Alcibiades, however, did not possess that degree of influence over the Persian, which he had pretended; it was evidently, therefore, his purpose to render the conference abortive, by making such demands for Tissaphernes, as the commissioners could not grant. But finding them disposed to concede much, he required on the part of the Persian monarch, the cession of all Ionia and the adjacent islands. Fearing, however, that the urgency of their affairs would oblige them to comply even with this demand, he required also that, along all the coasts of the Athenian dominion, the fleets of Persia should be allowed to sail undisturbed. Such a requisition satisfied the commissioners, that Alcibiades and his party intended nothing friendly to the Athenian republick, and they accordingly departed.

The artifices employed by Alcibiades, convinced the Athenians also, that his credit with the Persians was less than he represented it. The aristocratical party were, therefore, glad to get rid of a man whose ambition rendered him a dangerous associate; but they persisted with great activity in executing their purpose; and Phrynichus, who had opposed them only through hatred to Alcibiades, became an active abettor. When persuasion was found ineffectual, they recurred to violence. Many of the licentious demagogues were assassinated, and four hundred men, chosen from among the people, were appointed to conduct the administration of their country. These were to be men of dignity and opulence in the state, and assembled as often as they thought proper five thousand citizens, whom they judged most worthy of being consulted in the management of publick affairs; and thus was the Athenian democracy subverted, after it had subsisted one hundred years with unexampled publick glory, though with much intestine disorder.

B. C. 411. But the conduct of the four hundred tyrants, for such they certainly were, abolished every vestige of remaining freedom. Mercenaries from the islands of the Ægean sea were hired to overawe and intimidate the people, and to destroy the real or suspected enemies of the tyrants. They neglected the opportunity of attacking the Peloponnesians, enraged at the treachery and duplicity of Tissaphernes, and mutinous for want of pay and subsistence; but they sent a humiliating embassy to Sparta, to solicit peace on the most dishonourable terms. Their tyranny became odious in the city, and their cowardice contemptible in the camp at Samos. The generous youths, engaged in the defence of their country by sea and land, were indignant at the insults and outrages offered to their fellow citizens. The tyrants might probably inflict the same indignities on them, if suffered to proceed in their career, and the people neglected to vindicate their freedom. These several murmurs broke out at last into loud and licentious clamours, which the approbation of the Samians greatly promoted.

Activity and boldness were given to the insurgents by Thrasybulus and Thrasyllus, two officers of great merit, but not entrusted with a
share in the principal command. The abettors
of the new government at Samos were attacked
by surprise; thirty of the most criminal were
put to death; three were banished; and the
rest, submitting to democracy, received a free
pardon.

The first concern of Thrasybulus, who had
been appointed to the supreme command of the
armament, was to recal Alcibiades, who had
been deceived and disgraced by the tyrants, and
who was most capable of avenging the indignities and wrongs both of his country and himself.
Accordingly an assembly of the Athenian citizens, belonging to the armament, was convened
as the legal body of the commonwealth. And
the assembly assenting to the recal of Alcibiades,
Thrasybulus went to communicate the information to him, then residing with Tissaphernes,
and they returned together to Samos. Several
years had now elapsed since the eloquent son of
Clinias had spoken in an Athenian assembly.
He began by lamenting his calamities and accusing his fortune. His banishment, however,
though otherwise unfortunate, had procured
him, he said, the acquaintance and the friendship of Tissaphernes, who, by his entreaties,
had withheld the pay from the Peloponnesians,
and would, he doubted not, continue his good
offices to the Athenians, supply them with every
thing necessary for continuing the war, and even
assist them with a Phœnician fleet.

These flattering promises raised his credit
with the army, by whom he was immediately
appointed general; widened the breach between

Tissaphernes and the Spartans; and struck terrour into the tyrants of Athens, who were soon made acquainted with the speech of Alcibiades. Matters being thus settled, the Athenians at Samos already despised the efforts of the Peloponnesians. They prepared to revenge themselves on the four hundred tyrants at Athens; but Alcibiades dissuaded them from their purpose, and declared, that it would be proper to communicate first with Tissaphernes, show himself in the situation in which they had placed him, and consult the future arrangements. Accordingly he set off for Magnesia, anxious to prove to Tissaphernes the power he possessed among the Athenians, as he had been desirous to impress the Athenians with an opinion of his influence with Tissaphernes; and, as he could now be a valuable friend, or a formidable foe to either, he awed the Athenians with the name of Tissaphernes, and Tissaphernes with that of the Athenians. Upon the arrival of Alcibiades from Magnesia, he found the partisans of democracy, who had been inflamed with the report of the indignities and cruelties committed at Athens, ready to sail thither to take vengeance on their enemies, and to protect their friends. By these means Athens would have been plunged in the horrours of a civil war, and every remaining dependency of the commonwealth in Ionia, and on the Hellespont, would have submitted to the enemies of the republick. No man but Alcibiades was capable of preventing the people from committing this rash and destructive action; and he effectually checked the design; but at the same time he commanded it to be declared to the usurpers at Athens, that, unless they divested themselves of their illegal power, and restored the ancient constitution, he would sail with a fleet to Piræus, and deprive them of their authority and their lives.

When the message reached Athens, it contributed to increase the disorder and confusion of that city. The four hundred soon began to disagree among themselves, and divided into factions, which persecuted each other as furiously as they had persecuted the people before. The cruel and tyrannical measures, pursued by their colleagues, were opposed and condemned by Theramenes and Aristocrates: Phrynichus was publickly stabbed by one of the city guards: and the horrours of a Corcyrean sedition seemed ready to be renewed in Athens, when the old men, women, children, and strangers interposed for the safety of a city, which had long been the ornament of Greece, the terrour of Persia, and the admiration of the world.

To the duplicity of the satrap, and the treachery of their own officers, the Peloponnesians justly ascribed the want of pay and subsistence, and all the misfortunes which they suffered. Their resentment becoming violent and furious, they attacked and destroyed the Persian fortifications near Miletus, the garrison was put to the sword, and Astyochus, their own general, saved his life by fleeing to an altar. Nor were they appeased, until the guilty were removed, and an officer of approved valour and fidelity appointed to the command.

The dreadful consequences which must have resulted to the Athenians, had a large and powerful fleet appeared on their coast, during the late commotions and sedition in Athens, may be easily conceived from the terrour and consternation that were inspired by the sight of a squadron of forty-two-gallies commanded by the Spartan Hegesandridas. The friends of the constitution, and the partizans of oligarchy, had been convened in two distinct and separate assemblies; and the most important matters were in agitation, when the Peloponnesian fleet was discovered off the coast. Immediately the whole force of both parties in Athens united against the common enemy, and ran to Piræus as by mutual consent. Some went aboard the triremes that were afloat; others launched those that had been hauled on shore; and some prepared to defend the walls, and the mouth of the harbour. The Peloponnesians, however, made no attempt upon the Attic coast, doubling cape Sunium, sailed towards the island of Eubœa.

New alarm, however, then seized the Athenians; and to defend a country which formed their principal resources, and from which they could procure more plentiful supplies, than from the desolated lands of Attica, obliged them to sail in pursuit of the enemy, whom they next day observed near the coast of Eretria, the most considerable town of Eubœa. The inhabitants of the island had long desired an opportunity for revolting, and therefore supplied the Peloponnesian fleet abundantly with provision; but they refused to furnish a market for the Athenians. The commanders were therefore obliged to send detachments into the country, to obtain necessaries; when Hegesandridas seized this opportunity to attack them. Most of the ships were taken, and the crews swam to land, where many of them were killed by the Eretrians. After this defeat, the whole of Eubœa, except Oreus, immediately revolted to the Peloponnesians.

The consternation at Athens, when the news

of this misfortune reached the city, was greater than even from the complete defeat and destruction of the armament that sailed against Sicily. Corn, meat, every article of food, came principally from Eubœa. Attica itself was not half so valuable and productive to Athens, as that island. Nor was this the only distressing circumstance; if the enemy had pushed, with their victorious fleet, immediately for Piræus, they might have possessed themselves of the harbour. What might have happened beyond this is uncertain; but thus much, says Thucydides, might have been forseen, that nothing less than the return of the fleet from Samos could have saved Athens. And had the Athenian armament been compelled to quit the station they then occupied, the whole of Ionia, the Hellespont, and, in short, all the foreign dominion would have fallen into the hands of the enemy. It was not, however, on this occasion only, that the Lacedæmonians showed themselves accomodating enemies to the Athenians; and thus the misfortunes, which threatened the commonwealth with ruin, proved the prelude to its restoration ; for by the perfidious, or imprudent conduct of their commanders, the Lacedæmonians lost this seasonable opportunity of terminating the war with advantage and honour.

In the mean time, Theramenes encouraged the people to disburden themselves of those who had summoned, or, at least, who were believed to have summoned, the Peloponnesian fleet to the coast of Athens, that they might enslave their country. Antiphon, Pisander, and others most obnoxious to the friends of liberty, escaped ; and the rest submitted. The restoration of Alcibiades, and the approbation of the conduct of the troops at Samos, were then decreed; and the constitution was reestablished on its original principles, as founded by Solon. "And now," says Thucydides, "the Athenians, for the first " time, in the present age at least, modelled " their government right; which occasioned the " restoration of Athens."

During these transactions in the city, Tissaphernes acted the part between an open enemy and a treacherous ally. The Spartans, who had formerly neglected, now courted, the friendship and protection of Pharnabazus; and a numerous and powerful armament was sent to the province where he commanded. As soon as it was known, that the Peloponnesian fleet had sailed for the Hellespont, the Athenians, animated by the manly counsels of Thrasybulus and Thrasyllus, the generous defenders of their freedom, pursued the same course; and in the straits that join the Euxine and Ægean seas, the conflict began, and continued for a long time. In three successive engagements, the event of which became continually more decisive, did the Athenians, in the twenty-first year of the war, prevail over their Peloponnesian enemies. The first battle was fought in the narrow channel between Sestos and Abydus; in which Thrasybulus took twenty Peloponnesian ships, but lost fifteen Athenian gallies. The glory, however, remained entire to the Athenians.

A squadron of fourteen Rhodian vessels, near cape Rhegium, was intercepted by the Athenian fleet. While the islanders defended themselves with great bravery, Mindarus, the Spartan admiral, seeing their engagement, hastened to their assistance. The principal squadron of the Athenian armament attacked the Peloponne-

sians. Through the greater part of the day the
fight was maintained with various success in
different parts of the line ; but, towards evening, eighteen Athenian triremes were seen entering the strait from the south. This proved
to be the squadron under the command of Alcibiades. The Peloponnesians immediately fled ;
and, fortunately for them, the satrap Pharnabazus with his land-forces was at hand. He rode
into the sea, at the head of his cavalry, as far
as his horse would carry him, that he might relieve his distressed allies. Through his
assistance, the crews mostly escaped ;
but the Athenians carried off thirty triremes.

B.C.
410.

The Spartans now yielded possession of the
sea, which they hoped soon to recover, and retired to the friendly harbour of Cyzicus, that
they might repair the remains of their shattered
armament ; and the Athenians, profiting by
their victories, raised contributions from the numerous and wealthy towns in that neighbourhood. But meeting with very indifferent success
in their design, the several divisions returned
to Sestos ; nor could they expect that such strongly fortified places as Byzantium, Selymbria, Perinthus, on the European, or Lampsacus, Pari-
um, Chalcedon, on the Asiatic coast, would be
intimidated, without obtaining more decisive and
important advantages. It was therefore determined, chiefly by the advice of Alcibiades, to
attack the Peloponnesian fleet at Cyzicus. The
Athenian armament, coasting along the Chersonese, arrived at the small island of Proconnesus,
near the western extremity of the Propontis. A
heavy rain presently came on, which favoured
the purpose of surprising the enemy. As the

weather cleared, and they approached Cyzicus, they descried the Peloponnesian fleet manœuvring at such a distance from the harbour, that its return was already intercepted. The enemy, peceiving the Athenian armament so much stronger than they expected, were in great consternation; they confided not in the success of a naval action, but it was impossible for them to return to their port. A general engagement ensued, and the Athenians obtained a complete victory. The whole of the Peloponnesian fleet was captured, except the squadron from Syracuse, which was burned in the face of a victorious enemy, by the intrepid and enterprising Hermocrates. The circumstances and consequences of this victory were related in few but expressive words to the Spartan government, in a letter from Hippocrates, the second in command, which exhibits one of the most curious and authentic specimens of laconic writing : " Success has turned against us : Minda- " rus is slain : the men hunger : what to do we " know not." These four short sentences made the whole of the dispatch.

Alcibiades now raised contributions on the inhabitants of Cyzicus. The fleet then proceeded against Perinthus and Selymbria, and exacted from these places also large sums of money. Proceeding thence to Chrysopolis, in the Chalcedonian territory, near the entrance of the Euxine, Alcibiades caused that place to be fortified, and there established a custom-house for levying a duty of a tenth in value on all cargoes passing the strait. As this mode of collecting money required a force, he left, beside a garrison, thirty ships there, under the command of Theramenes.

In the mean time, the Peloponnesians, assisted by Pharnabazus, were busily employed in equiping a new fleet, the materials of which were easily procured in the Persian dominions. They were, however, deprived of the wise counsels of Hermocrates, who was degraded from his office, and punished with banishment, by the insolent populace of Syracuse. The conduct of Hermocrates is worthy of admiration : an assembly being called, he deplored his hard fortune, but recommended the most submissive obedience to the authority of the republick. He then requested the sailors to name temporary commanders ; but was answered, that he and his colleagues ought to continue in office. He again urged them, not to rebel against the government. " The time will come," he said, " when we " shall desire your support, to evidence the bat- " tles you have fought, the ships you have taken, " and the success that has attended you under " our command ; aud you will then bear testi- " mony to our conduct, upon all occasions, by " sea and land." The admonition had its full effect : nothing disorderly happened. The armament showed, however, that they would not have suffered any violence to their generals : they entered into an agreement upon oath, to exert themselves, on their return to Syracuse, for procuring their restoration.

For several years now the measures of the Athenians had been almost uniformly B. C. 408. successful ; but the twenty-fourth campaign was distinguished by peculiar favours of fortune. The Persians and Peloponnesians were repeatedly defeated by the Athenians, driven from their encampments and fortresses near the shore, and pursued into the country, which was plundered and desolated by the victors. The Athenians returned in triumph to attack the fortified cities, which had not yet submitted to the conquerors. Alcibiades displayed the wonderful resources of his extraordinary and enterprising genius in this kind of warfare. By gradual approaches, by sudden assaults, by surprise, by treason, or by stratagem, he soon became master of Chalcedon, Selymbria, and Byzantium. His naval success was also equally conspicuous. The enemy had fitted out several small squadrons, which without much difficulty he conquered; and these multiplied captures accumulated the trophies of the well-fought battles that we have already described. It was computed that Alcibiades, since assuming the command of the Athenian armament, had taken or destroyed five hundred Syracusan or Peloponnesian gallies; and his naval victories enabled him to raise such contributions, in the Euxine and Mediterranean seas, as abundantly supplied his fleet and army with all necessary subsistence and accommodation.

But while the Athenian arms were crowned with such glory abroad, the attic territory was continually harassed by the Spartan king, and the Lacedæmonian garrison at Decelia. They frequently, indeed, threatened the safety of the country; the desolated lands afforded no supplies; and the Athenians durst not venture without their walls, to celebrate their accustomed festivals. Alcibiades, therefore, hoped, that after so many foreign conquests, he might perhaps be able to alleviate the domestick sufferings of his country. He longed, also, to revisit his friends, relations, and native city, after having been absent six years; and he hoped likewise to enjoy

the rewards and honours, which the Greeks generally bestowed on successful valour.——
This celebrated voyage was performed
in the twenty-fifth summer of the war.

Notwithstanding, however, all the services he
had rendered the republick, there was still a
strong party in Athens inveterately inimical to
him. The cautious son of Clinias, therefore,
declined to land in Piræus, until he was informed the people had revoked the decrees against
him. Information from his confidential friends
reached him at sea, that he had been elected
general of the republick; and that the decree
respecting his banishment had been repealed.
Even after receiving this agreeable intelligence,
he was unable to conquer his well-founded dis-
trust of the inconstant and capricious humours
of the people. Nor would he approach the Attic shore, until he beheld, among the multitudes that had crowded from the city, his principal friends and relations, inviting him by their
voice and action. He then landed amidst the
almost universal acclamations of the spectators.
The general language was, that Alcibiades was
the most meritorious of the Athenian citizens;
that his condemnation had been the pernicious
measure of a conspiracy of wicked men, who
scrupled nothing to promote their own interest;
that his abilities were transcendent, and his liberality unbounded; that he had been compelled
to oppose his country, and his readiness and
eagerness to return to its service, proved his patriotick disposition. That with respect to the
danger of the state, men of his temper and inclination, could have no desire to innovate; for
the favour of the people gave him all the power
and preeminence, which he could possibly wish.

He had never oppressed any; but his opponents had destroyed and assassinated the most worthy men of Athens; and, if ever they appeared to possess any popular confidence, it was only when the death, or exile, of the great and leading men, left them, without competition, to enjoy the principal situations of the commonwealth.

While, however, these were the general sentiments and expressions of the people, a few were heard to murmur, that Alcibiades alone had occasioned all the past misfortunes and disasters of the republick; and it was to be feared he would still be the promoter of measures dangerous and hostile to the welfare of the commonwealth. His friends did not entirely confide in the protection, which the late established government could, or would, afford. They came, therefore, prepared to resist any attempt, that might be made against his person; and surrounded by them, Alcibiades proceeded to the city.

His first business was, to attend the council of five hundred; and then to address the general assembly of the people. Before both, he asserted his innocence, with respect to the sacrilegious profanation of which he had been accused, contrasted the situation of Athens, prior and posterior to his taking the command of the Athenian armament, apologized for his conduct during his banishment, and criminated his prosecutors. It was not difficult for Alcibiades, to plead his defence before judges, so favourably disposed to hear and to believe him; and the popular favour was so great, and so evident, that not a word was spoken in opposition to him.— But the transports of the people became immoderate, and they would have loaded their favourite with honours incompatible with the genius of a free republick, and which might probably have proved detrimental to his future safety. The crowns and garlands, and other pledges of publick gratitude, he thankfully received ; but respectfully declined the regal sceptre, and expressed his firm resolution, to support and maintain the liberty of Athens. The state, he said, did not stand in need of a king, but a general, who should possess undivided power, capable of restoring the ancient glory and splendour of the commonwealth. To this illustrious and exalted rank, which Themistocles and Cimon had formerly filled, Alcibiades might justly aspire. He was accordingly chosen commander in chief by sea and land, with supreme authority. The Athenians immediately equipped one hundred gallies, and prepared transports for containing fifteen hundred heavy-armed men, with a proportional body of cavalry.

The Eleusinian festival, a time set apart for commemorating and diffusing the temporal and spiritual gifts of Ceres, now approached. This goddess, whose festival was distinguished by appropriate honours, had introduced corn, wine, and oil among the Athenians, who had communicated them to the rest of Greece. Minerva who had given the olive, and was supposed to be the protector of Athens, was also rewarded with innumerable solemnities. In appointed days of the spring and autumn, various were the professions of gratitude expressed to the generous author of the vine. The worship of Ceres, indeed, returned less frequently, but in two particulars seemed calculated to excite reverence and awe ; by its seldom occurring, and by the

Eleusinian mysteries, those hidden treasures of wisdom and happiness, which were diffused on the initiated in the temple Eleusis. These mysteries are said to have expressed by external signs, the immortality of the human soul, and the rewards that will be bestowed in a future life on the virtuous and the good.

After Decelia had been occupied by a Lacedæmonian garrison, the Athenians were no longer masters of the road leading to Eleusis; and the mysterious procession having always passed by sea, many of the prescribed ceremonies were necessarily either omitted, or imperfectly performed. Alcibiades determined to wipe off the stain of impiety, which had long adhered to his character, by renewing this venerable procession in all its lustre. With the forces returned from Asia, added to the strength of the city, he undertook to conduct the peaceful ministers and votaries of the gods by land, and to protect them in the fullest performance of every accustomed rite. This accordingly he accomplished: the train went and returned without suffering any disturbance from the enemy; who, as it were by mutual compact, suspended hostilities at this season.

Soon after this meritorious enterprise, Alcibiades prepared to sail for Asia minor; and about this time Lysander was appointed to the command of the Peloponnesian fleet. It was a rule jealously observed by the Lacedæmonian government, that none should be admiral of the fleet above a year. Lysander, accordingly, in rotation was nominated commander: he had been educated in all the severe discipline of the Spartan state; he had spent his youth and manhood in those honourable employments, which properly became him; and it was not until the decline of life, that he assumed the command of the Peloponnesian fleet. Experience was added to his valour, and he had not yet lost the ardour and resources of that ambitious mind which animated his youth. His transactions with the world had taught him to soften the asperity and severity of the Spartan manners; to obtain by fraud what could not be gained by force ; and, in his own figurative language, to eke out the lion's with the fox's skin. This mixed character admirably suited the part he was called to act, in this crisis of publick danger.

Lysander, having received his command early in the winter, passed to Rhodes ; and proceeded with a squadron to Cos and Miletus, and thence to Ephesus, where, with the ships he had collected in the way, he found himself at the head of seventy triremes. But the assembling of such a force was a matter of little consequence, unless proper measures were pursued for holding it together, and enabling it to act with vigour. As soon, therefore, as he heard that Cyrus was arrived at Sardis, to take upon him the government of the inland parts of Asia minor, he hastened to pay his court to the young prince. Here he experienced a favourable reception, and Cyrus told him, that he had brought five hundred talents, or one hundred and twenty-five thousand pounds sterling, for carrying on the war against Athens; and that, if this sum should prove insufficient, he would expend his own revenue, and melt down and coin into money the golden throne upon which he sat.

This discourse gave great satisfaction to Lysander, and he requested that the seamen's wages might be raised from three oboli to an Attic drachma a day. Cyrus answered, that he had received express orders from his father, that the pay should continue on the ancient footing. Lysander, however, contrived, before he left Sardis, to procure the augmentation to the sailors, which induced the Athenian crews to desert; and thus while it increased the strength of Lacedæmon, enfeebled the armament of Athens. Cyrus gave him ten thousand daricks (about five thousand pounds sterling), with which he returned to Ephesus, and discharged the arrears due to his troops.

While Lysander was manning his vessels, and preparing them for action, Alcibiades attacked the small island of Andros; but meeting with more resistance than he expected, and being obliged to procure pay and subsistence to his troops, he sailed to the Ionian or Carian coast, with a view of raising contributions. He committed the principal armament to Antiochus, a man wholly unworthy of such an important trust, and commanded him to continue in the harbour of Notium, where the fleet then was, during his absence, and by no means to risk an engagement. No sooner, however, was Alcibiades departed, than Antiochus sailed towards Ephesus, approached the sterns of the ships of Lysander, and with the most licentious insults challenged the Spartans to battle; but Lysander had the prudence to delay the engagement until the presumption of the enemy had thrown them into confusion. When he perceived the Athenian vessels scattered in disorder, then he gave orders to the Peloponnesian squadrons to advance against the enemy. A few gallies were immediately launched and manned, and pursued the Athenian fleet. This being seen at Notium, a superiour force was instantly sent to the relief of Antiochus; upon which Lysander having led out the whole Peloponnesian fleet, the Athenians did the same with theirs, but in such haste, that they observed no order. Lysander began the action with his fleet regularly formed: the Athenians, one after another, endeavoured to get into the line, and for some time maintained an irregular contest; but at length they were obliged to retire to Samos, and lost fifteen vessels, with a considerable part of their crews. This was a very mortifying event for Alcibiades. He hastened back to his fleet, and, anxious to restore the tarnished lustre of the Athenian armament, sailed to the mouth of the harbour of Ephesus, and again offered battle; but Lysander declined to venture a second engagement with the superiour strength of Alcibiades.

The people of Athens, who expected to hear only of victories and triumphs, were not a little mortified, when they received the intelligence of this defeat; and as they could not suspect the abilities, they distrusted the fidelity of their commander. The enemies of Alcibiades immediately took advantage of the popular temper, and Thrasybulus arrived from the fleet, in order to impeach him. He represented the misconduct of Alcibiades as having ruined the affairs of his country. He had selected, he said, such friends as were the meanest and most worthless of men; and to such improper persons he had committed the command of the fleet, whilst he passed his time in the effeminate pleasures of Ionia, or raised contributions on the dependent cities, that he might maintain a fortress in the neighbourhood of Byzantium, which he had erected, to shelter him from the vengeance of the republick.

In the same assembly therefore, and on the same day, Alcibiades was accused, and almost unanimously condemned; and, that the affairs of the republick might not again suffer by the abuse of undivided power, they proceeded to elect ten generals. Among the newly appointed commanders, were Thrasyllus, Leon, Diomedon, Conon, and Pericles, men whose approved valour and love of liberty had recommended them to publick honours.

These had scarcely assumed the command of the Athenian fleet, when Callicratidas was sent to succeed Lysander, the Spartan Admiral. The character of the former was directly opposite to the ambitious and intriguing temper of the latter. On his arrival at Ephesus, Lysander told him that he resigned to him a fleet, which commanded the seas. "Pass then," replied Callicratidas, "along the isle of Samos (where the Athenians then lay) and surrender the armament to me at Miletus." Lysander endeavoured to elude this by saying, that he was no longer admiral. A cabal was formed against Callicratidas, by some of the principal officers in the armament, and among the allies; an universal discontent prevailed on account of the change which had taken place in the Spartan command. In order to bring matters to an issue, Callicratidas asked them, whether he should retain his authority, and they give him their zealous cooperation, or return home, and relate the present state of things in the Peloponnesian armament. Order was thereupon immediately established, and the commands of the Spartan government were obeyed.

This was not, however, the only difficulty, which the newly created admiral had to encounter; he repaired to Sardis, to demand the stipulated pay, but could gain no admission to the royal presence. The first time he went to the palace, he was told that Cyrus was at table. "It is well," replied he, " I shall wait until he has dined." He came a second time, but was still denied admittance. This behaviour might have deserved his resentment, but it chiefly excited his contempt. He left the royal city, despising the pride and perfidy of the Persian allies; and exclaimed, that he saw what would be the consequences of these quarrels among the Greeks; and that if he lived to return home, he would do his utmost to reconcile Lacedæmon and Athens.

The first operations of Callicratidas were directed against the isle of Lesbos, or rather against the populous and wealthy towns of Methymna and Mitylene, on the northern and southern divisions of the island. Methymna was taken by an assault, and the allies proposed the sale of the inhabitants: but Callicratidas, with a spirit of liberal patriotism, of which we meet with few instances in Grecian history, nobly declared, that where he commanded, no Greek should be made a slave.

He then threatened Conon that he would stop his adultery with the sea; and accordingly, the Athenian commander having sailed with a squadron of seventy ships to protect the isle of Lesbos, Callicratidas, discovering his strength, with a far superiour fleet intercepted the return of the armament to Samos. The Athenians fled towards the coast of Mitylene, but were so vigorously pursued by the enemy, that they entered the harbour together. Conon thus compelled to fight against numbers so superiour, lost thirty tri-

remes, and only saved the rest by hauling under
the protection of the battlements of the town.
Callicratidas, stationing his fleet in the harbour,
and sending for infantry from Methymna and
Chios, formed the siege of Mitylene both by
sea and land. After these successes Cyrus sent
supplies unasked for, and also a present for the
admiral. The supplies were accepted by the
Spartan, but the present he refused; observing,
that if Cyrus meant to be upon friendly terms
with the Lacedæmonians, he supposed he should
be included in the general favour.

Conon was now in a very distressing situation.
He embarked some of his bravest and most experienced seamen in two swift-sailing vessels,
one of which, eluding the vigilance of the enemy, escaped to the Hellespont, and informed the
Athenians of the misfortunes of their general.
This news soon reached Samos and Athens.
The importance of the object, which was no less
than the safety of forty ships, and more than
eight thousand brave men, excited the attention
and activity of the Athenians. A fleet of one
hundred and fifty sail was immediately equipped,
and manned; the assistance of their allies having added to their domestick strength, and all
the able-bodied men in the republick being pressed into the service.

This large and powerful armament instantly
sailed for Lesbos, to the relief of Conon. The
Spartan admiral did not decline the engagement.
Having left fifty triremes under the command
of Eteonicus, to continue the blockade of Mitylene, he went with one hundred and twenty ships
to meet the enemy. The same evening the
Athenians had advanced to the islands, or rather
rocks of Arginusæ; and both meditated a sur-

prise, which was rendered ineffectual by a violent tempest of rain and thunder. At the dawn the two armaments prepared to engage; but some experienced seamen, and the chief counsellors of Callicratidas, advised him not to hazard the weakness of the Peloponnesians against the superiour strength and numbers of the enemy. The generous and intrepid Spartan, with the spirit of a true disciple of Lycurgus, answered : " My death cannot be destructive to Sparta ; but my flight would be dishonourable both to Sparta and to myself." The fleets met, and the action was bloody and obstinate on both sides. Various evolutions then broke the regularity of order, and, nevertheless, the fight was maintained for some time with much equality. Callicratidas, who commanded in the right wing of the fleet, striking an enemy's galley with the beak of his ship, fell overboard and perished. Different turns of fortune prevailed in different parts of the battle ; but the Peloponnesians at length, were compelled to give way on all sides. Seventy of their gallies were taken, and the rest escaped.

B. C. 406. It was now the design of the Athenian admirals to proceed against Methymna, Mitylene, and Chios, and to attempt the recovery of the bodies of the drowned or slain. But Eteonicus, having notice of the defeat of the Spartan armament, gave orders to the galley to put to sea again, and to return by broad daylight into the harbour, with the crew attired with garlands, and proclaiming that Callicratidas had been successful against the Athenian fleet. This contrivance succeeded ; the Spartans returned thanks to the gods by hymns and sacrifices ; the sailors were enjoined to refresh themselves by a copious repast, and to profit by a favourable gale for sailing to Chios; while the soldiers burned their camp, and marched to garrison Methymna.

This place was now too strongly fortified, to be taken by assault; the Peloponnesian fleet had secured itself in its harbour; and the Athenians found it impossible to effect their designs. In the mean time at Athens the flattering intelligence, which had been received respecting the victory, was converted into disappointment and sorrow, when it was understood the fleet had returned to Samos, without attempting any thing besides. They lamented beyond measure the loss of the wreck, by which their brave and victorious countrymen had been deprived of the sacred rites of funeral; a circumstance viewed with considerable horrour, because, according to a superstitious tradition, their melancholy shades were supposed to wander a hundred years on the banks of Styx, before they were admitted into the regions of light and happiness.

Hence followed one of the most extraordinary, most disgraceful, and most fatal strokes of faction, recorded in history. The people by a decree deprived all their generals of their command, Conon only excepted. Protomachus and Aristogenes chose a voluntary banishment; but the rest returned to answer the charges brought against them. In matters of treason, perfidy, or malversation of men in power, the senate of five hundred, or rather the prytanes, that presided in the senate, performed the offices of the magistrate, while the collective body of the people, convened in publick assembly, executed the functions of judge and jury. The prytanes prescribed the form of action or trial, and admitted

'the accuser to implead, or impeach his antago-
nist. The people then, as judges of the fact,
gave their verdict, and as judges of the law,
passed their sentence or decree.

. But, in the present instance, the accused were
not allowed the usual forms of defence; and
each was permitted only to make a short speech
to the people. The commanders were accused,
tried, and condemned; and immediately delivered over to the executioner. Before they were
led to death, Diomedon addressed the assembly,
in a short but memorable speech. "I am
afraid, lest the sentence of death passed upon us
be hurtful to the republick. I would, therefore,
have you to employ proper means for averting
the vengeance of the gods. Our misfortunes
have deprived us of an opportunity for performing the sacrifices, which we had promised, in
behalf of ourselves and you, before the battle at
Arginusæ: and this just debt of gratitude we
exhort you to pay; for we are sensible, that the
assistance of Heaven enabled us to obtain that
signal and glorious victory." Diomedon having thus spoken, the six generals were executed;
but the cruelty of the Athenians was followed
by a speedy repentance, and punished by the
sharp pangs of remorse, which they endeavoured
to mitigate, but without effect, by inflicting a
well-merited vengeance on the worthless and
detestable Callixenus, who had been the chief
promoter of this unjust and tyrannical action.

. The removal and execution of the Athenian
admirals, and the defeat and death of Callicratidas, suspended the military operations on both
sides for some time. Two other commanders,
Philocles and Adimantus, had been joined in
authority with Conon. The former was a man

of a violent and ungovernable temper, unaccustomed to reflection, void of experience, and incapable of governing others or himself. The latter did not want humanity, but was destitute of spirit and activity, qualities for which the Athenians were in general so remarkable. He was careless of discipline, negligent of duty, and suspected of carrying on a treasonable correspondence with the enemy.

In the mean time, the Peloponnesian cause, after the death of Callicratidas and the dispersion of the fleet, seems to have been for some time neglected by Cyrus. The squadron, which had escaped from Mitylene, remained at Chios. Eteonicus, the commander, had rejoined it from Methymna; but he was without money, with which to pay the troops, and without resources. For some time, by hire and other methods, the soldiers, during summer, earned a comfortable subsistence; for the Greeks had been accustomed to live, when on military service, by their own means; and therefore at first this did not give them great uneasiness; but when autumn had advanced, their cloths were worn out, and with the increasing demands of necessity the means of earning were lessened. The approaching season of winter, therefore, afforded little hope of relief, and the most serious apprehensions were entertained. A conspiracy, in consequence, was formed by the troops, to make themselves masters of the island; and they determined to become rich at once, by seizing and plundering the large and wealthy capital of Chios.

This design, though formed in secret, was nevertheless openly avowed. The conspirators, that they might assume a distinction, which should enable them the better to know their asso-

ciates, who were very numerous, agreed that
every man of their party should carry a reed.
The intelligence of this plot did not reach Eteonicus, until it was hazardous to oppose the mutiny by open force; and if he destroyed them by
fraud, the obloquy and reproach of Greece would
be vented on him. He therefore selected fifteen
persons in whom he could confide, and arming
them with daggers, patrolled the streets of
Chios. The first person they observed to carry
a reed, was instantly put to death; and a crowd
assembling about the body, to know why the
man was slain, they were told it was for carrying
a reed in his casque. This information was
quickly communicated through the city. The
conspirators, unprepared, and ignorant of the
opposition they had to expect, hastened to throw
away the reeds, which exposed them to the dangerous assaults of their unknown enemies; and
thus, with the loss of only one man, a mutiny
was completely quelled, which, under a hesi-
tating commander, might have spread havock
and desolation over one of the most populous
and wealthy islands of the Ægean.

A congress of the Peloponnesian confederacy
was about this time held at Ephesus. Thither
the Chians, and all the Asiatic confederates, sent
deputies, commissioned for that purpose. In
this convention it was decreed, to send ministers
to Lacedæmon in the joint names of Cyrus, the
armament, and allies, to represent the present
posture of affairs, and to request that Lysander
might be reappointed commander in chief.

If we except Brasidas, we may safely affirm,
that no Spartan had ever so conciliated the
esteem of the allies as Lysander; no Spartan
was equally acquainted with the method of ren-

dering himself agreeable to a Persian prince:
for flattery and an insinuating address were the
principal, if not the only qualifications necessary
for obtaining the favour and esteem of a Persian
court; and these the severe discipline of Lycurgus had almost precluded from existing in
the Lacedæmonian commonwealth. The military and political conduct of Lysander had,
besides, been distinguished, and the success attending the engagement against Antiochus had
procured him great celebrity.

The Spartans, though inclined to comply
with the wishes of their allies, were, nevertheless much perplexed by an ancient law, enacted
in the jealousy of freedom, and still considered
of importance: namely, never to commit the
chief command of the fleet twice to the same
person. The consideration of the signal defeat
they had suffered, and of their inability to support and protect their Asiatic allies, or to contend with the Athenian armament, without the
assistance of Persia, contributed not a little to
induce them to relax in this point. They still,
however, nominally adhered to the law, while,
at the same time, they complied with the request
of Cyrus and of their Grecian confederates.
They invested Aracus, a weak and obscure man,
with the name of admiral, and sent Lysander
to command in Asia, under the appellation of
vice-admiral.

Lysander, arriving at Ephesus, made great
preparations to have a fleet able to oppose the
Athenian armament. Having, therefore, directed matters for this purpose, he hastened to
pay his compliments in person to the Persian
prince at Sardis. Absence, he found, had not
lessened his interest and esteem there. Cyrus

received him with the greatest demonstrations of joy, supplied him with money for satisfying the immediate expenses of the fleet, and, as he was about to make a journey to Suza, consigned the revenues of his wealthy provinces, during his stay there, to his esteemed Spartan friend. Such powerful and immense resources could not long remain unemployed in the active hands of Lysander. He returned to Ephesus, paid off the arrears of the seamen, and directed his attention to the means of prosecuting offensive operations against the Athenians.

In the mean time, so great had been his exertions, aided by an unfailing treasury that the fleet was already equal in strength to the Athenian armament. His emissaries had universally engaged, or pressed, the seamen on the Ionian and Carian coasts. Lysander, however, determined not to risk a general engagement, which no necessity of his present circumstances required. In all the towns on the Propontis and the Hellespont, which had submitted to the Athenian republick, under the command of Alcibiades and Thrasybulus, a Lacedæmonian faction still existed. The consequences, therefore, of giving efficacy to such a party, would probably be the accomplishment of two very important objects; the obstruction of the revenue that supported the Athenian fleet; and the recovery of the trade with the Euxine, which furnished the best supplies of corn.

For these reasons, the Hellespont was the point to which Lysander directed his principal attention. Desirous of avoiding the Athenian armament, he coasted along the shores of Asia, and, without receiving any interruption from the enemy, reached Abydos. Here his fleet rode in security in the harbour. The city was populous, and the body of infantry which it furnished was put under the command of Thorax, a Lacedæmonian. The important town of Lampsacus was then attacked; and the place, though bravely defended by the natives and Athenian garrison, was at length taken by storm. The city was abandoned to the licentious rapacity, the avarice, the lust, and fury of the conquerors, according to the barbarous and predominant custom of the age.

The government of Athens, after the violent and cruel proceedings occasioned by the spirit of party, in which the six brave and unfortunate commanders lost their lives, seems to have acted with supineness and languor. The dilatory and imprudent measures pursued by the fleet at Samos augured ill of the abilities of Tydeus, Menander, and Cephisodotus, who had been lately joined in command with the meritorious Conon and his unworthy colleagues. In the abilities of a commander, Conon was not inferiour to Lysander himself; and, but for the division of the supreme authority, the Athenian armament would have been superiour, in every respect, to the Peloponnesian. Confident of success, and flushed with victory, the fleet of Athens passed from Samos to the coast of Asia, and the dependencies of the Persian monarch. They then sailed for Ephesus, with the intention of offering battle to the enemy; but received intelligence that Lysander had already proceeded northward. In alarm for the dependencies of the commonwealth on the Hellespont, they immediately hastened after him. Lampsacus, was, however, taken before they reached Elæus. Staying, therefore, at this place only while they took refreshment, they proceeded to

Sestos, and arrived the same evening at Ægospotamos, over against Lampsacus.

This station was injudiciously chosen, as it afforded very insecure riding for the fleet, and was two miles distant from Sestos, the nearest town for furnishing them with provision. The strait between Lampsacus and Ægospotamos being only two miles wide, the arrival of the Athenian fleet was almost immediately known by Lysander. On the same night, therefore, his plan was formed, and his orders were issued. The morning no sooner dawned, than his crews had taken their meal, and repaired on board. Every thing was in readiness for action, but no movement was made. The sun was scarcely risen, when the Athenians, despising the inferiority of the Peloponnesian fleet, advanced in order of battle to the harbour of Lampsacus; and the enemy remaining motionless, the Athenians waited until the evening, and then returned in triumph, as the acknowledged masters of the sea. No sooner, however, had the armament of Athens withdrawn from before the harbour of Lampsacus, than Lysander sent two of his swiftest gallies after them, with instructions to the commanders to observe whether the enemy debarked, and to form some judgment of their immediate intentions, and then to hasten back with the information. This was punctually executed. In the mean time, Lysander kept his fleet in readiness for action; and not until he was assured that the enemy's motions indicated no intentions of attempting an enterprise, did he dismiss his troops, to procure refreshment. The next morning they repeated their insults, and the two following days also he prudently indulged their presumption.

Since the battle of Notium, on account of

which Alcibiades had been deprived of the command of the Athenian armament, and banished, he had resided in his castle on the Thracian Chersonese. The two hostile fleets of course attracted his attention, as they were both in the neighbourhood of his residence; and he was, at least, so far sensible of the welfare of his country, as to be uneasy at what he saw. Ægospotamos had only a beach on which the gallies might be hauled, or near which, in the shelter of the strait, they might safely ride at anchor. The ground was commodious for encamping; but, in the defects of the military system of that age, the troops went to Sestos, two miles distant, (as has been before observed) for a market: while on the other hand, the enemy at Abydos had the security of a harbour for their fleet, and a town for their people, where, that they might be always ready for every duty, they could procure what necessaries they wanted. Alcibiades went to the Athenian camp, modestly admonished his countrymen of their imprudence, and observed, that if they moved only to Sestos, they, as well as the enemy, would have the benefit of a town and a harbour, and where, equally with their present situation, they might fight whenever they pleased. This admonition of the illustrious exile was received with arrogance and disdain; and Alcibiades was reproached for presuming, while an outlaw of his country, to give advice to the admirals of Athens. Their conduct, indeed, too faithfully, corresponded, in every particular, with this insolence and folly.

Lysander, in the mean time, observed, that every day's experience of his inaction increased the negligence and confidence of the Athenians.

He was informed, by the vessels which he sent to watch their motions, that they did not confine themselves to the market of Sestos, but wandered into the country, to seek, or on pretence of seeking, provision. In the morning they failed not to offer battle to the Peloponnesian fleet, and in the afternoon returned again to their camp. On the fifth day, they advanced as usual to the harbour of Lampsacus and provoked the hostile fleet to an engagement, by more daring menaces than on any former occasion. Confident of success, they yielded without reserve to all the petulance of power and prosperity. They even debated among themselves, in what manner the Lacedæmonian prisoners should be punished, who had the misfortune to fall into their hands. The cruel Philocles proposed, that they should have their right hands cut off, that those enemies of the republick might be incapable of handling the oar, or brandishing the spear. This inhuman proposition, though opposed by Adimantus, was approved by the majority of his colleagues, and finally resolved on. After insulting the Peloponnesian fleet in the most mortifying and disdainful manner, they returned with an air of exultation and contempt, to their station.

Lysander then gave directions to the commanders of his exploring ships, that, if they observed the Athenians disembark and disperse as usual, they should hasten their return, and by the elevation of a shield communicate the intelligence. The advice boats, therefore, having followed the enemy to a convenient distance, noticed that they no sooner landed at their station, than the troops straggled about the shore, advanced into the inland country in quest of provision or amusement, and indulged in indolence, or revelled in disorder. Lysander had embarked the troops, cleared his ships, and made every necessary preparation, to avail himself of the opportunity of effecting by stratagem, what would have been difficult and dangerous to have attempted by force. The advice boats returned, the expected signal was made, and the fleet steered across the strait.

Conon endeavoured seasonably to assemble the strength of the Athenians but his advice was disdained by officers incapable and unworthy of commanding; and the seamen, unaccustomed, and unwilling to obey the commands of their leaders, despised his orders. At length, however, when it was too late, they became sensible of their errour. The Peloponnesians were upon them before any effectual and salutary measures of defence could be taken. The soldiers and seamen were equally dispersed; and most of their gallies were altogether empty, or manned with such feeble crews as were incapable of working, much less of defending them. The Peloponnesians, with their regular onset and disciplined valour, attacked the Athenian troops, as they flocked precipitately, and without order, to the shore. Those who fought were slain; the rest fled into the inmost recesses of the Chersonese, or sought protection in the Athenian fortresses scattered over that peninsula.

Conon's trireme, with seven others of his division, and the sacred ship Paralus, had their crews complete, and pushed off from the shore. One hundred and seventy-one gallies were seized by the enemy, at anchor or on the beach. No effort within the power of nine ships could have any other effect than to add the loss of them to that of the rest of the fleet. While the enemy, therefore, were intent upon their capture, Conon fled, unpursued, to the island of Cyprus. Three thousand prisoners were taken, among whom were Philocles and Adimantus; and Lysander returned with his invaluable spoil to Lampsacus, amidst the joyous acclamations of naval triumph. B. C. 405.

It now became a matter of serious consideration, how they might dispose of such a number of prisoners, beyond all common example of battles among the Greeks; the allies accordingly were assembled for consultation, and that animosity appeared in their proceedings, which the ancient manner of warfare was calculated to excite. The injustice and cruelty of the ambitious Athenians were copiously described, and maliciously exaggerated in this dreadful tribunal. "It would be tedious," they said, "to enumerate, though it was impossible to forget, the multiplied and abominable crimes, of which so many individuals and so many communities had been the innocent and unhappy victims. Even lately they had taken a Corinthian and an Andrian vessel, and thrown the crews down a precipice, and destroyed them. The gods had averted the odious and inhuman proposition of Philocles, of which the author and approvers were equally criminal; nor could those deserve pardon or mercy, who had no pity on the sufferings of others."

It was therefore instantly resolved, that all the prisoners, who were Athenian citizens, except Adimantus, should be put to death. The unarmed prisoners were then conducted into the presence of their armed judges, and, as a prelude to the inhuman massacre, Lysander sternly demanded of Philocles, what he ought to suffer for his intended cruelty. The Athenian replied with firmness and intrepidity, "Accuse not those whom it is in your power to judge, but inflict that punishment on us, which we, in your situation, would have inflicted on you." No sooner had he spoken thus, than Lysander began the execution, and killed that general with his own hand. The Peloponnesian soldiers followed the bloody and inhuman example of their commander. Of the three thousand Athenians, Adimantus alone was spared; and probably on this account it was asserted, that he had been corrupted by Lysander with the gold of Persia, and betrayed the fleet.

It might have been expected that the Spartan admiral after an event which gave him the complete command of the sea, would immediately have sailed to Piraeus, and assaulted the city, already grievously oppressed by the Lacedaemonian army at Decelia. But Lysander foresaw the numerous obstacles that would oppose his conquest of Athens, and therefore prudently restrained the ardour of the troops from the enterprise. The strongly fortified harbours of that capital, the long and lofty walls that surrounded the city, and above all, the ancient renown and actual despair of the Athenians, must, he was sensible, render the siege, if not fruitless, at least difficult and tedious.

On the coasts of Greece and Asia, and of any of the intermediate islands, there was no naval force capable of contending with the fleet of Lysander; nor, if we except the city of Athens alone, was there any fortified place in all those countries, sufficient to withstand the impression of his army. It was a design, therefore, deserving his ambition, and which his prudence

could not disapprove, to establish or confirm
the Lacedæmonian power and empire over those
valuable and extensive coasts. He had nothing
more to do than to direct the course of his victorious fleet, and to take possession. As soon
as he appeared between Byzantium and Chalcedon, the inhabitants of those places astonished and terrified by the dreadful misfortunes of
their Athenian allies, offered to capitulate. The
Athenian garrisons were allowed to depart; but
policy, more than lenity, prompted this measure:
Lysander looked forward to the conquest of A-
thens; and against the uncommon strength of
the fortifications, and other obstacles with which
he would have to contend, famine was considered as the most certain and efficacious weapon.
As, therefore, every augmentation of their
numbers would promote his purpose, he permitted all Athenian citizens to go to Athens,
but to Athens only.

In the mean time, the Paralus, arriving by
night at Piræus, communicated to the Athenians
such intelligence, as no other, perhaps, of the unfortunate fleet, without the protection of the sacred character of the ship, would have dared to
carry. The alarm and lamentations, commenc-
ing immediately in the vicinity of the harbour,
were quickly communicated through the town
of Piræus, and, passing from one person to another, reached the city. The consternation immediately became universal, and during that
night no person slept in Athens. Grief for the
slain, the best part of the Athenian youth, and
among whom every one had some friend or relation, was not the prevailing passion; this was
overborne by the dread of that fate, which threatened themselves; and thus every other feeling
was absorbed in personal considerations.

Even at this time, however, Athens was not destitute of able men, capable of directing the publick affairs in any common storm. But, exclusive of the incompetency of the republick, to oppose an equal force to that which would be brought against it, the endless strife of faction, and the violence of intestine tumult, had destroyed all coherence in the constituent parts of the government. Nothing now remained of that publick confidence, which, after the defeat of the Sicilian expedition, had enabled the leading men of the state to surprise all Greece with new exertions, and to regain the superiority of the sea. On the morrow, however, after the arrival of the Paralus, a general assembly was convened, and such measures were resolved on, as the exigency of affairs seemed to require. They expected an immediate siege by sea and land; and as it was impossible to raise a fleet able to oppose that of the Peloponnesians, they determined to block up all the ports except one, to repair the walls, to appoint guards, and to prepare every thing in their power to resist the enemy, and to sustain a blockade.

In the mean time, Lysander, having awed the Hellespontine cities into submission, sailed to the island of Lesbos, reduced Mitylene, and confirmed the allegiance of Methymna. Whilst he was extending his arms over the coast of Lydia and Caria, and the neighbouring islands, he sent Eteonicus with ten ships to the Thracian shores, who ravaged the maritime parts of Macedon, subdued the towns and cities of Thrace bordering on the coast, and rode triumphant in the Hellespont and Propontis, the Ægean and Euxine seas. Soon after the disaster of the Athenians at Ægospotamos, the fairest and most fa-

voured portion of the ancient world, submitted
with reluctance to the power, or voluntarily accepted the alliance, of Sparta.

During this long series of triumphs, Lysander
never lost sight of the reduction of Athens; an
object not only useful, but necessary, for completing his designs, and the victories he had already obtained. He therefore sent information
to Lacedæmon and Decelia, at the same time,
that he was ready to sail to Piræus with two
hundred gallies. The Lacedæmonians, as soon
as they received this intelligence, resolved to
make great exertions, that they might terminate
a war, which had continued for such a long series of years with little or no intermission. Their
allies were summoned to arms; and the whole
force of Laconia joining them, they marched toward Attica, under the command of Pausanias.
Agis now united the troops from Decelia to this
numerous and powerful army, and both proceeded to the gymnasium of Academus, close by
the city, where they fixed their quarters.

The Athenians, though destitute of allies, of
a fleet, of stores, and blockaded by a powerful
enemy by sea and land, made no proposals for
capitulating. In sullen and silent despondency
they beheld the formidable appearance of the
Peloponnesians on the sea and in the field, and
with all the means in their power they prepared
for a defence, which, at best, could only pro-
crastinate their final doom, and would be attended with nothing but present sufferings.—
When Lysander had blocked up the entrance of
their harbours, and no supplies could be procured for the city, famine soon began to be severely
felt by the Athenians. Still, however, they defended with vigour their walls and ramparts, pa-

tiently endured hardship and hunger, and beheld with obstinate unconcern the affliction of their wives and children. Disease and death now advanced among the unfortunate Athenians with increasing horrour; yet, even amidst this dreadful scene of woe, they punished Archestratus with the utmost severity for proposing a capitulation; and, at the same time, declared, that their independence and their lives should perish together.

But, notwithstanding the noble sentiments and melancholy firmness of the popular assembly, a numerous and powerful party of men existed in the state, who were governed by interest more than by honour; and the greatest enemies of the liberty of Athens flourished in the bosom of the commonwealth. The whole body of the senate was infected with the leaven of the five hundred; and not only Theramenes, but several other men of abilities and influence in the state, regretted the destruction of that tyranny, and the restoration of the democratical form of government. Amidst every shape of publick distress, the Athenians caballed, clamoured, accused, and persecuted each other; and the aristocratical faction, from the smallness of its numbers, being capable of acting with superiour concert and vigour, destroyed, by every base, cruel and illegal means, the friends and partisans of democracy.

A deputation, however, was at length agreed on between the two factions; and accordingly ministers were sent to Agis, the Spartan king, who commanded the blockade. The Athenians proposed an alliance, offensive and defensive with the Lacedæmonian commonwealth, which, in the language of the politicks of Greece,

meant nothing less than the subjection of Athens
to Sparta; and stipulated only for the preservation of their fortifications, and of their harbours.
Agis replied, that he had no power to treat, and
that proposals must be addressed to the administration at Lacedæmon.   Ministers were then
sent into Peloponnesus: but when they arrived
at Sellasia, on the borders of Laconia, they received a proud and haughty message from the
ephori, commanding their immediate return;
and informing them, that the terms they brought
were already known at Lacedæmon, and, if
they desired peace, they must procure more ample powers from Athens.

This answer being communicated in the city,
the Athenians were filled with despair.   They
now considered themselves as already condemned to slavery, if not to death, by their merciless
and implacable enemies; and even before another deputation could return with an answer
from Lacedæmon, many must perish with hunger. It was understood, that the Lacedæmonians
proposed among other things, that the long walls
for ten furlongs should be demolished.   There-
menes, whose character was extremely dubious,
ventured to offer, that, if the Athenians would
commission him to go to Lacedæmon, he would
undertake to bring certain information, whether
the Peloponnesians really intended to redude the
Athenians to slavery, or whether the demolition
of the walls were only required to insure political subjection. He named nine persons to be his
colleagues in this important mission, and flattered the people that they would procure some
moderate terms of accommodation. A decree
was therefore immediately passed by the Athenians in assembly, investing the embassadors with
full powers.

Having assumed the sacred badge of their inviolable character, they proceeded to the Spartan camp, held a conference with Agis the Lacedæmonian king, and then set forward on their journey towards Sparta. But when they arrived at Sellasia, the embassy was again met by an officer from the ephori; who would not permit them to proceed farther, until they had given assurance, that they were invested with indefinite authority, to treat for a peace with the Lacedæmonian commonwealth. When they reached Sparta, an assembly of the deputies of the Peloponnesian confederacy was convened, in which the fate of the Athenian republick was to be decided. The deputation from Corinth and Thebes vehemently contended, that no terms whatever should be granted the Athenians: the commonwealth of Athens, they said, which was the enemy of the common liberties of Greece, and had been so nearly successful in the horrid attempt to enslave or exterminate the whole nation, ought to be annihilated, and not suffered to exist. Many of the other deputies also supported the same opinion. The Lacedæmonians, however, whose administration was little subject to passionate counsels or hasty decisions, had previously considered the matter, and thought otherwise. Athens, if deprived of its navy, and of the revenue and power arising from transmarine dependencies, might, under an oligarchical government, become a necessary and valuable acquisition to Lacedæmon. The recollection of what had happened only a few years before, when almost the whole of Peloponnesus had united in war against them, might probably occasion an apprehension, that at some future period a balancing power might be wasted against Corinth, Thebes, or Argos.

With an ostentation, therefore, of regard for the common welfare and glory of the Grecian nation, the Lacedæmonians declared, that it would not become the Peloponnesian confederacy, and least of all the Spartans, to reduce to slavery a Grecian people, to whom the Greeks had been more than once beholden for the most important services, in the greatest and most imminent dangers that ever threatened their liberty. Accordingly it was proposed and resolved, that the conditions on which the Athenians should be permitted to retain their civil freedom, should be the following: that all their ships of war, except twelve, be surrendered; that the long walls and the fortifications of Piræus be destroyed; that all exiles and fugitives be restored to the rights of the city; that the Athenians consider the same states as friends or enemies, which should be respectively so to the Lacedæmonians; and that the Athenians send their forces wherever Lacedæmon should command by sea or land.

With these terms Theramenes and his colleagues hastened back to Athens. During the long absence of their ambassadors, the Peloponnesians had pressed the siege with redoubled rigour. The Spartans, reinforced by the Thebans and their other allies, had surrounded the city on every side. Lysander blocked up the harbours with the Peloponnesian fleet; and had made himself master of Melos, Cos, Ægina, and Salamis, islands so near to Athens, that they were almost regarded as a part of the Attic territory. Within the walls the greatest misery prevailed: the famine had become intolerable; but the diseases which it engendered were still more intolerable; and such numbers had already perished, that it was considered by the besieged as impossible to hold out many days longer.

No sooner, therefore, was the arrival of the embassadors announced at Athens, than people from every part of the city flocked about them in the most painful suspense, lest an irresistible and perhaps also an implacable enemy should still refuse to treat, and no other alternative remain than to perish with hunger, or submit to the mercy of those, from whom they scarcely hoped to receive any compassion. The information that a treaty had been concluded, gave relief for the night. The day following an assembly of the people was convened. Theramenes declared to the Athenians the terms, which, he said, were the best and most lenient, that himself and his colleagues could obtain; and such as in their present distressful and unfortunate situation, in his opinion, they would do well to accept. When these unexpected fruits of his boasted negotiation were produced, the people had no longer strength or spirit to resist, or even courage to die. A considerable body, however, pertinaciously declared, that they would never consent to the demolition of the walls.

But the principal leaders of the patriotick party had been destroyed by the perfidious snares of their opponents, who were prepared to bear a foreign yoke, provided they were allowed to exercise domestick tyranny. That odious and detestable faction was ready to approve the measures of Theramenes, however degrading and servile; and Theramenes himself might well influence the resolution of the assembly, by in-

forming them; that the severity of the Lacedæmonians, excessive as it seemed to be, was extremely moderate and lenient in comparison of
what was proposed by the furious and implacable Corinthians and Thebans. Arguments of
this nature he certainly might have made use of
if necessary, to justify his negociations with the
Spartans, and to persuade his countrymen to accept the terms offered them; but the full period of the three nine years having elapsed, which
according to the faithful and accurate history of
Thucydides, had been assigned by repeated oracles and predictions, as the continuance of the
Peloponnesian war, and of the greatness of
Athens, it seemed in vain to contend. The
treaty concluded by their embassadors was
therefore confirmed and ratified by the voice of
the aristocratical faction, and submitted to, rather than accepted by the majority of the popular assembly, with the silence and sullenness of
despair.

The acceptance of the offered terms being no-
tified to the besieging armament on the sixteenth
of May, the day on which the Athenians had
been accustomed to celebrate the anniversary of
the immortal victory of Salamis, Agis
took possession of Athens, and Lysander
with his fleet entered the harbour of Piræus. The walls and fortresses of the city of
Minerva, which the generous magnanimity of
its inhabitants, preferring the publick safety of
Greece to that of themselves, had abandoned to
the fury and resentment of a barbarian invader,
were ungratefully levelled to the ground by those,
to defend whom the Athenians had on former
occasions hazarded every thing near and dear to
them.

B. C.
404.

The domineering power of Athens, however had justly provoked resentment, and the demolition of its fortifications was a peculiar circumstance of rejoicing and triumph, throughout the whole of Peloponnesus. The enemy, with much parade, commenced this destructive operation at the sound of military musick, and with an eagerness and zeal almost incredible. They boasted that succeeding ages would consider the demolition of Athens, as the true æra of the freedom of Greece. No sooner, however, had they effected their purpose, and satiated their resentment, than they seemed to regret the injury they had done.

A magnificent festival concluded the day, in which the recitation of particular passages of the Grecian poets, formed, as usual, a principal part of the entertainment. The Electra of Euripides was rehearsed, and particularly that pathetic chorus, "We come, O, daughter of Agamemnon! to thy rustick and humble roof." The words were scarcely uttered, when the whole assembly melted into tears. The forlorn and helpless condition of that young and virtuous princess, who, having been expelled her father's house, was obliged to inhabit a miserable cottage, in want and wretchedness, recalled to their minds the dreadful vicissitude of fortune, which had befallen Athens. That city, once mistress of the sea, and sovereign of Greece, was deprived in one fatal hour of her ships, her walls, and her strength; and reduced from the pride and prosperity of her situation, to misery, dependence, and servitude. Nor did the Athenians make one memorable effort to brighten the moment of their destruction, and to make their fall illustrious.

Thus did the conquest of Athens, and the acknowledged superiority of Sparta, terminate the memorable Peloponnesian war of twenty-seven years. Lacedæmon, now allied to Persia, became decidedly the leading power of Greece; and aristocracy, or rather oligarchy, triumphed over the democratical form of government, in almost every commonwealth of the Grecian people.

END OF THE FIRST VOLUME OF THE HISTORY OF GREECE.

Stansbury and Gird, Printers.